D1739644

Illegitimacy

Illegitimacy

Shirley Foster Hartley

University of California Press
Berkeley / Los Angeles / London

University of California Press
Berkeley and Los Angeles, California
University of California Press, Ltd.
London, England
Copyright 1975 by
The Regents of the University of California
ISBN: 0-520-02533-4
Library of Congress Catalog Card Number: 73-83057
Designed by Jim Mennick
Printed in the United States of America

Contents

Tables

Figures

Preface

ILLEGITIMACY, generally viewed as a welfare problem or as a psychological problem of parents, may be studied as a societal phenomenon. Reasons for high or low levels of illegitimacy are related to differences in human group life. How is it possible that some social groups are able to organize so as to obtain conformity to the "principle of legitimacy," while other groups give lip service to the ideal when in fact their members produce up to 70 percent of all births out of wedlock?

The general scheme of analysis presented here should help us to understand illegitimacy in a variety of social settings. We are interested in examining how different societies promote or inhibit early and universal marriage, how groups may facilitate or limit extramarital sexual intercourse, how they influence the use of effective contraception or abortion, and how groups differ in pressure to marry when conception out of wedlock occurs. The analytical framework facilitates understanding at the societal, social, religious, or racial group level and even at the individual level.

Available cross-national data are assembled to allow comparisons over both time and geographical areas. For some countries the information is sparse and of questionable reliability; for others it is even more detailed than can be fully elaborated in this international overview. The utility of the theoretical scheme may be tested in future research.

This approach suggests that illegitimacy should be studied as the result of an interrelated chain of events allowing a number of alternatives to the production of births out of wedlock. At each stage in the chain a number of social forces influence individual decision making in such a way that social groups produce patterns of illegitimacy that are maintained over time and distinct cultural areas.

PLAN OF THE BOOK

Chapter 1 contrasts the ideal or "principle of legitimacy" found everywhere with an indication of behavioral variation evident among the nations of the world. It also reviews available research on some specific consequences of illegitimacy for the child, the mother, the father, and the social group. A working definition of the term *illegitimacy* and a brief survey of the various types of illegitimacy is included. Chapter 2 presents available international data on the most commonly used measures of illegitimacy: the number of births out of wedlock is used in the calculation of the ratios and rates that are most appropriate for comparative studies. Chapter 3 reviews the major theories previously proposed as explanations of illegitimacy in light of the cross-national data. The concatenated, multidimensional theory proposed by this author is developed in chapter 4.

The extent to which women in particular societies tend to be married or unmarried during part or all of the childbearing years is examined in chapter 5. Chapter 6 considers the extent to which unmarried women tend to participate in nonmarital sexual relationships and examines the differences in the proportions at various ages, wherever these data are available. A look at the societal influence on unmarried persons regarding knowledge about, availability of, and motivation to use contraceptives of varying efficiency is found in chapter 7. Societal variation in the tendency to marry during pregnancy is discussed in chapter 8. Finally, chapter 9 examines the group influence on the availability or restriction of abortion as an alternative to birth out of wedlock.

Chapters 5 through 9 specify a number of hypotheses related to each of the five factors examined in those chapters; concepts will be defined and operationalized so that the hypotheses may be tested as far as possible. Because the availability of data varies so greatly, some propositions may be tested more adequately than others; for some, data are available for all major nations, for others, case studies or examples must suffice. While no international study could hope to be complete, this scheme of analysis may be used by sociologists, demographers, historians, and welfare personnel in studying illegitimacy in their own nations. Chapter 10 will summarize the way in which societal levels of illegitimacy may be seen as a result of the restriction or promotion of alternatives to births out of wedlock.

The difficulties of multidimensional analysis are great. Yet only by going beyond simple propositions may we improve our understanding of illegitimacy and ultimately explain, predict, and even control it.

ACKNOWLEDGEMENTS

The author's early research profited from the advice of Kingsley Davis, Judith Blake, Calvin Goldscheider, and Nathan Keyfitz. Joseph Himes and Reuben Hill encouraged development of the initial theoretical formulation, which was presented at meetings of the International Sociological Association in Bulgaria, 1970. Professors John Finley Scott, Mary Grace Taylor, Neil Smelser, Nadia Youssef, and Peter Laslett made helpful suggestions on the entire first draft of the manuscript, and Phillips Cutright and Harriet Presser contributed advice based on detailed illegitimacy and fertility research. Ms. Mary Grace Kovar, Survey Statistician with the U.S. Public Health Service, and Ms. Stephanie Ventura, of the Division of Vital Statistics, made detailed comments based on their experience in fertility research within the United States. Christopher Tietze, M.D. and Emily Moore, Ph.D., made a number of comments on the abortion chapter and offered recent references. Professor George Roberts was most helpful in obtaining Jamaican statistics. The author remains responsible for the final product.

1. Introduction

ILLEGITIMATE reproduction, or the bearing of children out of wedlock, presents an interesting problem for the social scientist who wants to understand the effects of norms or rules on human social life. On the one hand, we have the ideal of legitimate reproduction, which is found everywhere. On the other hand, we have the reality of variations in human behavior, which are manifest in measures of illegitimacy.

THE "PRINCIPLE OF LEGITIMACY" AS AN IDEAL

With hundreds of societies in the world having varied beliefs and customs, different environmental problems, and differences in group size and organization, the principle of legitimacy comes as near as any social rule to being truly universal. Why should people care whether or not children are born within socially recognized family units? And why does behavior often contradict verbalized ideals, with some educationally and economically advanced nations reporting up to 15 percent of births as illegitimate and with the less-developed countries of the world reporting from 0.0 to 74 percent of all births out of wedlock?

The sociological interest in illegitimacy does not follow from a moral commitment to the principle of legitimacy, and it does not necessarily reflect a concern for the welfare of the mother and child. It follows instead from a series of fundamental questions about the way societies maintain themselves through the bearing and rearing of future generations. How are the young of each society to be integrated into a complex, ongoing system of human relationships? Who is to provide the physical, economic, and emotional support for the mother during her period of pregnancy and child rearing? To what extent does the social group require and how does it provide a male link between the mother-child pair and the larger society?

The questions raised are related to our knowledge about human socialization. We know that the first few years of life are crucial to the future development of each individual and that human infants do not develop their genetic potential without the ongoing help of concerned adults. We also know that schooling does not compensate for deficiencies in early training and that the delegation of parental tasks to others is incredibly difficult and expensive. No wonder, then, that patterns of mating and child rearing are a major concern of human societies and their members. Illegitimacy is an important subject of study precisely because the social organization of reproduction and the socialization of future generations is important to the survival and progress of each society. Social arrangements are not equally successful at those tasks.

The basic problem in the case of births out of wedlock is the assignment of a sociological father to the biological pair of mother and child. It is advantageous to have a sociological father to the extent that there is any sexual division of labor. And, of course, the sexual division of labor is never more complete than during the period of childbearing, suckling, and rearing. Since the female is biologically tied to the child, through the period of pregnancy and lactation, it is her period of maximum dependency, as well as a time of complete helplessness for the infant.

Even among some subhuman species the survival of the mother and offspring depends on the support of the father, while for other species the biological role of the male is "to impregnate the female and then to disappear. And yet in all human societies the father is regarded by tradition as indispensable" (Malinowski, 1930:13). Scott (1972:581) suggests that:

> the problems of reproduction in human society are rooted in physiology. Humans are primates, and primate infants are extremely helpless and dependent. Except as there exists some agent which feeds its infants and protects them from harm, the human species will disappear. And the human infant is not only dependent but also extremely ignorant. Human intelligence and its cultural elaboration through human social organization is the key to man's domination of all other species. But humans—indeed all primates—raised in social isolation remain remark-

ably stupid and unable to cope with their environment.... Man's potential for learning is of course great. But without a rather specialized environment for learning he learns next to nothing.

No wonder so many different social organizations and institutions have been created to facilitate the development of raw human potential. One concomitant of the organization of the family as a social institution is what Bronislaw Malinowski called "the principle of legitimacy." He stated that:

> the most important moral and legal rule concerning the physiological side of kinship is that no child should be brought into the world without a man—and one man at that—assuming the role of sociological father, that is, guardian and protector, the male link between the child and the rest of the community.... The form which the principle of legitimacy assumes varies according to the laxity or stringency which obtains regarding prenuptial intercourse; according to the value set upon virginity or the contempt for it; according to the ideas held by the natives as to the mechanism of procreation; above all, according to whether the child is a burden or asset to its parents.... Broadly speaking, an unmarried mother is under a ban, a fatherless child is a bastard. This is by no means only a European or Christian prejudice; it is the attitude found amongst most barbarous and savage peoples as well. (1930:13)

The principle of legitimacy developed out of Malinowski's work as an anthropologist studying primitive groups, in particular the Trobriand Islanders. As a proposed universal sociological law, it required further research and testing. Almost twenty years later, George Murdock (1949) gathered together and summarized the vast literature, produced by hundreds of investigators, on 250 societies of the world. Although 70 percent of those societies allowed some form or occasion for sexual license, none of them accepted childbirth out of wedlock. No matter how varied the definitions and rituals of marriage and kinship structure, virtually all societies distinguish between legitimacy and illegitimacy of birth and apply penalties to unmarried parents and, in many cases, to illegitimate children. Illegitimacy, therefore, involves the absence of legitimacy, but the most important aspect is not a "formal law," but the recognition by the social group of the rights and responsibilities of parenthood.

The related social sanctions vary, but those of a primitive group lacking written language or legal codes may be even more forceful than those of contemporary societies with their complex legal systems.

The rule of legitimacy has been challenged from time to time by two basic sets of data. Studies of matrilineal groups, such as Kathleen Gough's of the Nayar of Kerala, are often cited as an exception to the rule. However, Gough (1959) disputes these interpretations of her original field reports. She claims that although the women are relatively independent of husbands and fathers, the notion of fatherhood is not lacking in such societies and marriage does serve to establish the legitimacy of children. In matrilineal systems of kinship, the mother's brother serves as the sociological father: hence illegitimacy is impossible as long as a mother has a natural or classificatory brother. Moreover, matrilineage itself is quite rare and not easily adapted to modern conditions.

A second challenge to the principle comes from some of those who have studied illegitimacy in the Caribbean area. Because births out of wedlock make up so large a proportion (from 40 to as high as 74 percent) of all births in that area, some authors have concluded that such births are expected and accepted as normal. These authors have inferred beliefs and values from behavior. But the values, beliefs, and expectations of human beings are not necessarily consistent with their actions, and the study of human behavior must take this complexity into account. The important point is that research in the Caribbean by Judith Blake (1961) and others (summarized by William Goode, 1961) all remind us that the ideal of legitimacy prevails, even though it is not always adhered to in practice.[1]

ILLEGITIMACY AS A CONCEPT

DEFINITION

Illegitimacy is broadly defined as the state of being of illegitimate birth (from the Latin *illegitimus* or "not in accord with the law"), that is, born outside a legal marital unit. Because laws develop from

---

[1] Similarly, the miscellaneous sexual relationships or alternative family forms accepted by some contemporary groups should not be interpreted as acceptance of illegitimacy. Very few individuals prefer that children be born without a unit committed to child care. The only unit obligated to the long years of care is the recognized family.

the culture of the society or are imposed on it by some group, and because words and their meanings are socially determined, it would be surprising to find any concept defined uniformly by all the human groups around the world. What we are primarily interested in is the fact that all societies define some births as occurring within and others outside of socially approved and recognized—that is "legitimate"—units. We therefore use the societal definition and records of illegitimate births.

Because the label "illegitimate" is given by the social group and because it carries some negative connotations, some people have suggested that to do away with the burden on the illegitimate child we need only do away with the word. But the situation itself would not thereby be eliminated, and as long as it remains worthy of notice, a new expression would arise to denote it. The term of reference is less important than the condition and its consequences. If we were to eliminate the label "illegitimate," as many nations no longer use the term "bastard," we would not significantly alter the child's situation, "Indeed, overconcern with nomenclature carries with it the danger that a legislature, having outlawed an unpleasant word, may come to think that it has solved an unpleasant problem" (Krause, 1971:21).

TYPES

Although we do not now have enough data to distinguish which types of illegitimacy prevail in each of the societies of the world, we will briefly present two well-known typologies. Determining the relative importance of different types for specific social groups requires detailed national studies.[2]

The general rule of legitimacy was amplified by Kingsley Davis (1939b) to tie it more closely to a number of specific rights and obligations as well as to connect it to the general theory of the family as a social institution. He relates the disapproval of illegitimacy directly to the social concern for reproduction within an organized system of cooperative behavior that will guarantee the care and

---

[2] Adulterous illegitimacies in England (Hartley, 1969b), consensual unions in Jamaica (Hartley, 1969a), and historical concubinage in Japan (Hartley, 1969a, and 1970b) have been examined through available data.

socialization of children. Davis distinguishes five specific norms of childbirth, which, when violated, form nine major structural types of illegitimacy.

The first norm is simply that procreation should come after the parties are married. The form of illegitimacy that results when this rule is violated is illegitimacy by fornication. The second norm forbids adulterous procreation. Violations may take three forms: one-sided adultery with the illegitimate mother married, one-sided adultery with the illegitimate father married, and "symmetrical" adultery, in which both parents are married to other persons.

A third group of cases go against the law of nonincestuous procreation. Violations may be in the form of brother-sister, father-daughter, or mother-son incest. Intercaste illegitimacy violates the fourth norm of caste endogamy where this prevails. Celibate illegitimacy would violate the fifth principle of nonreproduction of celibate groups where these exist.

William Goode has more recently suggested that the types of illegitimacy might be increased in number and rearranged according to the increasing degree of likely social disapproval. "The ordering also follows roughly the degree of apparent disruption in the social structure caused by the illegitimacy. . . . This tentative ranking will have to be qualified by empirical research, especially directed toward ascertaining *who* or *which* categories of persons disapprove more or less of each type of illegitimacy." Goode's (1964:23) ordering of types according to increasing disapproval or disruption is as follows:

1. Consensual union
2. Concubinage where it is institutionalized (traditional China and Japan)
3. Lower-class illegitimacy
4. Liaison of nobleman with mistress in preindustrial Western society
5. Childbirth during betrothal
6. Casual relationship, followed by marriage
7. Adulterous, only the man being married
8. Union of a person in a celibate status with either another celibate or a noncelibate
9. Adulterous, only the woman being married
10. Adulterous, both parties being married
11. Union of upper-caste women with lower-caste man

12. Incestuous, brother-sister
13. Incestuous, father-daughter
14. Incestuous, mother-son

No matter how one prefers to rank the types of illegitimacy, the relative importance of the forms varies from society to society and from one historical period to another. It is an example par excellence of a socially determined category.

We will view illegitimacy as a societal rather than a purely individual[3] phenomenon. In order to discover the societal factors that contribute to reported levels, we must conduct a detailed examination of societies in which illegitimacy is low as well as high, and those in which illegitimacy is decreasing, as well as those in which it is increasing. Studies of contributory factors and of effects are hampered by a scarcity of data, yet we will bring together both direct and indirect indicators of underlying causes and consequences of illegitimacy.

RESEARCH ON THE EFFECTS OF ILLEGITIMACY

It is not possible to sort out the independent effects of illegitimacy from the confounding effects of interrelated factors such as rejection of pregnancy, not really wanting the child, the poor health care of the mother, lack of a stable father figure, etc. Yet, it is in part because these factors are often closely interconnected that human groups tend to prefer that children be born within, rather than outside of wedlock.

We have noted that neglected children, deprived of friendly human interaction, do not develop their capacities for physical, social, and verbal maturation. There have been extreme cases in which children who were relatively isolated from human contact before being found at about six years of age had not developed the capacity to sit or crawl, much less walk or talk or do anything else considered "normal" for a young child (Davis, 1948:204 ff.). The human, as compared to subhuman animals, has not only a much longer period of complete dependence but also a much greater learning capacity. The more

---

[3] See the plethora of social casework or interview studies that focus on the psyche of the unmarried mother, especially Young, 1954; Cattell, 1966; and yearly reports of the National Council on Illegitimacy; also Chaskel, 1967; Jones et al., 1966; and Perlman, 1964; among others.

complex the culture, the more there is for each individual to acquire. Human interaction and the adequacy of basic language learning are crucial for our ability to think, to plan ahead, to create, to invent, to become fully human. We have a number of indications that human interaction differs, on the average, for children born in and out of wedlock. Although we lack data on the specific consequences of illegitimacy for all societies, we do have some research results that may offer clues as to why people do prefer legitimacy.

CONSEQUENCES FOR THE CHILD

The fact that a child has been born out of wedlock does not mean that he will not grow up to be a useful member of society. Nor are children born within wedlock assured a trouble-free childhood and smooth transition to adult status. However, the *probabilities* of a healthful, satisfying, and productive life are vastly different for the two categories.

1. In every nation for which data are available, the probability of fetal or infant mortality is higher for illegitimate than for legitimate maternities (U.N. *Demographic Yearbook*, 1965). Although mortality differentials for the two have narrowed greatly in recent years in the medically advanced nations, infant mortality rates in the United States are 73 percent higher for children of unmarried mothers than for legitimate children (U.S., H.E.W., 1971:3).[4] This is related to the fact that unmarried mothers averaged fewer visits to medical doctors during pregnancy than married women even within the lowest income category (U.S., H.E.W., 1968b:6).

2. General health and emotional stability may be impaired for children born out of wedlock. In the United States, median birth weight is lower for both white and nonwhite illegitimate births than for legitimate babies, and the percentage of immature infants (weighing 2,500 grams or less) is higher for illegitimate than for legitimate

---

[4] The difference was less pronounced for nonwhites than for whites, because nonwhites have had far higher infant mortality rates than whites regardless of legitimacy status.

My appreciation to Ms. Stephanie Ventura of the Natality Statistics Branch, U.S. Department of Health, Education, and Welfare for pointing out that "the differential in fetal mortality by legitimacy status for the population other than white is relatively small."

births (U.S., H.E.W., 1968a:65).[5] In addition, syphilitic infants have been markedly more frequent among those born out of wedlock.

Edward Pohlman (1967:148-50) has summarized dozens of research reports indicating that emotional upset during pregnancy has many negative effects on the fetus, infant, and child. As we will see below, unwed mothers are consistently classified as overanxious, neurotic (at least following pregnancy), or even psychotic. Whether the emotional strain affects the fetal environment or only the interaction between mother and child, there is a high probability that these offspring will have continuing emotional problems.

In "A Study of the Adjustment of Teenage Children Born Out of Wedlock" the Welfare Council of Toronto and its District (1943:5-20) found that 47 percent of these 92 young people were described as "maladjusted." As early as age 14 or 15, over 20 percent had had outstanding behavior problems called to the attention of authorities. Unfortunately the report did not offer evidence on percentages for legitimate teenagers.

Another study contrasted legitimate and illegitimate Negro children of comparable economic and social circumstances in grades 4 through 12. All were recipients of "aid to dependent children" in one county in Missouri. The legitimate children were found to rate higher than the illegitimates on I.Q. tests, age-grade placement, subsets of the California Test of Personality, teachers' ratings, and academic grades. The only variable examined that did not differ was school absence. Most important was the finding that differences were consistently greater among the older children (Jenkins, 1958). This implies that children disadvantaged by birth out of wedlock are less likely than children of comparable circumstances to develop their innate capacities, and thus they fall farther behind their peers each year.

A follow-up study of requests for legal abortion that were refused by the Swedish authorities found (21 years later) that the unwanted children had been very much overrepresented by births out of wedlock that were never legitimized. In spite of the excellent social services of Sweden, researchers found that indicators of an insecure childhood appeared two to five times more frequently among the children whose mothers had been denied abortions than among a sample matched

---

[5]If it had been possible to control for social class, these differences might have been reduced.

in other respects (Forssman and Thuwe, 1971). Unfortunately, the measures of insecurity were not separately specified for the subgroup of illegitimate births. Nevertheless, the "unwanted" classification is revealing in itself. In at least one group of unwed mothers who were asked, 90 percent declared that the child was unwanted (Hill and Jaffe, 1965).

3. Although adoption seems to offer a happy solution, in most societies, only a small proportion of illegitimate children are adopted or later legitimized by the marriage of the parents. The number of adoptions (including legitimate as well as illegitimate children) and legitimations vary from country to country, but they are typically in the minority, often affecting only about 5 percent of births out of wedlock (see U.N. Sub-Commission, 1967:216 ff.). It appears that the smaller the proportion of births that occur out of wedlock in a given country or for a subgroup, the higher the proportions adopted. In the United States recent increases in the illegitimacy rate have led adoption agencies to liberalize their policies, reducing parental age and financial requirements, yet in 1967 there were 2.5 million illegitimate children in the country awaiting adoption ("Parent Shortage," 1967). While "desirable" infants may be in short supply, less attractive, older, or ethnically or racially different children remain unwanted for the most part.

4. Although the state may supply monetary support, the amount is usually less than a steadily employed father would earn. Furthermore, money is only one of many contributions of a father to his family. The lack of a stable father figure, the completion of a nuclear family, cannot be overcome by government fiat. Nor can the state or its social service agents daily enact the role of father. Just as the child needs the emotional and financial support of the father, most mothers need his emotional and financial support in order to feel adequate to fulfill their roles.

5. Children from fatherless families exhibit a number of deleterious effects (Benson, 1968). Boys from fatherless homes have been found by a number of researchers to be less vigorous, less well adjusted in their peer relations, more likely to strive for compensatory masculinity, more immature, more anxious about sex, and more effeminate than boys who had consistent fathering (Winch, 1949; Stephens, 1961; Lynn and Sawrey, 1959; Sears, 1951; McCandless, 1967; Wynn, 1964). A cross-cultural study (Mischel, 1961) found that a greater proportion

of fatherless children were impulsive and chose immediate rewards over those that must be delayed. Girls from fatherless homes showed greater dependence on their mothers than girls from homes in which the father was present (Lynn and Sawrey, 1959).[6] Using the technique of "anonymous confession," Siegman (1966) found that antisocial behavior of the sort likely to get a youngster into serious trouble was reported more often by father-absent young men than by those whose fathers had been in the home. Siegman suggests that the absence of the father may lead the young boy to confuse being "good" with being feminine; to be masculine, he must be "bad." John Clausen (1961) notes that a disproportionate number of prostitutes, drug addicts, unwed mothers, and other deviants came from homes lacking a *stable* male head—a larger category than that of "father absence" alone.

6. Research also indicates that the "natural" father is unlikely to maintain any consistent relationship with the mother and child out of wedlock. A follow-up study of mothers who kept their babies (Reed and Latimer, 1963) showed that less than 10 percent of the fathers had consistently kept in touch with the mothers and children for even a few months after the birth out of wedlock. Only 12 percent contributed any financial support and then usually only as required by court order.

7. The unwed mother, then, is likely to be the main agent of socialization for the child born out of wedlock. Yet Harrison Gough (1961) found unwed mothers to be among the least adequately socialized persons (scoring above only women in jails) on his scale of socialization. As will be evident in chapter 3, I do not agree with those studies that find all unwed mothers pathological in some sense. Yet it is not realistic to suppose that unmarried mothers in general would be most adequate to help their offspring mature into constructive group members. Furthmore, researchers comparing unwed mothers who kept their babies with those who surrendered them have found that the former tend to be lower in intelligence, lower in ego strength or emotional stability, and more submissive (W. C. Jones et al., 1966:201-17 and James P. Cattell, M.D., 1966:95-104). The least competent of unwed mothers, then seem to be those who elect to maintain control over their children.

---

[6]For qualifications to the above, see the review by Herzog & Sudia (n.d.) who note that some fatherless families are cohesive and warm.

8. Recent research on the "battered-child syndrome" indicates that children born out of wedlock are the ones most likely to be abused. In a study of 313 cases, Simons and Downs (1966) found that children born out of wedlock were about three and one-half times more likely to be among the abused than their proportion in the population.

9. Devereaux (1960:15) reports that in primitive societies an unwed mother "may be required to kill her own child, or cannibalism may be imposed on the child of a prohibited union. . . . In other groups the child may face ridicule, or lack social status—a name and place in the tribal group."

CONSEQUENCES FOR THE MOTHER

Among primitives, a woman with a child may find chances of marriage enhanced, unaffected, or severely impaired depending on tribal traditions. Although numerous tribes permit premarital sexual license, an unmarried mother is sometimes in such disgrace that she may be killed or beaten or otherwise shamed.

In contemporary societies, the majority of unwed mothers are very young. Often the girl must drop out of school, or she may lack interest in schooling even if able to continue. There is little chance for the young unwed mother to develop fully the skills that would be useful to herself and the child (see Campbell, 1968:238). The more complex the society, the more disadvantaged in this respect is the young unwed mother and her child.

In an 18-month follow-up study of 262 unwed mothers who kept their babies, Sauber and Rubinstein (1965) found that the problems of the mother varied according to their ages. Overall they expressed a need for counseling services, more adequate housing, income adequate to maintenance, educational continuity and child care services. No one suggests that the woman's situation in life is improved by the addition of a child out of wedlock.

Research indicates that being alone and lacking a secure commitment on the part of the child's father affects the mother's self-esteem (Jones et al., 1966; Vincent, 1961; Cattell, 1966). And we know from a series of studies that the child's self-esteem is directly related to that of the mother (Coopersmith, 1967).

Even where financial support is not a problem, the emotional warmth, security, and consistency so important in child rearing are less likely to be available to the illegitimate child than to the legitimate child. The unwed mother may even expect the growing child to provide emotional support for *her* and may interpret the child's crying as a personal rejection.

Although a recent study indicates that the anxiety or neurosis of the unwed mother follows rather than precedes pregnancy (Pauker, 1969), almost all studies comment on the very high anxiety levels of unmarried mothers. The fact that those who keep their children have even higher levels of neurosis on the average than those who give them up for adoption holds little promise for the future of these mother-child relationships.

It is easy to suggest that society ought to provide more services to help the unwed mother and her child, and often that is possible and true. Yet no matter how fine the services provided, "society" is an abstraction and can provide only the most abstract and impersonal fathering.

CONSEQUENCES FOR THE FATHER

Studies of the unwed father are far less common than those of unwed mothers, in part because the father is so much less visible. In fact, for every thirty studies of unwed mothers, there is only one of unwed fathers (Vincent, 1962a:451). The unwed father is a "problem" for social welfare agencies only if he is known to them. In that case he has, in addition to the normal emotional problems of fatherhood, the very real distress of possible "court action, potential long-term involvement, loss of schooling and ultimate socioeconomic achievement, unfavorable publicity that could hurt him or his family socially and financially, and so forth" (LaBarre, 1969:25). In addition "industrialization and technological advance both put a very high premium on more and more education. There are notoriously fewer and fewer jobs for the unskilled and semiskilled, and young people who do not or cannot accept the challenge of further personal discipline and more education are doomed to a substandard socioeconomic status" (ibid.). The young man may have been using sex to try to prove his masculinity and maturity; yet "ultimate maturity in human beings always consists in taking responsibility for others in some form or other" (ibid., p. 26). "Flight into purely pseudoadult-hood [through sex] can be dangerous to all concerned" when youthful identity problems are aggravated by parenthood (ibid.).

In a study of over 1,000 cases, Vincent (1962b) concludes that contrary to common assumption, unmarried fathers experience fairly intense conflicting feelings toward the females they impregnate and the children they beget. Because they commonly take advantage of anonymity and irresponsibility does not mean that they lack problems of remorse and guilt; shirking of responsibility may make them feel robbed of masculinity. Unmarried fathers resolve their feelings partly by devising derogatory stereotypes about the unwed mother.[7] If he moves on without taking responsibility, however, his irresponsibility may be reinforced and repeated.

The Scandinavian countries have made a consistent attempt to hold fathers responsible for their children out of wedlock. Beginning early in this century, Denmark, Finland, Norway, and Sweden passed laws stating that sexual relations with the mother are enough to establish a maintenance order for child support (U.N. Sub-Commission, 1967). The child is also entitled to the father's name. Only in Norway was the father's responsibility settled in 100 percent of the cases (Nelson, 1953). Norway is one of the few countries registering a long-term decline in births out of wedlock. Yet the law sanctioning the mother's sexual partner was liberalized in 1956, and there has since been a slight rise in rates and ratios of illegitimacy.

CONSEQUENCES FOR THE SOCIAL GROUP OR SOCIETY

The survival and development of the individual human being as well as the continuity of a society and its cultural pattern, depend on the socialization process. Social control over child care and thus over the social unit responsible for it has become more important to the extent that the human animal in its evolution has come to depend increasingly on culture (knowledge, beliefs, norms, and values) rather than instincts or drives. The society has come to depend on

---

[7] Faulting the mother is especially appealing for men who fathered children when they were in the armed services stationed abroad. Recognizing that they are unlikely to be held responsible for the children produced, servicemen may be unconcerned about preventing conceptions. The thousands of fatherless children remaining after every major war are a long-term reminder of those difficult years.

the effectiveness of socialization, on how well the child acquires the values, attitudes and behavior of his community and family. Thus, the community has an interest in its members' choices of mates and in the conditions of childbirth and child rearing.

As Judith Blake suggests, "the question of alternative modes of meeting the societal need for reproduction and child training is as important for our understanding of human society as is the question of alternative economic and political systems" (1961:21). However much variety we find in societal patterns of family stucture and however individuals are designated as the sexual role models, it has been suggested that "always and everywhere children of both sexes need both male and female role models" (LaBarre, 1969:26). Children moreover need warm, stable relationships so that they may learn a sense of trust in the human environment (See Spitz, 1964; Erikson, 1963). The tasks of early childhood socialization— (1) the provision of nurture and loving care, and the training and channeling of physiological needs; (2) the teaching of language, perceptual skills, and so forth; (3) the orienting of the child to his world of kin, neighborhood, community, and society; (4) the transmitting of cultural and subcultural goals and values; (5) the promotion of interpersonal skills; and (6) the guiding of the child toward self-actualization (Clausen 1968:138ff.)—cannot be carried out as well by unwed mothers. On the average these women are less secure emotionally and less well socialized to the larger human group (Gough, 1961), more ambivalent and inconsistent in named values or goals (Vincent, 1961), and limited in community and even neighborhood relationships. They typically spend 5 to 18 hours a day watching television and frequently limit their reading to the comics in the newspapers (see Reeder, 1965). Eighty-two out of 118 mothers who kept their babies reported that they had no hobbies or creative interests (Reed and Latimer, 1963). Even when the grandmother helps with the care of the child, there may be a questionable repetition of the mother's own socialization. There is in these cases a "conflict between the physical creation of children and the development of capable and responsible adults" (Blake, 1961:21).

If a society recognizes the disadvantages of socialization by the unwed mother and tries to provide alternatives, problems and costs multiply alarmingly. For example, we know that large, well-run, hygienic and nutritionally superior institutions are detrimental to the development of children (Spitz, 1964). Yet, there are never enough foster homes for those in need, and group homes for children are incredibly expensive to staff.[8]

If we accept the interdependence of human group life, it becomes clear that a loss of potential for any individual becomes a loss for the whole group. Because births out of wedlock do not typically lead to a maximization of human potentialities, we should attempt to understand the phenomenon and its the causes at the societal level.

Furthermore, since population growth for the world as a whole, and for less-developed nations in particular has reached unprecedented levels (Hartley, 1972), it is important to examine segments of fertility that might be reduced. As we will see in chapter 2, there are many nations in which births out of wedlock contribute 25 to 75 percent of all births. If we add births conceived out of wedlock but legitimated before birth to those issuing as illegitimate, the proportions of these typically unplanned births are sizable even in many of the advanced, westernized nations (see chapter 8 and Hartley, 1971). A reduction in these births would lessen the problems associated with population growth of the world. And, in more general terms, increased acceptance of responsibility for parenthood is absolutely necessary to further the idea of and progress toward population limitation.

CROSS-NATIONAL FOCUS

The cross-national study of illegitimacy takes us away from the more traditional psychological and social service approach to the social group, or societal, level of analysis. The fact that measures of illegitimacy—rates, ratios, and numbers—do not vary randomly but are patterned according to their social environment means that illegitimacy may be treated as a "social fact"[9] or societal phenomenon, rather than as the "deviant" or idiosyncratic behavior of individuals.

---

[8] The problems surrounding these alternatives are a part of the reason social groups seem to prefer establishment of parental responsibility. (Experiments in communal child rearing in the Israeli Kibbutzim arose from very rare commitments similar to those of an extended family, and yet even these have led over time toward the more traditional nuclear family form.)

[9] A social fact as originally described by Durkheim (1962) and exemplified in his classic *Suicide* involves a manifestation of collective life external to any individual, yet influencing the behavior of individuals as a part of the collectivity.

In other words the subject requires sociological, rather than strictly psychological, research and analysis. The various levels and trends of births out of wedlock may be seen as a reflection of the patterns of human group life—the social structure—and the related beliefs, values, and expectations—the culture—of a whole society or of a subcultural group within it.

International concern about illegitimacy is implied in a series of studies begun in 1927 by the League of Nations (1929, 1932, 1939). The United Nations has collected and published national data on births out of wedlock in those editions of the *Demographic Yearbook* featuring birth statistics, and its Sub-Commission on the Prevention of Discrimination and Protection of Minorities published *The Study of Discrimination Against Persons Born Out of Wedlock* in 1967. Such broad-based interest in this question on the part of national representatives—even of those countries unable to contribute reliable data—indicates the universal level of concern about illegitimacy.

Even with the expertise of these international organizations and their summary list of 29 factors leading to births out of wedlock, we have not had a scheme of analysis capable of drawing together the myriad variables related to the diverse levels of births out of wedlock. I believe the model established in chapter 4 will be useful to future investigations as more detailed national data become available.

2. International Levels and Trends: An Overview

THE MASS of data available for the international study of illegitimacy provides the reader with the opportunity to find broad patterns and to study the range of variation in the different measures used. Over seventy countries have reported information on the percentages of birth out of wedlock, and more than forty have provided data for the computation of illegitimacy rates. The data presented in this chapter provide us tools for understanding illegitimacy at the societal level and constitute an integral part of the total study, to be used as reference material throughout the later chapters.

These statistics reveal many surprises. Poor countries, for example, are as likely to register low as high levels of illegitimacy. Similarly, the notion that industrialization and urbanization tend to increase illegitimacy may go unchallenged without reference to the figures. Chapter 3 will use the information presented here to question many traditional notions about the causes of births out of wedlock.

PROBLEMS ENCOUNTERED IN INTERNATIONAL COMPARISONS

There are two drawbacks in any attempt to make worldwide comparisons of illegitimacy. In the first place, for many of the countries of the world, there are no available statistics on any of the several measures of illegitimacy. Secondly, the information that is available may be assumed to be of less than perfect accuracy and comparability.

AVAILABILITY OF DATA

The Population Division of the United Nations has facilitated a variety of international comparative studies. The annual publication, beginning in 1948, of the *Demographic Yearbook* (especially of those volumes detailing fertility), has made the present study possible. Over seventy major nations have provided some data on illegitimacy, yet many cannot do so. In response to a special *Study of Discrimination Against Persons Born Out of Wedlock*, the 33 countries listed in Table 1 reported that they had no data available on illegitimate births. While many of these were small nations, many were also among the largest in the world, e.g., India, Pakistan, and the Soviet Union (U.N. Sub-Commission, 1967:216-24). Mainland China, not then a member of the United Nations, likewise offers no information on illegitimacy to the world community.

Table 1. Nations Reporting No Data Available on Births Out of Wedlock

Afganistan	Nepal
Burma	Niger
Cameroon	Nigeria*
Ceylon	Pakistan
Cuba	Philippines*
Ghana	Republic of Korea
Guatemala*	Republic of Vietnam
Hungary*	Romania*
India	Sierra Leone
Iraq	Sudan
Ivory Coast	Thailand
Jordan	Turkey
Kenya	Uganda
Laos	Union of Soviet Socialist Republics*
Lebanon	United Republic of Tanzania
Malaysia	Western Samoa
Mali	

SOURCE: U.N. Sub-Commission (1967: 216–24).

* These nations have furnished some statistical data on illegitimacy in other sources.

ACCURACY AND COMPARABILITY

The statistical information that is available on worldwide illegiti-macy does not allow an absolutely accurate comparative analysis because of the different bases and methods used for the compilation of statistics in the many nations. In most countries, the figures refer to live births, while in some they refer to total births, including stillbirths. On some occasions (e.g., Brazil) the information is supplied with reservations on its value. Finally, it should be noted that there are many countries in which the registration of births does not cover the total population. In some cases the exclusion of particular (tribal) groups is deliberate; in other cases there is inadvertent nonreporting by relatively isolated rural groups or a difference in registrations of in- versus out-of-the-hospital deliveries.

In considering the implications of the international comparisons of illegitimacy, it should be noted that social attitudes toward illegitimacy govern the amount of concealment that may be practiced and, thus, the accuracy of the basic figures. Where consensual unions are widespread there is less incentive to conceal births out of wedlock; hence the resulting illegitimacy ratios may be closer to true proportions than they are in the areas where such unions are frowned on. We must realize, therefore, that international comparisons are not entirely trustworthy as *absolute* measures of illegitimacy.

How, then, is it possible to study illegitimacy as a societal phenomenon? Should we wait for more perfect counting before we begin our analysis? On the contrary, since we are dealing with populations in the millions and births in the thousands, hundreds of thousands, and even millions, it is unrealistic to hope for complete accuracy. Many of our most thought-provoking sociological studies (e.g., suicide, crime, and delinquency) work with imperfect data, some of which is concealed. Finally, interest in and research on social phenomena often stimulate improvement in the collection of relevant information.

Therefore, if allowances are made for under registration and reporting, the available data can give a good idea of the problem in relative terms. It is certainly unlikely that the illegitimacy figures of any country are *lower* than the official data given. In view of the complexities of recording vital statistics (and gathering census information), it is fortunate that we do have some data on births out of wedlock for over seventy of the major countries of the world. The United Nations has not only stimulated the gathering and reporting of demographic data but also encouraged the improvement of techniques of obtaining information. Where the United Nations demographers have reason to question the reliability of specific data reported by member nations, some indication is made to this effect.[1] The quality code is usually heavily dependent on the member country's own evaluation, however.

---

[1] Notations on questionable data are indicated in figure 1.

Although there are some deficiencies and distortions in the international data, available information is adequate in most cases, and excellent in some, for our comparisons of illegitimacy over time and space.[2]

OPERATIONALIZING ILLEGITIMACY

In the introductory chapter we examined a general definition of illegitimacy and discussed the social source of labeling and attributing meaning to concepts. Illegitimacy is taken to be the state or condition of having been born out of wedlock, that is, to parents who are not married to one another. Legitimacy, its opposite, is the state of having been born within wedlock, *having specified rights and obligations.* Legal statutes merely formalize social recognition that is the basis of family identification. Allowing that some portion of all births out of wedlock will be unknown, our "operational" definition of illegitimate births will be those that are registered or recognized[3] and reported as such by local or national government agencies. Phillips Cutright has taken an exhaustive look at the criticisms and evidence relating to the quality of the illegitimacy reporting in the United States. He concludes (1973a:432) that the "alleged differences in the concealment of white and nonwhite illegitimate births are less than one might suspect. The count of (illegitimate) births . . . appears to be . . . reasonably accurate."

Consensual unions, involving persons who are living together as man and wife without any socially recognized form of marriage, cannot be considered legal unions unless they are redefined. Offspring of these unions are, therefore, considered illegitimate unless a reregistration of birth occurs after the marriage of the parents.[4] The meaning of "consensual" unions varies form from one social group to another.

---

[2] In a general discussion of the problems encountered in international comparisons, Davis suggests that "even incorrect information about something important is better than none at all, at least when its defects are approximately known and therefore are subject to correction." See Kingsley Davis (n.d.).

[3] Even in places where registration does not allow, much less require, indication of illegitimate status there are a number of ways of recognizing births out of wedlock on birth registration forms. See Beth Berkov (1968).

[4] In Trinidad and Tobago, for instance, where "living" arrangements and consensual unions involve a significant proportion of the population, during the period from 1959 through 1963 there occurred 6,760 such re-registrations, or about eleven per hundred births out of wedlock. See United Nations Subcommission (1967).

 me these unions may be short lived, for the most part, while
her places, or for other persons, the unions may endure until
the death of one of the partners. The usual indication of a consensual
union is that there is no social or legal commitment and no social
control to channel the rights and duties of partners, much less their
offspring. (We will discuss information on consensual unions in some
detail as we examine theories related to such unions in chapter 3).

MEASURES OF ILLEGITIMACY

There are three commonly used indicators of the level of illegitimacy in a society.[5] These are the absolute *numbers* of illegitimate
births, their *ratio* or relation to all births, and their *rate* per 1,000
unmarried women in the childbearing ages. The three measures offer
diverse information, and they may actually move in opposite directions. That is not to say that the measures themselves are independent
of one another; they all have one quantity in common—the number
of illegitimate births—but two involve computations that use different
denominators.

NUMBER

The absolute number of illegitimate births is normally obtained
from a registration system designed by the national government. We
have already noted the problem of definiton and registration of births
out of wedlock and our necessary reliance on the data that is provided
by each nation. The absolute number of births out of wedlock is
of greatest concern to social welfare directors and staff within each
country. These persons are employed in helping to meet the needs
of mother and child, and the extent of their task is largely determined
by the absolute numbers involved.

For international comparisons absolute numbers are less useful
than relative indices of illegitimacy, because total populations, their
fertility levels, and the proportions of women unmarried all vary

---

[5] See Hartley (1969a:28-29) for formulae to compute other illegitimacy measures
not presently in use: crude illegitimate birth rate, total illegitimate fertility rates, and
gross illegitimate reproduction rates. Arthur Campbell has suggested another illegitimate birth rate (per 1,000 women 15 to 44), See Kiser et al., (1968: chapter 8).

so greatly among nations. It is important to recognize that numbers could increase or decrease even while ratios and rates remained stable. For instance, with stable rates and ratios population increase alone would mean increasing numbers of births out of wedlock. Therefore, when we refer to illegitimacy levels or trends we will be referring not to absolute numbers but to the measures (ratios and rates) relative to total births or to unmarried women in the population. The numbers of illegitimate births clearly are crucial to the computation of the relative indices of illegitimacy.

RATIO

The illegitimacy ratio is the most frequently used measure in making comparisons of illegitimacy among nations or over time. The ratio is usually expressed as the percentage of all births that are illegitimate, or the number of births out of wedlock per hundred births. It is important to note the specific usage of each country, however, as some nations report the ratio as the number of illegitimate births per *thousand* live births.

Computation

The usual calculation is as follows:

The illegitimacy ratio = The number of illegitimate births ÷ the number of illegitimate plus legitimate births (total births) X 100

$$\text{or, } R = \frac{I}{I + L} \times 100$$

The advantage of the ratio is that it indicates the proportions of *all* births that occur outside legal marital units. The measure is independent of the overall level of fertility or differences in proportions of women who are unmarried. It reveals the extent to which illegitimacy maintains its relative importance, even as fertility in general increases or decreases. For the more developed countries we can see the relative contribution of illegitimate births over a long history of declining fertility, or we can compare the importance of births out of wedlock across nations independent of their high or low levels of total fertility.

The disadvantage of the ratio is that it depends not only on the number of illegitimate births, but also on the number of legitimate births. These, in turn, depend on a number of variables: the age at marriage, the proportion of women married, the amount of the reproductive period spent after or between marriages, and a series of factors governing the exposure to conception (e.g., use or nonuse of contraception, periodic abstinence, fecundity, or infecundity) and successful parturition (Davis and Blake, 1956:211-235). These variables are also patterned over time and space though subject to gradual changes and even some radical shifts, as in wartime. Thus, a shift in any of the variables that would lower legitimate births would force an increase in the ratio even if there were no increase in the number of births out of wedlock.

Recent Data for Nations

Ratios for all major nations for which there are current data are reported in figure 1. I have indicated those nations for which data may be unreliable or for which reporting covers only a portion of the nation. The most immediately apparent feature of the graph is the very great variation in the percentages of births reported as occurring out of wedlock, with Egypt and Syria actually reporting 0.0 and Jamaica 74.1 percent of all births out of wedlock. As we look more closely at the details, the patterning of ratios for nations within geographical areas stands out. Those countries with the very highest illegitimacy ratios, ranging from 41 to 74 percent of births out of wedlock, are the Central American and Caribbean nations. Following these, and ranging as low as 17 and as high as 53 percent of all births illegitimate, are the South American countries. The European nations range downward from about 15 to 1 percent illegitimate. Even within Europe there tends to be a patterning, with the Catholic nations of southern and western Europe lower on the range. For the world as a whole the lowest ratios, from 0.0 to 0.9, are reported by industrial Japan and Israel and the Moslem countries of Africa and the Middle East.

This geographical patterning is curious in itself, and ought to give us some clues in our attempt to find the causes of illegitimacy. But how consistent are the ratios over time? No doubt there has been

Figure 1. Illegitimate Births as a Percentage of Total Live Births in 70 Countries; Rank Order of Ratios for Latest Available Year

Percentage of total births

Year	Country	Percentage
1964	Jamaica	74.1
1967	Panama	70.0
1965	Guatemala	67.4
1968	El Salvador	67.2
1957	Honduras[1]	64.5
1968	Dominican Rep.[1]	61.8
1967	Nicaragua[1]	53.4
1967	Venezuela[1]	53.2
1965	Peru[1]	48.9
1967	Martinique	48.2
1968	Paraguay[1]	43.0
1967	Guadeloupe	41.6
1967	Trinidad & Tobago	41.1
1966	Mozambique[1]	34.3
1962	Surinam	34.1
1963	Angola[1]	32.6
1966	Ecuador[1]	32.2
1967	Iceland	30.0
1966	Argentina	26.4
1967	Costa Rica	25.8
1967	Colombia[1]	23.4
1965	Puerto Rico	23.2
1968	Mexico	22.5
1967	Reunion	20.2
1963	Uruguay[1]	20.0
1967	Chile	17.7
1958	Bolivia[1]	17.2
1969	Sweden	16.3
1968	New Zealand	13.0
1960	Brazil[2]	12.9
1968	Austria	12.0
1967	East Germany	10.7
1966	Denmark	10.2
1968	United States	9.7
1968	Bulgaria	9.6
1970	England & Wales	8.3
1967	Yugoslavia	8.3
1967	Canada	8.3
1967	Australia	7.7
1951	Indonesia (Euro)	7.5
1968	Portugal	7.4
1968	Scotland	7.4
1956	Congo, D.R.[1]	6.7
1967	France	6.1
1968	Norway	5.6
1967	Czechoslovakia	5.4
1967	Finland	5.1
1968	Hungary	5.0
1968	Poland	4.9
1968	West Germany	4.8
1968	Switzerland	3.8
1956	Morocco (So.)[1]	3.8
1968	No. Ireland	3.8
1968	Ireland-Eire	2.6
1967	Belgium	2.5
1967	Philippines[1]	2.5
1967	Italy	2.0
1968	Netherlands	2.0
1968	China-Taiwan	1.6
1968	Spain	1.4
1964	Albania	1.4
1968	Greece	1.1
1967	Japan	0.9
1968	Israel	0.6
1965	Tunisia[1] (Moslem)	0.3
1968	Mauritius	0.3
1965	Algeria[1] (Moslem)	0.2
1961	Nigeria[2] (Lagos)	0.1
1967	U.A.R. Egypt[1]	0.0
1955	U.A.R. Syria[1]	0.0

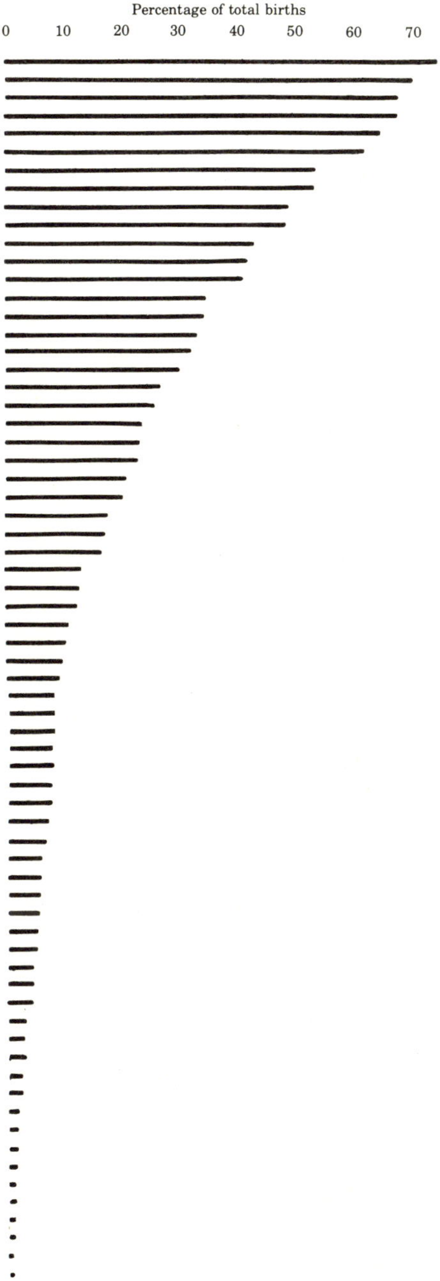

[1]Data are of unknown reliability.
[2]Refers to data from less than the entire country.
SOURCE: U.N. *Demographic Yearbook* (1965 and 1969: table 20) and the Statistical Yearbooks or Vital Statistics of those nations with more recent data.

some variation in the rank ordering of countries with historical records of illegitimacy. If such changes were widespread, the utility of the data given at any one time would be small. What can we learn from the historical records of illegitimacy?

Changes in Illegitimacy Ratios Over Time

In order to examine the ratios over time it is necessary to subdivide the numerous nations offering information in some meaningful way. Since we have already seen in figure 1 that the rank ordering of ratios tends to fall into a geographical or continental pattern, I have organized the following tables and graphs of illegitimacy ratios over time into major geographical divisions. In studying the accompanying graphs it is important to notice the differences in scale of each graph. For instance, the graph for African countries shows one group of ratios from 0.0 to 7.2 and another group from 30.0 to 40.0.

One of the first questions arising as one examines the graphs is whether the visible changes predominate over the stability or patterning of the ratios. In order to obtain a general idea of the extent of change over time, I computed a rank order correlation. Starting with the rank ordering of countries of the world according to their most recently available illegitimacy ratios, as in figure 1, it was possible also to rank most of those nations according to their ratios for 1949 (or alternatively 1950 or 1951 where 1949 was not reported). Paired rankings were thereby obtained for 51 countries. The Spearman rank correlation coefficient computed for these is .89, a correlation that would occur by chance in less than one case in a thousand.[6] The statistical test confirms in a more precise manner what is evident from an examination of the tables: the ratios do not vary at random but are patterned for each country and even for some geographical-cultural areas.

Middle America and the Caribbean: The countries of Middle America evidence a real split in the levels of reported illegitimacy ratios. Mexico and Costa Rica indicate that about 25 percent of all births are registered as illegitimate. These two countries report very

---

[6] I have preferred the ordinal over the interval test of statistical significance, since the interval measure implies a level of precision that cannot be assumed for all ratios listed.

Figure 2. Middle America, Percentage of Live Births Illegitimate, 1949–68

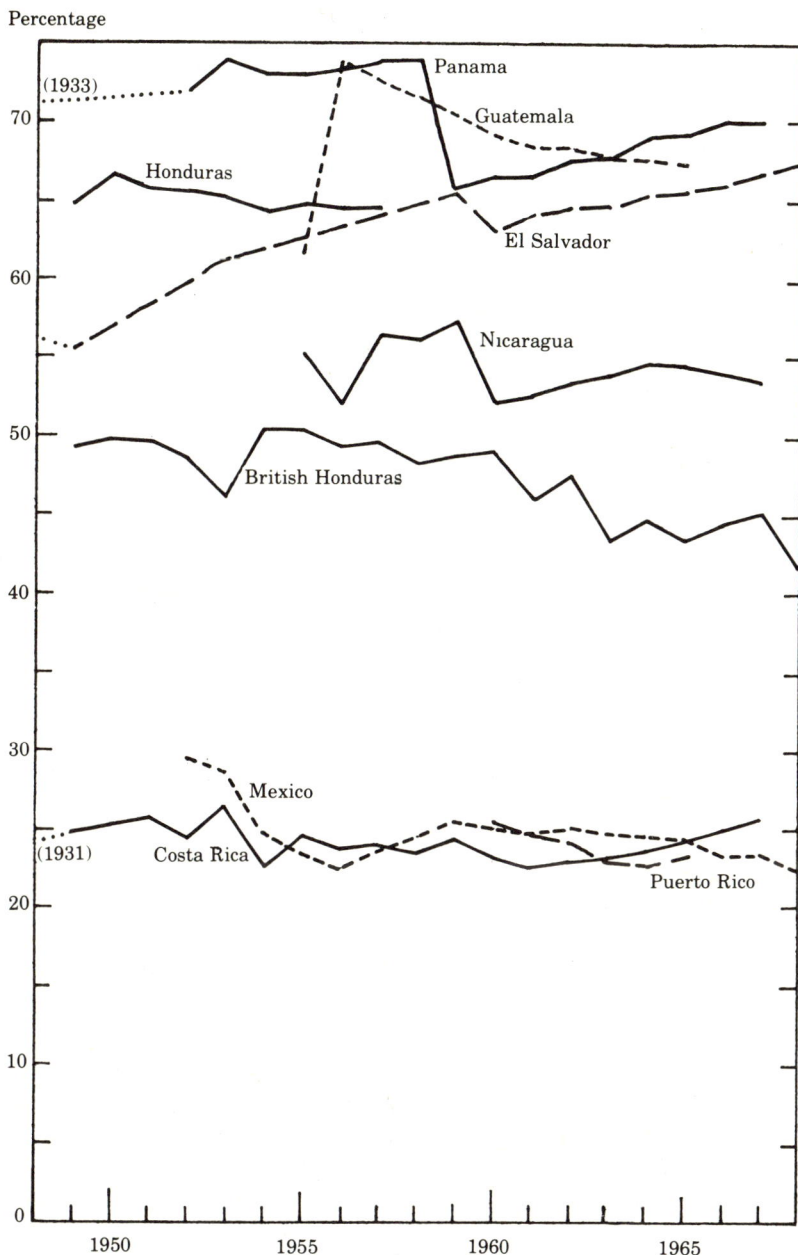

Figure 3. Caribbean, Percentage of Live Births Illegitimate, 1949–68

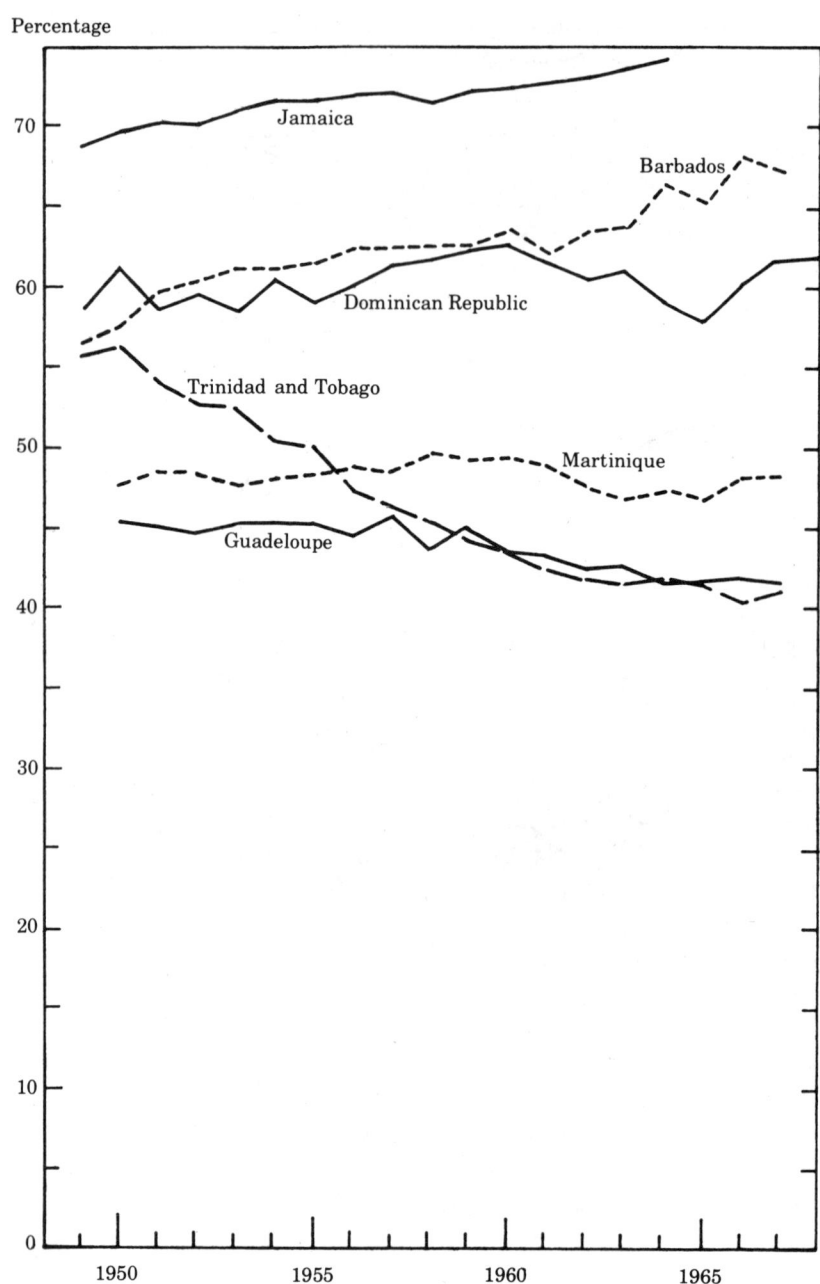

stable ratios over time, at least after a small Mexican decline in 1954. The other countries of the area report far higher illegitimacy ratios, more closely resembling those of the Caribbean area than those of their giant Mexican neighbor.

The data for Honduras, British Honduras, and Nicaragua are considered by United Nations demographers to be of questionable reliability. It is significant, however, that even though less than 90 percent of births are thought to be registered, illegitimate births form a high proportion of those that do get recorded. Because Panama and Guatemala report data with some discontinuities over time, their information would also need further verification before it could be assumed to represent an accurate picture of the levels of illegitimacy. At this point we can only (1) pass on the illegitimacy ratios as reported by each country, (2) note the gulf between the lower and higher levels for the nations reporting, and (3) call for more adequate gathering and reporting of information and more detailed subsequent analyses.

Except for Trinidad and Tobago, the trends for ratios in the Caribbean, wherever changes are occurring, are toward a slight increase in the already extremely high ratios. Are these very high percentages of births out of wedlock simply the result of differences in marriage patterns? Is the consensual union merely a nonlegal equivalent to marraige? If so, why do the governing bodies of these nations record births to such unions as illegitimate? We will be examining the details of illegitimacy in Jamaica, and although we expect that there would be some similarities with other countries in that area, we cannot know where there is concordance and where there are differences without more detailed information on each. A number of the tiny islands of the area included in table 2 have not been graphed; it is enough to note a similarity in patterning.

In Trinidad and Tobago, the *only* political unit with a steady decline in illegitimacy ratios, the crude birth rate has also dropped sharply. Is it possible that the general increase in available means of population control has effected a greater proportional control over births out of wedlock?

In contrast the percentage of all births illegitimate in Jamaica has been slowly increasing, while the crude birth rate was also rising. In an earlier study I found that the increase in age-specific illegitimacy

Table 2. Middle America and Caribbean,

Country	Early Data	1949	1950	1951	1952	1953	1954	1955
Antigua		68.2	68.3	67.5	67.6	66.8	67.8	68.0
Antilles		64.5	65.1	65.0	64.9	64.6	64.9	65.0
Barbados		56.5	57.6	59.7	60.1	61.0	61.0	61.5
Bermuda		27.4	32.9	28.1	29.7	30.6	32.4	32.7
British Honduras*		49.3	49.8	49.5	48.4	46.0	50.2	50.2
Canal Zone					3.2	3.5	3.0	2.7
Costa Rica	(1931) 22.5	24.9	25.1	25.7	24.2	26.3	22.7	24.6
Dominica		62.4	63.7	67.7	64.9	67.8	66.9	67.3
Dominican Republic*		58.8	61.1	58.6	59.5	58.6	60.6	59.0
El Salvador	(1921–25) 59.0	55.6	. . .	. . .	. . .	61.3	. . .	. . .
Grenada		67.7	69.1	68.6	69.6	69.1	69.7	71.9
Guadeloupe			45.2	45.0	44.8	45.2	45.2	45.2
Guatemala	(1928) 52.5							61.7
Honduras		64.9	66.6	65.7	65.6	65.1	64.2	64.6
Jamaica		68.8	69.8	70.2	70.1	70.9	71.6	71.6
Martinique			47.8	48.5	48.3	47.7	48.0	48.2
Mexico		. . .	. . .	. . .	29.3	28.7	24.9	23.3
Netherlands Antilles*		21.3	20.1	21.2	20.1	21.3	21.8	24.2
Nicaragua*					. . .	. . .		55.2
Panama	(1921–25) 70.6							
	(1933) 70.5	. . .	. . .		71.9	73.9	73.1	73.0
Puerto Rico								
St. Kitts-Nevis								
(St. Christopher-								
Nevis) and Anguilla		72.6	68.5	69.1	66.3	68.1	70.4	66.7
St. Lucia		68.6	68.5	69.0	69.4	69.1	71.1	71.3
St. Vincent		72.9	71.8	68.0	73.3	75.9	76.6	77.2
Trinidad and Tobago		55.8	56.2	54.0	52.8	52.4	50.3	50.0

SOURCES: Data prior to 1948 from Wimperis (1960: tables 2a and 2b, Appendix). Data after 1948 from U.N. *Demographic Yearbook,* (1959; 1965: table 20; 1969: table 21).
*Data are of questionable reliability.

rates accounted for the entire rise from 30.9 to 38.1 in the Jamaican crude birth rate between 1948 and 1957 (Hartley, 1969a:159).

Why are the numbers, rates, and ratios of births out of wedlock not declining in all of these countries? Education and contraceptive technology have become more widespread, and economic development, though slow, has made some progress. All these would lead to the expectation of decline in both legitimate and illegitimate fertility.

South America: Within the South American countries that have been studied in detail there were obvious and huge internal differences apparent for Chile, Ecuador, Brazil, and Venezuela (Vergara, 1965; Arriaga, 1968). Perhaps similar regional or cultural differences would

Percentage of Live Births Illegitmate, 1949–68

1956	1957	1958	1959	1960	1961	1962	1963	1964	1965	1966	1967	1968
67.3	65.9	66.6	63.5	63.7	62.0	63.7	62.5	65.0	64.2			
62.3	62.3	62.6	62.6	63.6	62.0	63.5	63.8	66.4	65.2	68.1	67.3	
30.2	27.1	26.2	27.7	27.5	25.8	27.7	26.0	26.4	27.5	31.4	30.9	33.4
49.3	49.5	48.1	48.8	49.0	46.0	47.6	43.4	44.9	43.5	44.7	45.1	41.7
1.2	3.4	3.5					5.0	5.0	6.1	5.3	4.2	5.2
23.8	24.0	23.5	24.3	23.1	22.8	23.0	23.3	23.8	24.3	25.0	25.8	
66.7	67.6	68.6	67.9	· · ·	64.0	66.6	63.9	64.6		65.8		
60.0	61.4	61.6	62.2	62.6	61.5	60.5	61.0	59.0	57.9	60.1	61.7	61.8
· · ·	· · ·	· · ·	65.4	63.0	64.1	64.7	64.7	65.3	65.7	66.0	66.9	67.2
69.5	71.7	70.2	69.9	67.5	67.7	66.8	65.5	67.8	67.3	70.6	70.2	71.7
44.4	45.7	43.6	45.0	43.5	43.3	42.3	42.7	41.7	41.6	41.9	41.6	
73.8	72.6	71.6	70.4	69.1	68.5	68.3	67.9	67.8	67.4			
64.4	64.5											
71.9	72.0	71.6	72.2	72.4	72.7	73.0	73.6	74.1				
48.8	48.5	49.5	49.2	49.2	48.9	47.5	46.8	47.2	46.9	48.1	48.2	
22.5	23.6	24.4	25.4	25.0	24.7	25.1	24.9	24.6	24.4	23.2	23.4	22.5
22.2	24.0	23.4	23.8	24.9	24.2	25.2	26.6	26.4	28.4	30.0		
52.1	56.3	56.0	57.2	52.1	52.6	53.4	53.9	54.7	54.5		53.4	
73.4	73.8	73.9	65.7	66.5	66.5	67.6	67.9	69.0	69.2	70.0	70.0	
			25.4	24.7	24.1	23.0	22.9	23.2				
66.0	68.9	68.2	69.7	67.3	66.8	69.0	69.8	70.8	70.1	69.4	74.0	74.9
60.7	72.8	72.0	72.0	70.4	66.1		61.5					
77.8	78.6	77.5	79.2	73.3	74.6	76.9	75.4	75.6				
47.3	46.4	45.3	44.2	43.5	42.5	41.9	41.5	41.9	41.5	40.3	41.1	

also appear in the detailed data for the others. One might expect pronounced cultural differences on the continent that are unrelated to the national boundaries.

Among the nations of South America the range in ratios is the most widely spread of any continent. Chile reports a low of 17.7 percent illegitimate while French Guiana records 64.9 percent of all births as out of wedlock. Between these, the remaining South American nations are rather evenly distributed.

Only four of the South American countries show any great change in ratios over the time span indicated. Paraguay, Bolivia, Uruguay, and Chile all report a considerable drop in ratios early in the period, with only Bolivia exhibiting a continued decline in the level of illegitimacy after 1953. The degree of stability in reported ratios for the other nations is noteworthy in itself.

ain we must point out that the registrations, not for births out of wedlock alone but for all births, are of questionable reliability in at least seven of the thirteen countries (as starred in table 3) of South America, and for the Amerindian population of Guyana, formerly British Guiana (see also Collver, 1965).

Europe: There are so many more statistics available for Europe than for any other geographical area, both in historical coverage and in the numbers of countries reporting on illegitimacy, that it becomes difficult to deal with the information. Historians have been analyzing the records of local communities or parishes as far back as the middle of the sixteenth century (see Peter Laslett, 1973:260 and Edward Shorter, 1971). In bringing together the available data, Shorter (1971:238) finds that: "Starting around the mid-eighteenth century a dramatic increase in the percentage of illegitimate births commenced all over Europe: illegitimacy further accelerated around the time of the French Revolution, and continued to increase until approximately the mid-nineteenth century." A peak in illegitimacy ratios appears to occur for many regions of Europe at about the time that our data for whole nations begins. Table 4 lists the European ratios as far back as the 1876 to 1880 period. Five year averages are indicated until 1930; beginning in 1938, yearly data are reported. This information is listed for 27 countries for at least a part of the historical time span.

To display the ratios over time visually with a minimum of confusion, the European nations have been organized according to geographical and cultural similarities. The British Isles, then, may be viewed as distinct from the Scandinavian, the West-Central, Eastern, and Southern European countries. The similarities and differences within and among these groups should be noted.

Except for Eire, the countries of the British Isles are a part of the United Kingdom, and they share some similarities in both social structure and culture. It is interesting that Northern Ireland and Eire, having rather different religious and political orientations, nevertheless report almost identical illegitimacy ratios over the last twenty years or so. Both had slight increases in illegitimacy during the Second World War, but not nearly so great as the peaks in ratios evident for England and Wales, and Scotland. We have a great deal of detailed data available for England and Wales that allow an

Figure 4. South America, Percentage of Live Births Illegitimate,1949–68

Percentage

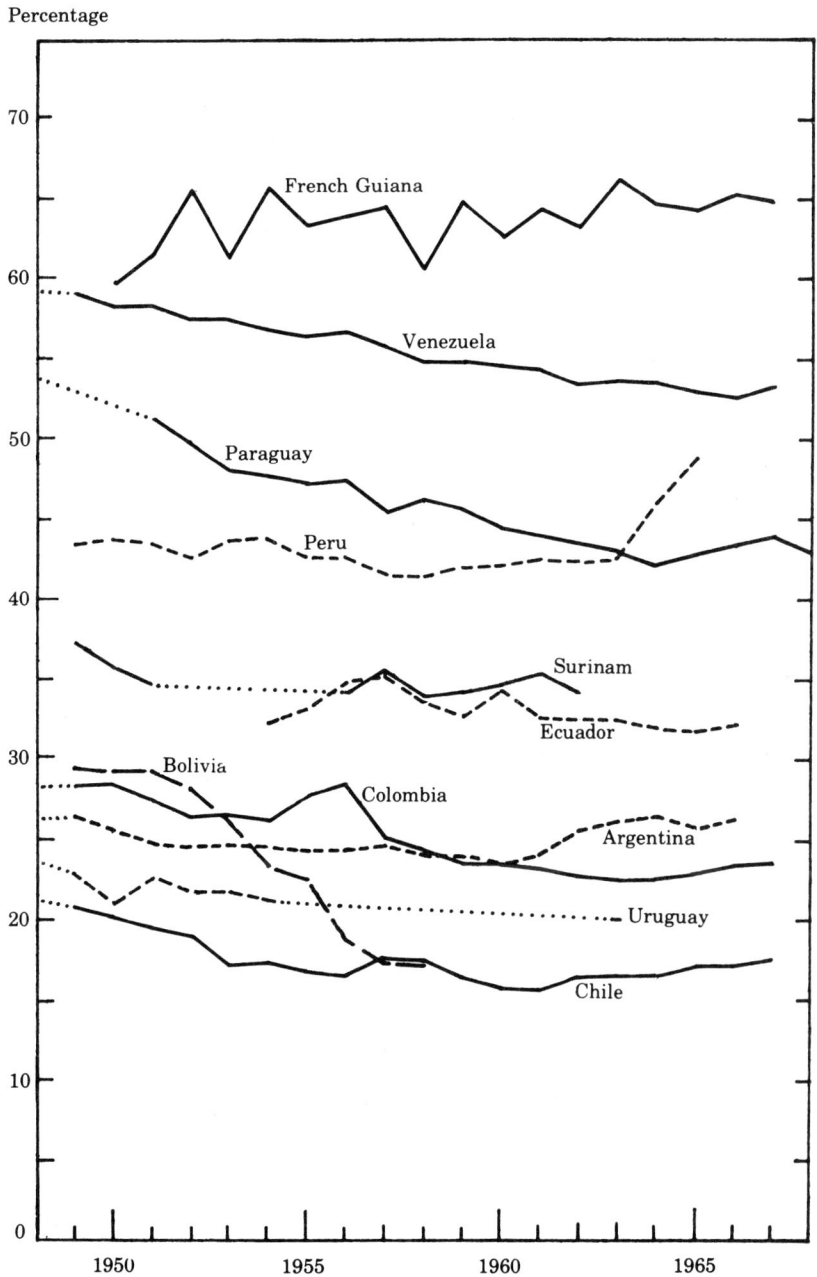

Table 3. South America, Percentage

Country	1921–25	1933	1949	1950	1951	1952	1953	1954	1955
Argentina		25.8	26.4	25.6	24.9	24.7	24.7	24.6	24.2
Bolivia			29.6	29.2	29.2	28.1	26.1	23.3	22.7
Brazil									
Federal District			13.1	13.8	13.4	12.4			
State of Guanabara									11.8
Total									
British Guiana									
Britannique			40.2	37.5	36.1	34.7	35.7	36.1	34.9
Amerindian*			. . .	. . .	. . .			41.4	42.2
Chile	36.2	31.7	20.9	20.2	19.7	19.0	17.2	17.4	16.9
Colombia*		28.0	28.1	28.3	27.4	26.5	26.7	26.1	27.8
Ecuador*								32.3	33.1
French Guiana*				59.8	61.5	65.4	61.3	65.7	63.2
Paraguay*	70.3	66.5			51.2	49.9	48.0	47.7	47.2
Peru*			43.5	43.7	43.5	42.8	43.8	43.9	42.8
Surinam			37.2	35.8	34.9	. . .			. . .
Uruguay*	28.8	28.6	22.9	21.0	22.5	21.9	21.8	21.1	
Venezuela*		59.5	59.0	58.1	58.2	57.5	57.3	56.9	56.3

SOURCES: U.N., *Demographic Yearbook* (1959; 1965: table 20; 1969: table 21); U.N. Sub-Commission (1967: 216); Wimperis (1960).

* Data are of questionable reliability.

analysis of the extent to which their wartime peak was due to increases in conceptions out of wedlock and/or to a decreased probability of getting married following conception (see chapter 8). Following the war, declines in ratios continued for about twelve years in Scotland, England and Wales and even longer in Eire and Northern Ireland. Recent increases in the percentage of births out of wedlock seem to be a return to the levels of 100 years ago in Scotland, but for England and Wales the rapid rise in illegitimacy far surpasses anything indicated by the historical reports, challenging the wartime peak, but without the disruptions of that period. As we may see in some detail, the rise in England occurs in spite of a significant decrease in the proportion of women who are unmarried. (This means that there has been a far greater increase in the illegitimacy rate than in the ratio exhibited here.) Each of these factors will be a part of the analysis carried out in later chapters.

The Scandinavian countries of Northern Europe report percentages of births out of wedlock that vary according to their own peculiar histories. Finland, for instance, has its own distinctive pattern with a peak in ratios in 1940 following the Russian takeover in 1939 and of Live Births Illegitimate, 1921–68

1956	1957	1958	1959	1960	1961	1962	1963	1964	1965	1966	1967	1968
24.3	24.7	24.0	23.9	23.5	24.0	25.6	26.1	26.4	25.8	26.4		
18.9	17.4	17.2										
12.2	9.4	10.8	11.5	12.9								
			8.4	7.6								
34.1	36.2	36.0	34.1	33.6	23.8	49.6	19.2	25.7				
39.0	33.5	41.0	43.9	45.1	39.5	51.5	26.1	32.6				
16.4	17.6	17.3	16.4	15.9	15.8	16.4	16.5	16.6	17.1	17.1	17.7	
28.5	25.1	24.5	23.7	23.5	23.1	22.8	22.6	22.6	22.9	23.3	23.4	
34.8	35.1	33.6	32.7	34.2	32.7	32.5	32.5	32.0	31.9	32.2		
63.9	64.5	60.7	64.8	62.9	64.3	63.2	66.1	64.8	64.5	65.2	64.9	
47.4	45.5	46.1	45.8	44.3			43.0	42.1	42.9	43.3	44.0	43.0
42.7	41.7	41.5	42.0	42.1	42.6	42.4	42.6	46.0	48.9			
34.2	35.3	34.0	34.3	34.7	35.3	34.1						
							20.0					
56.4	55.9	54.9	54.9	54.6	54.2	53.5	53.7	53.6	53.0	52.7	53.2	

repeating an earlier, somewhat lower peak in the 1920s. A second World War II peak occurs in 1945, and although Denmark also peaks in 1945, the Scandinavian countries do not show the violent wartime jump in illegitimacy ratios that is indicated by the major European belligerents. An interesting paradox is found in the reported decline in Icelandic ratios at precisely the time of peaking in ratios in Sweden, during 1911 to 1930. The increase in ratios over the last ten years in Denmark and Sweden looks very much like the rapid rise evident for England, yet the Swedes and Danes have had very much higher historical ratios than have been reported for England. It is curious that Finland and Norway have had very much lower ratios than their neighbors, and that Norway, in particular (and Finland to a lesser extent), evidences a long slow decline over eighty years, with a very recent upturn.

Some even earlier historical records (Tomasson, 1971) indicate that Sweden had only about 2 percent of all births registered as illegitimate from 1749 to 1760, with slight but steady increases each decade until our data begin for 1876-1880. The early records for Finland also indicate very low proportions of births out of wedlock, again with small increases up to the beginning of our data. The earliest records for Norway indicated higher initial illegitimacy ratios than either

Table 4. Europe, Percentage of Live Births Illegitimate, 1876–1968

Year	Austria	Belgium	Bulgaria	Czechoslovakia	Denmark	Finland
1876–80	13.8	7.4			10.1	7.3
1881–85	14.5	8.2			10.0	7.0
1886–90	14.7	8.7			9.5	6.5
1891–95	14.6	8.8			9.4	6.5
1896–1900	14.1	8.0			9.6	6.6
1901–05	12.8	6.8	0.4		10.1	6.5
1906–10	12.2	6.3			11.0	7.0
1911–15	23.6	6.4			11.4	7.8
1916–20	24.5	6.9	1.2	10.1	11.3	8.1
1921–25	21.0	5.6	1.2	10.0	10.6	8.8
1926–30	25.6	4.4		10.7	10.9	8.1
1938	20.9	2.5	2.9	7.8	9.0	6.6
1939	16.2	2.4	3.1	7.7	8.7	7.7
1940	13.8	3.1	3.1	6.3	8.8	9.3
1941	13.2	3.0	3.0	5.5	8.6	6.0
1942	14.2	2.4		5.1	8.5	6.9
1943	16.0	2.6		4.4	8.9	6.4
1944	20.3	3.4	2.4	4.6	9.2	7.4
1945	25.5	4.2		9.9	9.9	7.0
1946	24.5	3.8		8.9	7.9	6.0
1947	20.2	3.1		8.5	8.0	5.6
1948	19.1	3.1		7.6	7.7	5.6
1949	20.7	2.6	2.6	6.5	7.4	5.5
1950	18.3	2.6	2.0	6.0	7.4	5.2
1951	17.6	2.3	2.5	5.4	7.0	4.9
1952	16.5	2.3	2.1	5.0	6.7	4.7
1953	15.9	2.2	3.7	5.1	6.8	4.5
1954	15.5	2.1	4.8	5.3	6.7	4.4
1955	14.4	2.1	6.4	5.3	6.6	4.2
1956	13.5	2.1	7.2	5.4	6.8	4.2
1957	13.3	2.0	7.4	5.4	6.9	4.3
1958	13.2	2.0	7.6	5.1	7.2	4.0
1959	13.3	2.1	7.7	4.9	7.3	4.1
1960	13.0	2.1	8.0	4.8	7.8	4.0
1961	12.6	2.0	8.0	4.5	8.0	4.1
1962	12.0	2.1	8.1	4.5	8.3	4.0
1963	11.6	2.2	8.4	4.7	8.9	4.2
1964	11.3	2.3	8.8	4.9	9.3	4.4
1965	11.2	2.4	9.4	5.1	9.5	4.6
1966	11.4	2.5	9.6	5.3	10.2	4.8
1967	11.5	2.5	9.7	5.4	11.1	5.1
1968	12.0		9.6		11.1	5.3

Year	France	Germany		Greece	Hungary	Iceland	Irish Free State (Eire)
		United					
1876–80	7.2	8.7			7.3	22.6	
1881–85	7.8	9.2			7.9	20.2	
1886–90	8.3	9.2			8.2	20.4	
1891–95	8.7	9.1			8.5	17.7	
1896–1900	8.8	9.0			9.0	15.5	
1901–05	8.8	8.4			9.4	13.9	
1906–10	8.9	8.8			9.4	13.0	
1911–15	8.7	9.9			9.2	13.2	
1916–20	12.0	11.7			9.8	13.1	
1921–25	8.7	10.8		1.2	9.6	13.3	2.6
1926–30	8.4	12.2		1.3		14.4	3.0
1938	6.3	7.7		1.4	8.4	23.7	3.3
1939	6.3	7.8		1.4	8.7	23.7	3.2
1940	7.1				8.5	25.6	3.2
1941	8.1				8.6	24.3	3.5
1942	7.7					24.6	3.7
1943	7.9					25.1	3.8
1944	9.4					25.4	3.9
1945	10.5	Eastern	Western			24.0	3.9
1946	8.7		16.4		8.1	25.9	3.9
1947	7.6		11.9			25.6	3.4
1948	7.2		10.2			26.6	3.3
1949	7.0	11.9	9.3		8.3	25.2	3.1
1950	7.0	12.8	9.6	3.1	8.5	27.9	2.5
1951	6.8	13.2	9.5		8.4	27.5	2.5
1952	6.8	12.8	8.9		8.1	25.2	2.5
1953	6.7	12.9	8.6		8.2	25.4	2.1
1954	6.4	13.1	8.3		7.8	27.6	2.1
1955	6.3	12.8	7.7	1.5	7.0	26.5	2.0
1956	6.3	13.1	7.3	1.4	6.6	25.2	1.9
1957	6.2	13.1	7.7	1.5	6.4	24.9	1.7
1958	6.1	12.1	6.7	1.3	5:7	25.5	1.6
1959	6.1	11.8	6.5	1.3	5.7	25.4	1.6
1960	6.1	11.4	6.1	1.2	5.5	25.3	1.6
1961	5.9	10.9	5.8	1.2	5.5	25.3	1.6
1962	5.9	9.9	5.4	1.2	5.4	24.5	1.8
1963	5.9	9.1	5.1	1.2	5.3	25.1	1.8
1964	5.9	9.4	4.8	1.1	5.2	26.7	2.0
1965	5.9	9.8	4.6	1.1	5.2	26.9	2.2
1966	5.9	10.0	4.4	1.0	5.1	28.4	2.3
1967	6.1	10.7	4.5	1.0	5.0	30.0	2.5
1968			4.8	1.1	5.0		2.6

Year	Italy	Netherlands	Norway	Poland	Portugal	Romania	Russia
1876–80	7.2	3.1	8.4				2.8
1881–85	7.6	3.0	8.1				2.7
1886–90	7.4	3.2	7.5		12.3		2.7
1891–95	6.9	3.1	7.1		12.2		2.7
1896–1900	6.2	2.7	7.4	6.1	12.1		2.7
1901–05	5.7	2.3	7.0		11.6		
1906–10	5.2	2.1	6.6		10.2	9.0	
1911–15	4.8	2.1	7.0		12.7	7.9	
1916–20	4.8	2.2	7.0	3.1	13.0	9.0	
1921–25	4.9	1.9	6.9	7.5	12.6	9.8	
1926–30	5.1	1.8	7.0	5.9	14.3	9.1	
1938	4.1	1.4	6.0		15.6	9.3	
1939	4.1	1.3	6.2		15.7	9.2	
1940	3.8	1.4	6.4		15.7	9.2	
1941	3.9	1.7	6.9		15.1		
1942	3.8	1.7	7.3		14.1	8.2	
1943	3.8	1.8	7.5		13.4		
1944	4.6	2.0	7.3		13.0		
1945	5.2	3.5	7.4		12.6		
1946	3.8	2.5	5.8		12.3		
1947	3.7	1.9	5.3		12.1	11.9	
1948	3.5	1.7	4.9		11.8		
1949	3.4	1.6	4.0		11.8		
1950	3.4	1.5	4.1		11.8		
1951	3.9	1.4	4.0		11.6		
1952	3.4	1.4	3.7		11.5		
1953	3.3	1.3	3.6		11.2		
1954	3.2	1.3	3.5		10.9		
1955	3.1	1.2	3.4	4.7	11.0		
1956	3.0	1.2	3.5	5.6	10.6		
1957	2.8	1.2	3.7	5.3	10.5		
1958	2.7	1.2	3.6	5.2	10.5		
1959	2.5	1.4	3.6	5.0	10.1		
1960	2.4	1.3	3.7	4.5	10.0		
1961	2.4	1.4	3.7	4.3	9.3		
1962	2.2	1.5	3.8	4.2	9.0		
1963	2.2	1.6	3.9	4.1	8.7		
1964	2.0	1.7	4.2	4.1	8.4		
1965	2.0	1.8	4.6	4.5	8.3		
1966	2.0	2.0	4.9	4.6	8.1		
1967	2.0	2.1	5.1	4.9	7.9		
1968		2.0	5.6	4.9	7.4		

Year	Spain	Sweden	Switzer-land	England and Wales	Northern Ireland	Scotland	Yugo-slavia
1876–80		10.0	4.7	4.7		8.5	
1881–85		10.2	4.8	4.8		8.3	
1886–90		10.3	4.7	4.6		8.1	
1891–95		10.5	4.6	4.2		7.4	
1896–1900	4.9	11.3	4.5	4.1		6.8	
1901–05	4.4	11.9	4.3	3.9		6.4	
1906–10	4.6	13.5	4.5	4.0		7.1	
1911–15	4.8	15.4	4.7	4.3		7.2	
1916–20	5.8	14.5	4.5	5.5		7.6	
1921–25	6.0	14.9	3.7	4.3	4.3	6.8	4.9
1926–30	6.1	16.0	4.1	4.5	4.7	7.3	4.7
1938		12.7	3.5	4.2	4.5	6.1	4.8
1939		12.4	3.5	4.2	4.7	6.0	4.8
1940		11.8	3.8	4.3	4.6	5.9	
1941	4.8	10.9	3.8	5.4	4.8	6.6	
1942	5.4	9.2	3.4	5.6	4.9	7.1	
1943	5.9	8.8	3.2	6.4	5.5	7.6	
1944	6.2	9.0	3.2	7.3	5.6	7.9	
1945	6.3	9.6	3.5	9.3	5.4	8.6	
1946	6.2	9.3	3.4	6.6	4.4	6.6	
1947	5.5	9.4	3.5	5.3	3.8	5.6	
1948	5.7	9.3	3.7	5.4	3.6	5.8	
1949	5.7	9.2	3.6	5.1	3.7	5.5	
1950	5.2	9.5	3.8	5.1	3.4	5.2	
1951	5.2	10.0	3.5	4.8	3.1	5.1	
1952	5.1	10.0	3.5	4.8	3.3	4.8	
1953	4.8	9.8	3.6	4.7	2.8	4.6	
1954	4.6	9.8	3.7	4.7	2.9	4.5	
1955	4.2	9.9	3.6	4.7	2.4	4.3	7.7
1956	3.8	10.2	3.7	4.8	2.7	4.2	8.2
1957	3.3	10.1	3.8	4.8	2.4	4.1	8.8
1958	2.9	10.2	3.6	4.9	2.3	4.1	8.9
1959	2.4	10.4	3.8	5.1	2.4	4.2	8.7
1960	2.3	11.3	3.8	5.4	2.5	4.4	8.7
1961	2.3	11.7	4.0	6.0	2.5	4.6	8.4
1962	2.1	12.4	4.2	6.6	2.4	4.8	8.2
1963	1.9	12.6	4.1	6.9	2.6	5.2	8.5
1964	1.8	13.1	4.2	7.2	3.0	5.4	8.4
1965	1.7	13.8	3.9	7.7	2.9	5.8	8.3
1966	1.6	14.6	3.8	7.9	3.1	6.4	8.3
1967	1.5	15.1	3.9	8.4	3.6	6.9	8.3
1968	1.4	15.8	3.8	8.5	3.8	7.4	
1969		16.3		8.4			
1970				8.3			

SOURCES: Wimperis (1960: tables 1 and 2a, Appendix); U.N., *Demographic Yearbook* (1959; 1965: table 20; 1969: table 21).

Figure 5. British Isles, Percentage of Live Births Illegitimate, 1876–1968

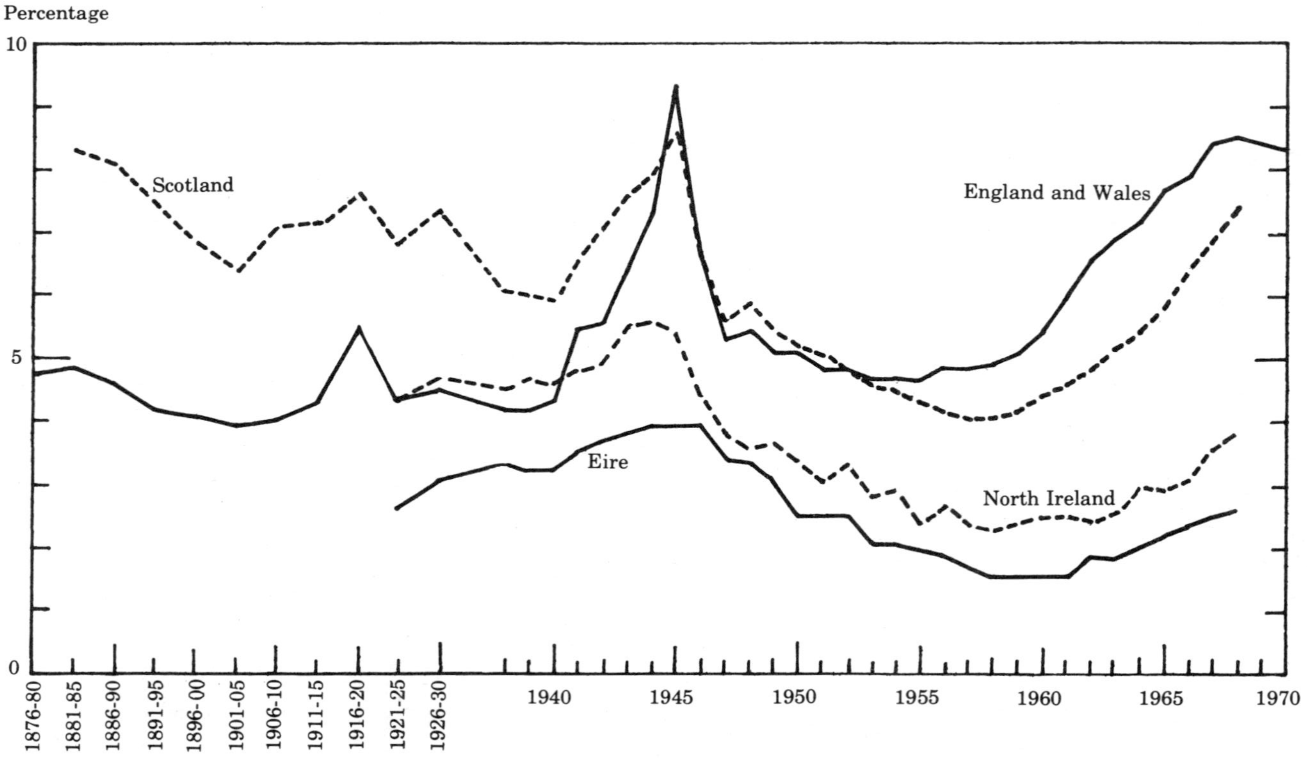

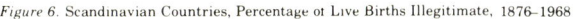

Figure 6. Scandinavian Countries, Percentage of Live Births Illegitimate, 1876-1968

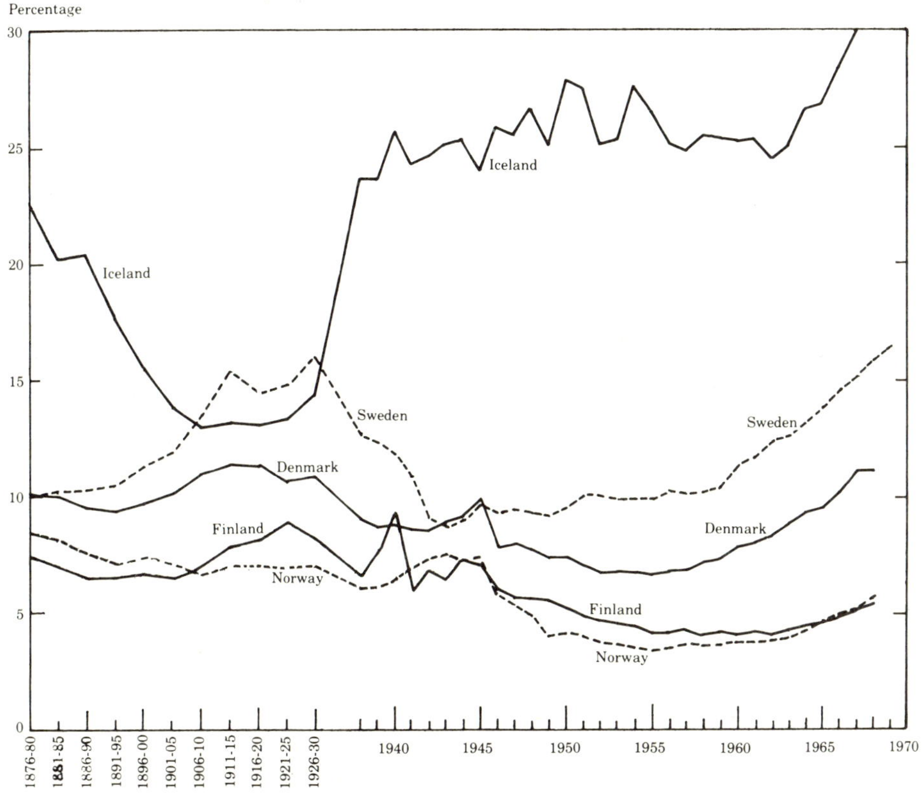

Sweden or Finland, peaking at about 8 percent from 1840 through 1880. The records for Denmark begin with the first decade of the nineteenth century, with over 7 percent of all births out of wedlock. Tomasson has begun an analysis of differences within the Scandinavian region, but has not yet examined all of the several variables to be presented below. To what extent would changing patterns of marriage, nonmarital coitus, use of contraception, and abortion or marriage during pregnancy explain these trends?

West-Central Europe seems almost to be composed of two subgroups of countries with regard to percentages of births out of wedlock. Both Switzerland and the Netherlands report relatively stable ratios over the nearly one hundred years of record. These range from 1 to 3 percent for the Netherlands and from 3.2 to 4.8 percent for

Figure 7. West-Central Europe, Percentage of Live Births Illegitimate, 1876–1968

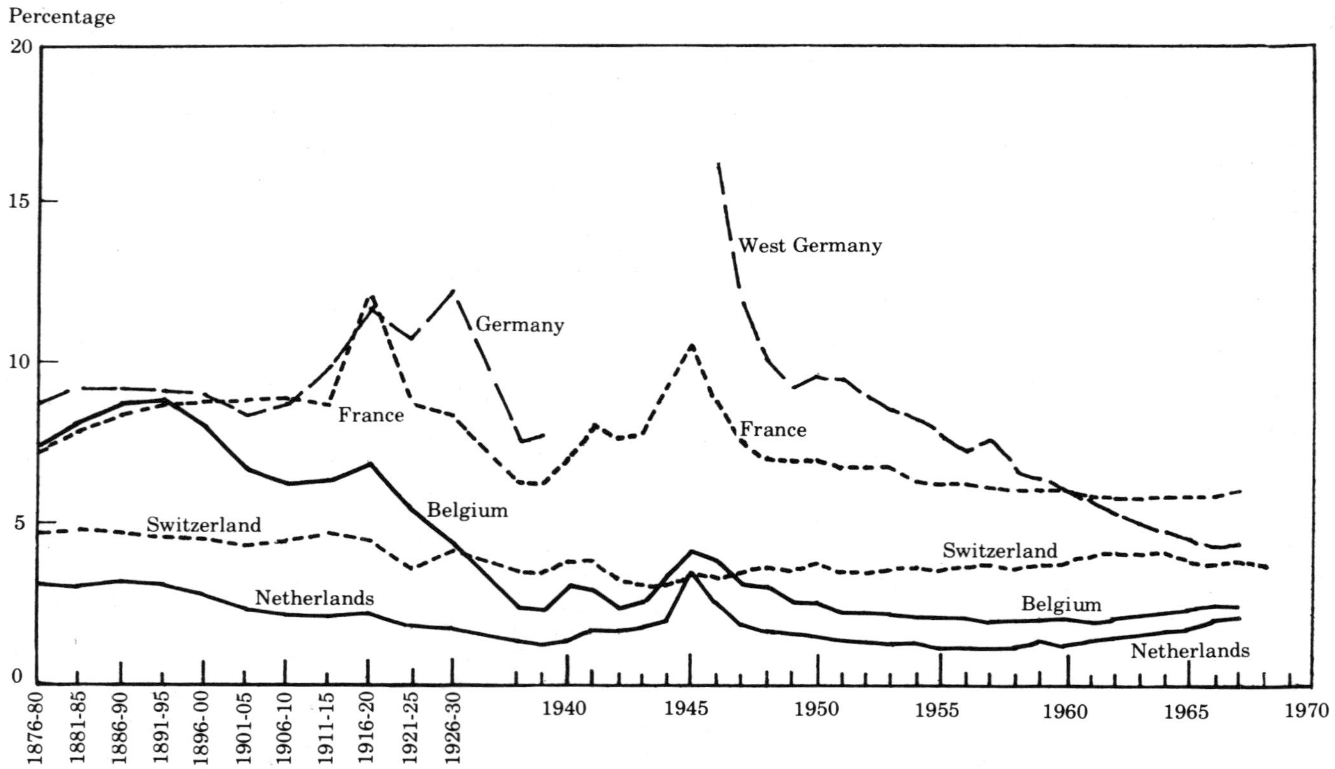

Switzerland, one of a very few European countries that does not report a wartime jump in 1945. Belgium's very early reports indicated illegitimacy ratios of 7 to 9, but these declined throughout the early third of the twentieth century to about 2.5 percent, maintained, except for two wartime peaks, in the following years. Thus, while Belgium's ratios now resemble those of its northern neighbor, in the last century its percentages of births out of wedlock more nearly resembled those of its neighbors to the south and east.

Both France and Germany exhibit illegitimacy ratios that reflect the disruptions of two world wars fought on home territories. Although I will discuss the factors associated with the wartime rise in illegitimacy in England and Wales, I have not researched details for each country whose data are presented. One may hope that area specialists will use the mode of analysis to determine precisely which of the multidimensional factors to be reviewed are involved in the changes in observed measures of births out of wedlock. Why should it be that the ratios continued to decline beyond prewar levels in West Germany, while for France and most of the other belligerents the postwar decline either leveled out or began another upswing? It is important to note that there is a break in the data for Germany in the early 1940s followed by a separation of eastern and western regions following the war. What factors might be involved in the different patterns of east and west that result in ratios for the eastern portion about double those of West Germany?

Few of the countries of Eastern Europe have reported illegitimacy ratios over the entire period under consideration. The East German data show a continuation of the unified German ratios. Yet, as noted, they are very much higher than those of West Germany or of the other Communist bloc nations. Russian ratios are only available for a short time before 1900. Information for Poland was spotty until a regular reporting began in 1955. Austria is difficult to graph with Europe, since until recently its percentages of births out of wedlock were very high (up to 25 percent of all births) and fluctuated dramatically (see table 4). Austrian ratios declined steadily for 20 years after the war and have recently been about half as high as during the peak years, although they are still among the highest of Europe.

Figure 8. Eastern Europe, Percentage of Live Births Illegitimate, 1876–1968

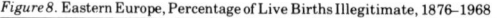

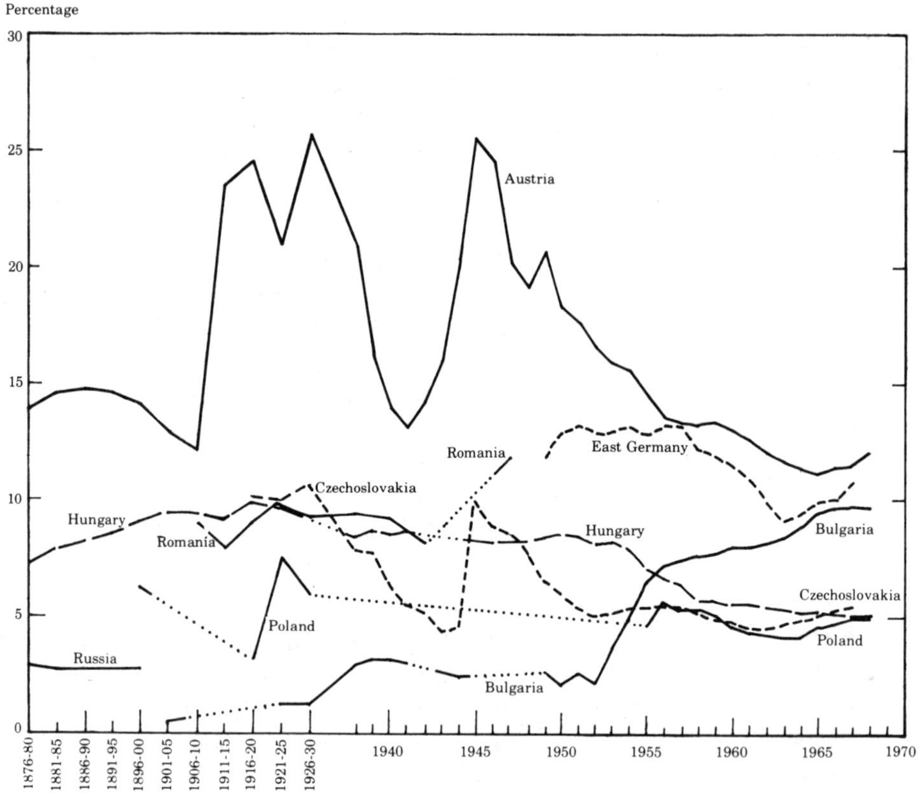

Czechoslovakia reports a wartime peak in illegitimacy, while Hungarian data are missing for those years so that greater stability appears there, from 1876 through 1950, with a decline thereafter. Hungary, Czechoslovakia, and Poland have recently reported very similar illegitimacy ratios, apparently leveling off at about 5 percent of all births. Some experts had expected that with legalized, easily obtainable, and frequently used abortions, births out of wedlock might become insignificant in numbers and proportions. What happened in Japan has evidently not been repeated here.

Bulgaria appears to be the paradox of the East European group. Historically low proportions of births out of wedlock (1 to 2 percent) gave way to incredibly rapid increases beginning in 1953, continuing to recent reports of over 9 percent. Bulgarian ratios show a surprisingly rapid increase during a time when the other nations of the area report decreases or a leveling out.

Southern Europe again seems to offer a pattern of similar ratios of births out of wedlock for three countries and two significant exceptions. Greece has the lowest and most consistently low illegitimacy ratios of this group, among the lowest of the world, excepting, of course, those years of internal disruption for which data are unavailable. Italy and Spain, whose reported information begins at different dates, seem to travel similar paths over time, with ratios declining over the long run to less than one-third of their earliest reported levels. It would be easy and convenient to ascribe these declines to the influence of the Roman Catholic Church. But, then, why should the ratios have been higher in the earliest reported years, and even more puzzling, why would Catholic Portugal record so much higher ratios of births out of wedlock? At least the declines reported for Portugal paralled those of Italy and Spain, even though at a much higher level, while Yugoslavia records ratios almost twice as high in the latter half of the twentieth century as are reported for the 1920s and 1930s. Illegitimacy ratios in present day Yugoslavia, a union of some historically very distinct cultures, may offer a composite of very different internal patterns of births out of wedlock. All of these offer a challenge and opportunity for further analysis.

For Europe as a whole, the wartime peak of 1945 and to some extent the peak for the period 1916 to 1920 are the most common dislocations to be found in the illegitimacy ratios. Only Switzerland, Bulgaria, and Sweden appear unaffected. To what extent are the wartime peaks a result of the loosening of sexual morals? Although that explanation is most often assumed by the general public and dramatized in books and films, we will see evidence for England and Wales in chapter 8 indicating surprisingly little change in the number of premarital conceptions that result in childbirth. The proportion of these legitimated by marriage before the birth of the child, was, however, drastically reduced during the war years and reached an all-time low in 1945 (see table 24).

The variations in levels of illegitimacy in Europe over time dramatize the need for detailed case studies (for the purpose of specifying causes in particular countries) along with the international overview (in order to correct the tendency to generalize from single studies).

Figure 9. Southern Europe, Percentage of Live Births Illegitimate, 1876–1968

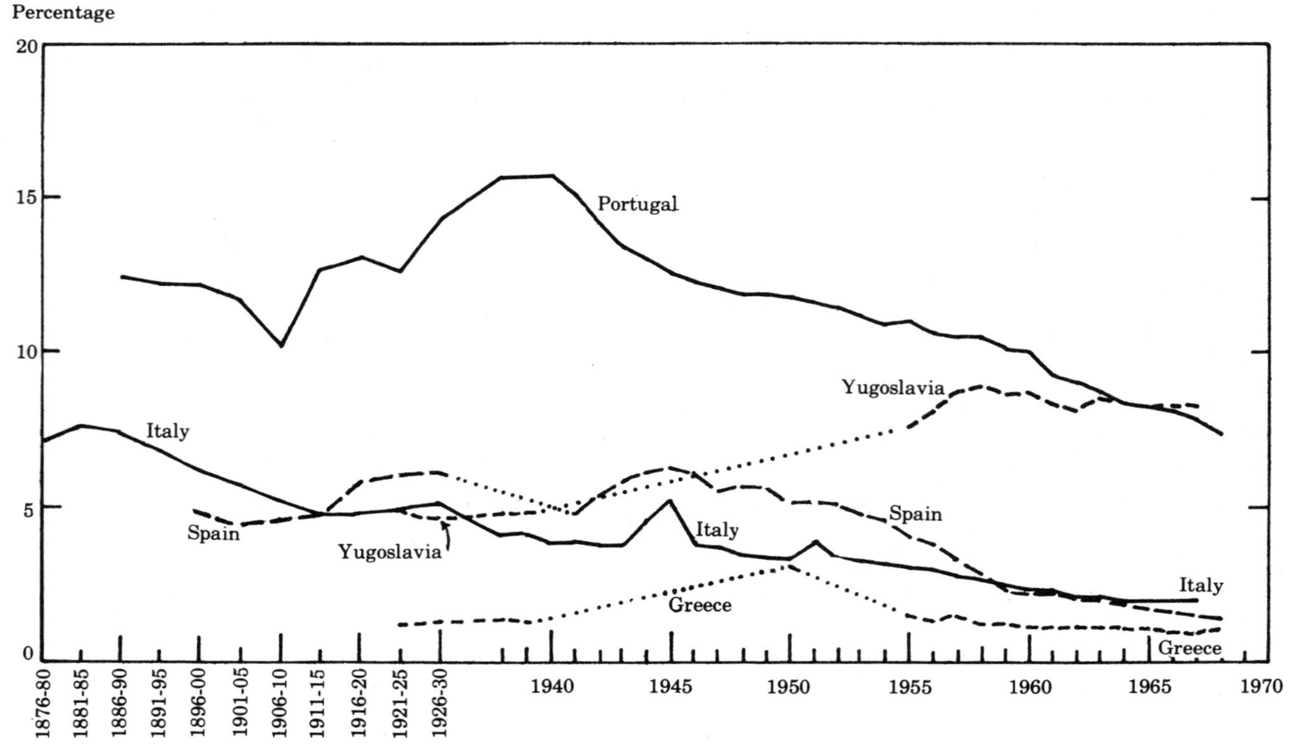

Percentage

North America and Australasia: Whether from the common English cutural heritage, similar social organization, or other factors yet to be discovered, the statistics on the percentage of births that are recorded as illegitimate are amazingly parallel in the four countries of North American and Australasia and the "mother country," England. The very recent rapid rise in the percentage of births out of wedlock is almost identical in all five nations. It should be noted, however, that the very sharp jump in the percentages of births occurring out of wedlock in New Zealand between 1961 and 1962 is in large part a result of the inclusion for the first time of the Maori population in total figures. From 1962 on, the Maoris are an inseparable part of the population statistics and birth data. Therefore,

Figure 10. North America and Australasia, Percentage of Live Births Illegitimate, 1876–1968

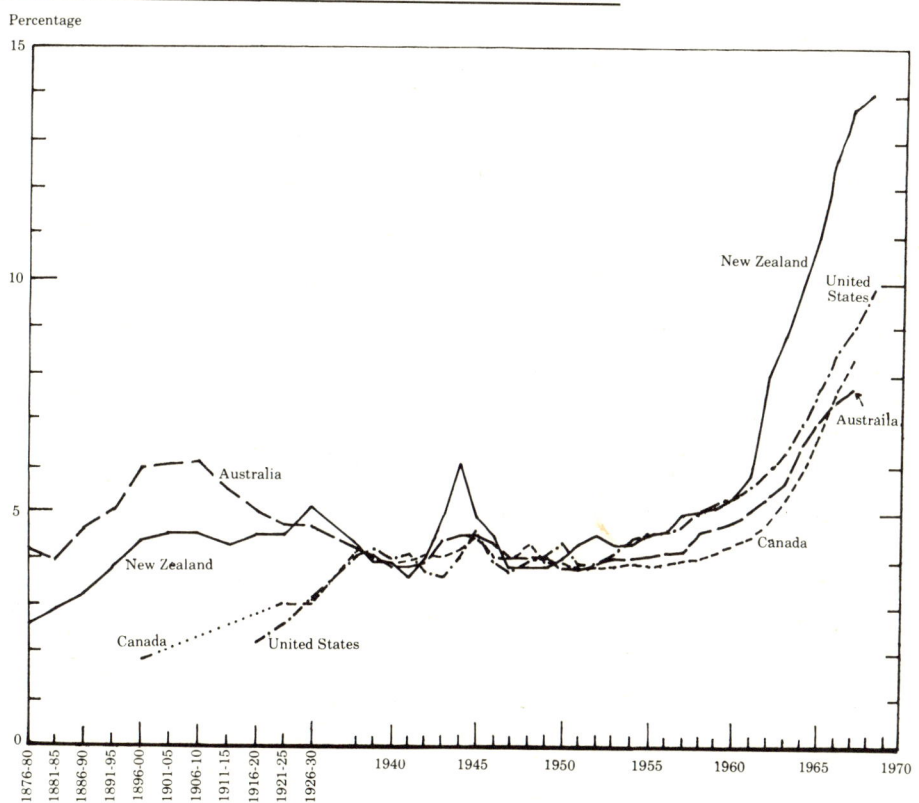

Table 5. North America and Australasia,
Percentage of Live Births Illegitimate, 1876–1968

Years	Canada	United States	Australia	New Zealand
1876–80			4.2	2.3
1881–85			3.9	2.9
1886–90			4.6	3.2
1891–95			5.0	3.8
1896–1900	1.8*		5.9	4.4
1901–05			6.0	4.5
1906–10			6.1	4.5
1911–15			5.5	4.3
1916–20		2.2	5.0	4.5
1921–25	3.0*	2.6	4.7	4.5
1926–30	3.0	3.1	4.7	5.1
1938	4.2	4.1	4.2	4.3
1939	4.0	4.2	4.1	3.9
1940	3.9	4.0	3.8	3.9
1941	4.0	4.1	3.8	3.6
1942	4.1	3.7	3.9	4.0
1943	4.0	3.6	4.4	4.8
1944	4.2	4.0	4.5	6.0
1945	4.5	4.6	4.5	4.9
1946	4.1	3.9	4.3	4.4
1947	4.0	3.7	4.0	3.8
1948	4.3	3.9	4.0	3.8
1949	3.9	4.0	4.1	3.8
1950	3.9	4.3	3.8	4.0
1951	3.8	3.9	3.8	4.3
1952	3.8	3.9	3.9	4.5
1953	3.8	4.1	4.0	4.3
1954	3.9	4.4	4.0	4.3
1955	3.8	4.5	4.1	4.5
1956	3.9	4.6	4.2	4.6
1957	4.0	4.7	4.2	4.9
1958	4.0	5.0	4.6	5.0
1959	4.2	5.2	4.7	5.1
1960	4.3	5.3	4.8	5.3
1961	4.5	5.6	5.1	5.8
1962	4.8	5.9	5.4	8.0
1963	5.3	6.3	5.7	8.8
1964	5.9	6.9	6.5	9.9
1965	6.7	7.7	7.0	10.9
1966	7.6	8.4	7.4	11.6
1967	8.3	9.0	7.7	12.7
1968		9.7		13.0

SOURCES: Data prior to 1948 from Wimperis (1960: tables 2a and 2b, Appendix). Data after 1948 from U.N., *Demographic Yearbook* (1959; 1965: table 20; 1969: table 21). *Percentage for Ontario Province in 1900 with about 40 percent of all births in Canada from *Canada Yearbook* (1900: 582). The 1921–25 data from *Canada Yearbook* (1965: 194).

we do not know what proportion of the pronounced rise is attributable to persons of European heritage, on whom the data were based before 1962. Because the rise had been going on for eight years before, and continues after, the addition of the Maoris, we certainly cannot attribute the entire increase to that portion of the population.[7]

In fact, the United States data are also a composite of two rather distinct populations. Tables 10 and 11 indicate the long-term differences, with illegitimacy ratios for the nonwhite population averaging 7 to 10 times the ratios for whites. Although the gap between the two groups has been narrowing in recent years, the data still indicate two categories with different levels and trends in the production of children out of wedlock.

One cannot know in how many nations similarly wide internal differences contribute to the national figures without a more explicit internal analysis of each of the countries than will be possible here.

Asia: It is difficult for us to imagine the countries in the table for Asia as a geographical unit, because they are spread one-third of the distance around the world. But there appears to be more similarity in their ratios of children born out of wedlock than is the case for many continental entities. Except for the European population of Indonesia, the illegitimacy ratios are quite low, averaging below 3 percent for the most part. Furthermore, many of these nations, already at the low end of the international rank ordering of ratios, indicate slight reductions in the percentage of illegitimacy over time. The most pronounced reduction has been occurring in Japan since 1900. How is it possible in a country that has had institutionalized concubinage and has been undergoing profound dislocations, such as rapid urbanization and industrialization, wars and their aftermath, that we find a prolonged decline in the illegitimacy ratio? Because it is such an interesting case, and because the Japanese supply excellent, detailed data, we will refer to their situation in several of the chapters to follow (see also Hartley, 1969a; 1970b).

---

[7] Maori births in 1962 made up 11.8 percent of all births, and if we assume the illegitimacy ratio for "Europeans" had increased from 5.8 to 6.5, then the Maori ratio was 19.7 percent illegitimate in that year. Since the Maori view of sex, marriage, and children is said to be quite typically Polynesian (J. Metge, 1967:97-101), such a ratio would not be at all surprising. I am indebted to Campbell Gibson for this estimate and the detailed data on New Zealand.

Table 6. Asia, Percentage of Live Births Illegitimate, 1949–68

Country	1900	1949	1950	1951	1952	1953	1954	1955	1956	1957	1958	1959	1960	1961	1962	1963	1964	1965	1966	1967	1968
Cyprus*		0.9	0.7	0.7	0.6	0.6	0.8	0.5	0.4	0.3	0.2	0.3	0.2	0.3	0.2	0.1	0.2	0.2	0.1	0.2	0.3
Indonesia		6.7	7.1	7.5																	
Israel		..	0.1	0.2	0.3	0.2	0.3	0.3	0.4	0.4	0.2	0.2	0.3					0.4	0.6	0.6	0.6
Japan	8.8	2.5	2.5	2.2	2.0	1.9	1.7	1.7	1.6	1.5	1.4	1.3	1.2	1.2	1.1	1.1	1.0	1.0	1.1	0.9	
Macao*		2.7						0.6	0.6	0.3	0.3	0.2	0.2	0.3	0.2	0.1	0.3	0.2	0.2	0.2	
Philippines*					3.0	2.4			2.3	1.6	1.5	0.9	0.7	1.5	1.2	1.6	3.3	2.8	2.7	2.5	
Ryukyu Islands										3.7	3.3	3.6	3.6	3.3	3.4	3.4	3.6	3.4	3.7	3.1	3.5
Syria							0.0	0.0													
Taiwan		2.5	2.4	2.6	2.7	2.6	2.5	2.4	2.7	2.2	2.2	2.0	1.8	1.4	1.3	1.2	1.3	1.3	2.6	1.7	1.6

SOURCE: *Demographic Yearbook* (1959, 1965: table 20; 1969: table 21).

Figure 11. Asia, Percentage of Live Births Illegitimate, 1949–68

Percentage

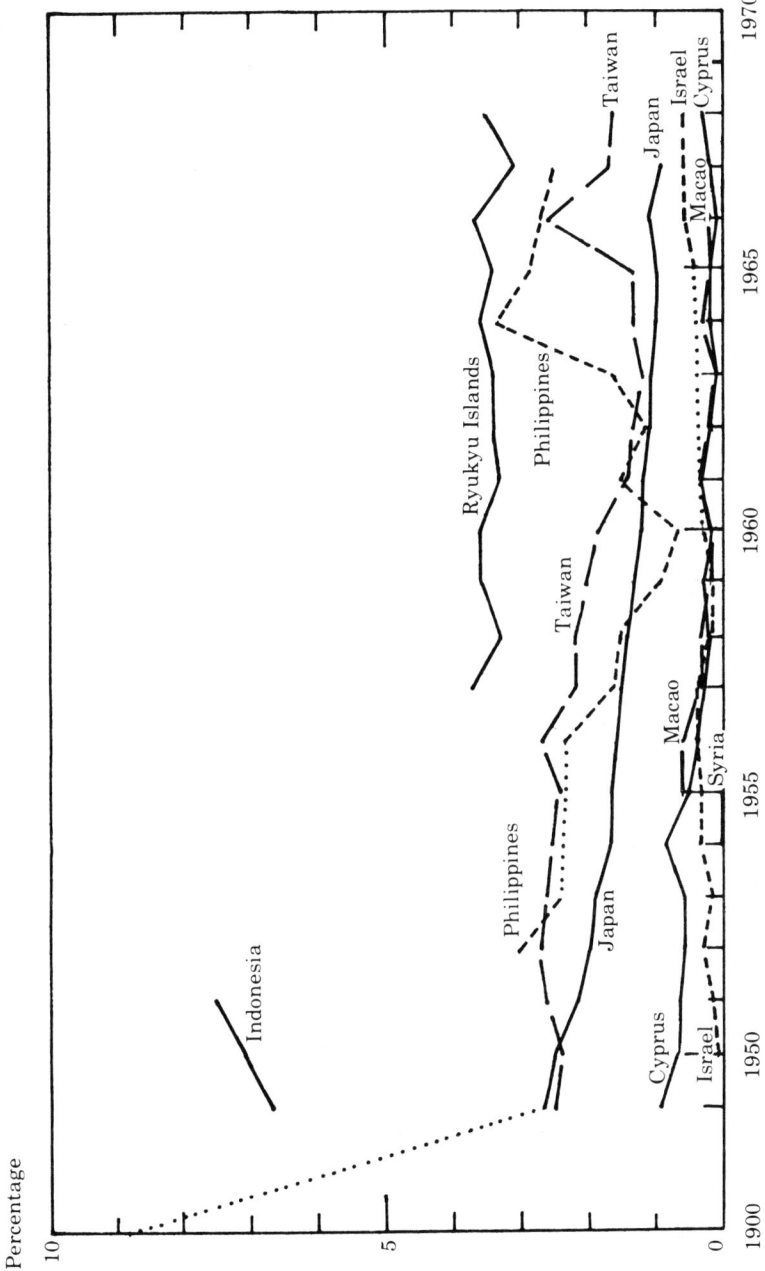

Africa: The available data from Africa are difficult to assess. As the table indicates, the United Nations has questioned the reliability of the reported illegitimacy ratios from most of the African nations. Many have only recently begun to collect birth and population statistics, and it would be unrealistic to expect that these would be accurate immediately. If we assume the data reported to be the best or even the only available estimate, some tentative comparisons are in order.

The data illustrated on the African table seem to be divided into three groups. First, there is a group of nations or segments of the population of nations that are reported to have between 30 and 40 percent of all births reported as illegitimate. These are all among the southernmost nations of the African continent: Angola , Mozambique, and the colored (mixed) populations of the Union of South Africa and southwest Africa. A second group of nations reports 4 to 7 percent of births as illegitimate. These include the two Congos, African Guinea, the Central African Republic, Dahomey, Southern Morocco, and the European populations of Algeria and Tunisia. A third group with very low reported illegitimacy ratios is made up of the white populations of southern African nations on the one hand, and the Moslem populations of several North African nations on the other. These groupings have many geographical and cultural similarities, but a detailed analysis would require the attention of African specialists.

William Goode (1963) claims that illegitimacy was rare in the old African marriage system, and indeed among both matrilineal and patrilineal peoples the relevant arguments and court cases often centered about the question of who had the *right* to a child born under deviant circumstances, rather than who had the responsibility for it. A high value was placed on children, who tend to be viewed as assets in agricultural societies, and there was far more emphasis on the *social* definition of kinship than on the biological continuity of a lineage. Goode suggests that in the new circumstances of urban life or in plantation settlements several factors unite to increase illegitimacy. An unbalanced sex ratio due to differential migration of the sexes and the kinship structure's inability to perform its normal activities both led Goode to predict a rise in illegitimacy for a while but a drop in the next two decades (Goode, 1963:174-185; see also UNESCO, 1956).

Figure 12. Africa, Percentage of Live Births Illegitimate, 1949–66

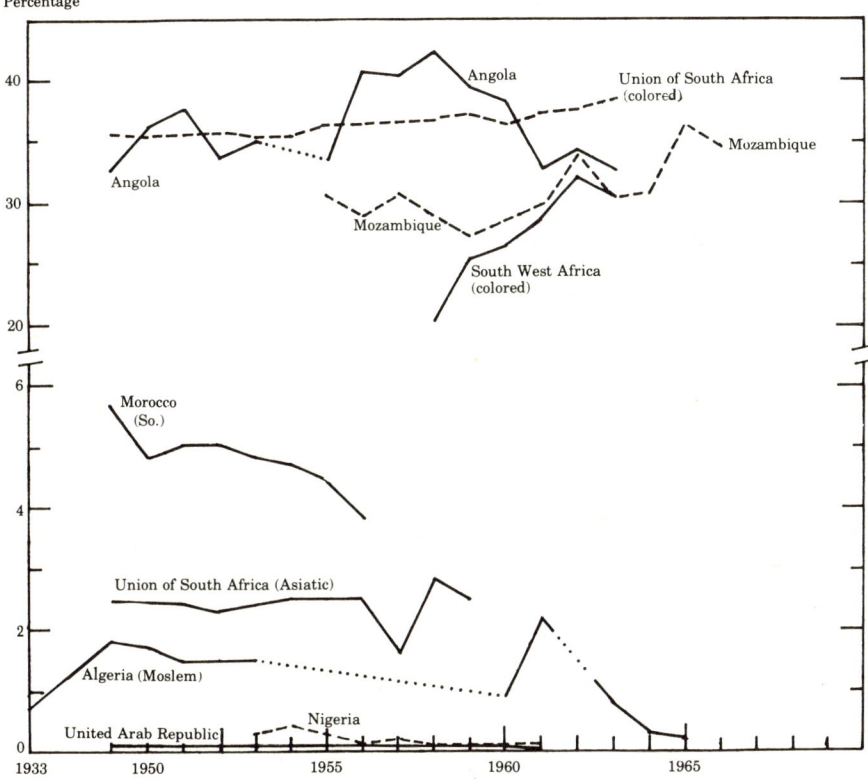

Percentage

Again we are limited by the scarcity of information, but the data on the African graph do not confirm Goode's prediction of the early 1960s. The only change is found in the declines of illegitimacy ratios among Europeans in Algeria and Tunisia and the general population of Southern Morocco. Nigeria and Egypt, the two most populous nations of Africa, report amazingly low and stable illegitimacy ratios, with the very low Nigerian ratio recorded only for the capital city. The higher ratios for native and colored populations of southern Africa do not show the predicted pattern, although the time period from 1949 to 1968 and the small number of countries reporting make any firm conclusions impossible at this time.

Table 7. Africa, Percentage of Live Births Illegitimate, 1949–68

Country	1933	1949	1950	1951	1952	1953	1954	1955
Algeria								
European	7.4	6.1	6.3	6.3	5.6	6.4	4.8	5.4
Moslem*	0.7	1.8	1.7	1.5	1.5	1.5		
Angola*		32.9	36.2	37.9	33.6	35.0		33.4
Central African Republic*								
Congo* (Brazzaville)								
Congo, Democratic Republic*							(	
Dahomey*								
Guinea*								7.2
Mauritius								
Morocco* (So)		5.7	4.8	5.0	5.0	4.8	4.7	4.4
Mozambique*								30.6
Nigeria						0.3	0.4	0.3
Reunion				18.5	19.2	19.4	19.0	19.5
Southern Rhodesia (European)		1.3	1.5	1.1	1.2	1.1	1.3	1.1
South West Africa								
Coloured*								
White		1.1	1.3	0.8	1.0	0.5	1.0	0.9
Union of South Africa								
Asiatic		2.4	2.4	2.4	2.3	2.4	2.5	2.5
Coloured		35.6	35.2	35.4	35.7	35.4	35.6	36.1
White	2.7	1.7	1.6	1.6	1.7	1.5	1.3	1.2
Tunisia								
European		5.7	6.1	5.4	4.3	4.5	4.5	4.3
Moslem								
United Arab Republic								
Health Bureaus* (Egypt)		0.1	0.1	0.1	0.1	0.1	0.1	0.1
Zambia (European)								

SOURCE: United Nations, *Demographic Yearbook* (1959; 1965: table 20; 1969: table 21.)

 * Unreliable or questionable data.

 † Average percentage over two or three years.

GENERAL ILLEGITIMATE FERTILITY RATE

We shift focus now to another indicator of illegitimacy, the rate. We are no longer examining the proportion of all births within a country that are registered as illegitimate. Now the question is: To what extent do the persons "at risk"—that is, the unmarried women within the childbearing ages (those single, widowed, divorced, and even separated where these are known)—actually produce children

1956	1957	1958	1959	1960	1961	1962	1963	1964	1965	1966	1967	1968
3.7	3.1	2.7	2.4									
				0.9	2.2		0.8	0.3	0.2			
40.8	40.6	42.2	39.5	38.3	32.8	34.2	32.6					
			(	4.8	)†							
				(	5.8	)†						
6.7	)†											
					4.1							
							0.6	0.5	0.4	0.4	0.3	0.3
3.8												
28.9	30.6	28.9	27.1	28.3	29.7	33.9	30.5	30.9	36.4	34.3		
0.1	0.2	0.1	0.1	0.1	0.1							
20.0	19.3	19.6	20.1	19.6	18.8	19.7	19.6	20.3	19.9	20.3	20.2	
1.1	1.3	1.7	0.6		1.3	1.8	2.6	0.6	0.8	0.7	1.6	1.2
		20.3	25.4	26.7	28.6	31.0	30.5					
1.0	0.7	1.1	1.7	1.2	1.9	2.1	2.2					
2.5	1.6	2.8	2.5									
36.3	36.6	36.8	37.1	36.3	37.2	37.7	38.5					
1.5	1.8	1.6	1.9	1.9	2.2	2.3	2.5					
3.9												
			0.3						0.3			
0.1	0.1	0.1	0.1	0.1	0.1	0.0			0.0	0.0	0.0	
			0.2		1.1	1.1	1.9					

out of wedlock? To find out, we need to know the number of
illegitimate births and the number of unmarried women in the fertile
years. The formula is:

$$\frac{\text{General}}{\text{Illegitimate Fertility Rate}} = \frac{\text{Number of Illegitimate births}}{\text{Number of unmarried women aged 15 to 44}} \times 1000$$

The general illegitimacy rate, then, gives us the number of births per thousand unmarried women of a specified age group.[8] A rank ordering of the general illegitimate fertility rates for all nations supplying data for the computations, is graphed in figure 13. The rates range from 1 to 209.9 illegitimate births per thousand unmarried women for the countries and years indicated. The rates may be transformed into probabilities; in Angola, Guinea, and El Salvador the probability that an unmarried woman between the ages of 15 and 44 would produce a child was one in five for the given year, while in Japan and Israel the probability of such a birth was only one in a thousand.[9]

The advantage of the rate as a measure of illegitimacy is that it relates the illegitimate births to the *potential* mothers of illegitimate children. The rate is particularly useful where the proportion of women unmarried varies over time. Using the rate it becomes possible to note the extent to which the unmarried category maintains or changes its reproductive behavior. The illegitimacy levels of several nations may also be compared without weighting the high or low proportions of women "at risk" in the countries (see chapter 5).

The disadvantages of the rate as an indicator of levels of illegitimacy include the problems of scarcity of data, the problem of consensual unions, and the differential treatment of the category "married but separated."

The general illegitimate fertility rates reported in figure 13 are not available for as many nations as was true of the ratios. Many of the less-developed nations of the world have only recently begun to take censuses. Some have not yet asked for or reported the marital status of their citizens or have reported only gross categories of married or single over age 15.[10]

----

[8] The rate used for detailed studies usually has unmarried women aged 15 to 44 in the denominator. United Nations reports, however, have tended to use unmarried women aged 10 to 49. Understandably the unmarried category is greatly inflated if the 10- to 14-year-old group is included. Rates up to 60 percent lower than otherwise are thus reported. Yet, so few births are actually contributed by those 14 and under or 45 and older that the 15- to 44-year-old range seems preferable.

[9] These probabilities would err in not taking into account the typically small proportions of multiple births and instances of two single births by one woman in one calendar year.

[10] Age-specific illegitimacy rates, for five-year age categories, require even more detailed data but are most useful in examining national variations in illegitimacy (Hartley, 1966, 1969b, 1970b). Some age-specific rates are reported below.

Figure 13. General Illegitimate Fertility Rates by Rank Order
for 46 Countries (Latest Available Year)

Date	Country	Rate	0	50	100	150	200
1955	Guinea	209.9					
1960	Angola	209.4					
1961	El Salvador	206.6					
1961	Venezuela	190.3					
1960	Jamaica	189.5					
1961	Honduras	185.1					
1960	Panama	170.4					
1962	Ecuador	136.3					
1961	Peru	125.8					
1960	Mexico	112.6					
1964	Colombia	92.9					
1960	Iceland	85.6					
1960	Puerto Rico	78.4					
1960	Argentina	60.9					
1955-57	Congo, Dem. Rep.	49.4					
1960	Chile	48.3					
1968	Austria	28.1					
1961	Yugoslavia	26.0					
1965	Bulgaria	25.3					
1961	New Zealand	24.1					
1965	United States	23.5					
1960	Portugal	22.2					
1964	England & Wales	20.2					
1960	Sweden	19.7					
1961	Canada	17.9					
1961	Australia	17.8					
1960	Denmark	17.1					
1960	Poland	15.3					
1962	France	14.5					
1961	West Germany	13.0					
1960	Hungary	12.4					
1966	China (Taiwan)	11.9					
1960	Norway	9.2					
1960	Finland	8.5					
1960	Ryukyu Islands	8.2					
1960	Switzerland	7.1					
1961	Belgium	5.6					
1960	Spain	4.9					
1961	Italy	4.2					
1955	Albania	3.6					
1960	Netherlands	3.6					
1961	Ireland	3.5					
1961	Greece	2.2					
1960	Philippines	1.9					
1964	Japan	1.6					
1961	Israel	1.3					

SOURCES: Computations from the number of births by legitimacy and total births, numbers of unmarried women aged 15–44; that is, those single, widowed, and divorced (and separated, when numbers available) from U.N. *Demographic Yearbook* (1959, 1962, 1963, 1965, 1969, 1970).

Increasingly, however, countries are providing a great variety of detailed information. For instance, some nations have a national register of the entire population,[11] or take surveys between census years, or have excellent registrations of vital statistics in addition to the census data. These allow computations of illegitimacy rates not only for census years (when marital status by sex and age is categorized) but also between census years.

The classification of marital status varies greatly around the world. I know of no country in which a census taker would challenge the respondent for proof of the stated legality of a marriage. A number of countries where consensual unions are frequent provide a separate count of these. In some countries these unions may be stabilized or "socially legitimated" by religious or tribal ceremonies but remain unrecognized in distant civil registers. In other countries such unions are, in the main, indicative of casual mating.

Another source of noncomparability among nations is the category "legally married but separated." Some national bureaus report these persons within the broader category "single, widowed, and divorced" and some include them with the married respondents, while others record the distinct category.[12] Our study depends on the national census bureaus and their reports for the necessary data. Wherever possible (e.g., Japan), those reported "separated" are included with the single, widowed, and divorced. In most states of the United States "separated" is not even legally defined, so that those legally married but separated would be included in the married category. The problem probably is not very important in this country, because a pilot study indicated that the overwhelming majority of illegitimate births are to women who have never been married (Kiser et al., 1968:133).

CORRELATION BETWEEN RATIO AND RATE

The three most commonly used measures of illegitimacy offer different information. The numbers of births out of wedlock indicate

---

[11] A population register provides for the continuous recording of information about events that occur to each individual on a current basis. Virtually complete coverage is provided in Taiwan, Israel, Japan, Belgium, Bulgaria, Czechoslovakia, Denmark, Finland, the Federal Republic of Germany, Iceland, Italy, Netherlands, Norway, Sweden, and the Soviet Union (Shryock and Siegel, 1973: Part I:34).

[12] A detailed study of England and Wales revealed that these persons contributed a significant proportion of all illegitimate births and should, therefore, for our purposes, be included with those "at risk" of bearing a child out of wedlock (Hartley, 1969b).

the extent to which individuals in a given country may be affected. For international comparisons or comparison over time, the ratio and rate are most useful, the ratio signifying the proportion of all births that are illegitimate in a given year and the rate indicating the extent to which unmarried women have produced children in a given year. Although the number of births out of wedlock plays a part in all three measures, the ratio and rate, with different denominators, may and sometimes do vary independently of one another:

1. Raising (or lowering) legitimate fertility rates would lower (or raise) the illegitimacy ratio if illegitimacy rates remained constant.

2. Any change in the percentage of women married would lead to a change in the ratio if legitimate and illegitimate fertility rates remained constant.

3. Changes in the proportions of women at specific ages could affect changes in the general illegitimate fertility rate and the ratio in opposite directions; e.g., a great increase in young women 15 to 19 could lower the general illegitimacy fertility rate (for women 15 to 44) even if age-specific rates remained stable; at the same time increased numbers of births out of wedlock could increase the ratio (percent of all births that are illegitimate).

Although ratios and rates may and sometimes do vary independently, the rank orderings for those countries for which we have data are actually very highly correlated. There are 44 countries listed both in rank order of ratios (figure 1) and of rates (figure 13). Comparing these one finds only a few countries with widely different ranks on the two measures of illegitimacy. Nationalist China (Taiwan), which ranks thirty-first on rates and thirty-ninth on ratios, has a general illegitimacy rate similar to that for Hungary and France, but with a small proportion of women unmarried and higher legitimate fertility, the percent of all births recorded as illegitimate is very small.

A similar situation is evidenced by the Democratic Republic of the Congo, ranking fourteenth out of forty-four on rates and twenty-sixth on ratios. The rate at 49.4 is very close to that of Chile. The very different ratio is indicative of the much smaller proportion of women unmarried and higher legitimate rates in the Congo as compared to Chile.

Finally, both Sweden and Denmark have much lower rankings on illegitimacy rates than on ratios. This is possible because of a reverse in the demographic situation prevailing above: a higher than the average European proportion of unmarried women aged 15 to 44 and a low set of age-specific legitimate fertility rates. It is notable that illegitimacy rates for England and the United States in 1964 and 1965, respectively, are higher than the Swedish rate of 1960. Yet the Swedes, with a greater proportion of women unmarried produce a relatively high percentage of births out of wedlock.

Comparing the rank orders for the 44 countries with both rates and ratios produces a Spearman rank correlation coefficient of $+.95$ significant at the .001 level,[13] which demonstrates a high relationship between these two most important measures of illegitimacy for these countries. This means that although we must recognize the possibility of deviant cases—the independent variation of rates and ratios—we are able to make some cautious inferences about the relative ordering of countries on their rates of illegitimacy, even if we have only the more often reported ratio with which to work. For instance, we can assume that Middle Eastern countries, which have low illegitimacy ratios, would also have very low rates of illegitimacy; on the other hand, South and Central American countries reporting very high ratios (i.e., Nicaragua and Paraguay) would also be expected to rank high on an ordering of national rates of illegitimacy. Thus ratios can give us some clues to the probability of correspondingly high or low rates where these data are not directly available.

AGE-SPECIFIC MEASURES

Few persons would expect, after reflection, that the ratios and rates just presented would be uniform for women throughout thirty or more childbearing years. How do the percentages of births out of wedlock vary for younger and older age categories? To what extent do unmarried women differ by age in the probability of producing an illegitimate child? Age differences themselves vary somewhat over time and space.

---

[13] Similar rank orderings would occur purely by chance in less than one case in a thousand. The Pearson Product-Moment Correlation was also computed with an r of $+.93$ statistically significant at the .001 level.

Age-Specific Ratios

During the rise of illegitimacy in England and Wales over the last thirty years, the percentage of births out of wedlock rose for each age group listed by the registrar general. Table 8 shows the ratios or percentages of births out of wedlock for specific age groups of mothers. In 1964, while 7.2 percent of all births were illegitimate, over 22 percent of all births to women under age 20 were out of wedlock. Comparison estimates based on the partial data of the United States are included for the white and nonwhite categories for 1964. Although young mothers had the highest percentage of illegitimate births of all age groupings, this is due in part to the overwhelming preponderance of unmarrieds in the youngest age category. Their illegitimacy rate is actually lower than that for the next four age groups.

Table 8. Illegitimate Birth Ratios by Age of Mothers, England (and Wales) and United States

Age Group of mother	Illegitimate Live Births per 100 Live Births				
	England and Wales			United States 1964	
	1938	1964		White	Nonwhite
Under 20	17.7	22.6	(15–19)	9.8	49.8
20–24	5.4	7.4		3.2	23.4
25–29	2.7	4.5		1.6	16.7
30–34	2.4	4.7		1.4	15.1
35–39	3.2	5.7		1.7	14.8
40–44	3.9	7.3		$\Big\{$ 2.1	13.8
45 and over	3.8	9.9			
All ages	4.0	7.2		3.4	26.4

SOURCES: Great Britain, General Register Office (1938: pt. II, pp. 110, 174; 1964: pt. III, p. 69); U.S., H.E.W. (1968a: table 17).

Age-specific Illegitimate Fertility Rates

Age-specific rates may be computed for any country that reports legitimacy status at birth by age of mother and marital status by five-year age groups. For most nations and time periods, births out of wedlock per thousand unmarried women are typically lower for the youngest age group than for all the other categories below age 40. Table 9 exhibits the age-specific rates for four countries, allowing a series of comparisons to be made:

Table 9. Illegitimate and Legitimate Fertility Rates by Age

Age Group	England and Wales 1964	Japan 1964	Jamaica 1957	Chile 1960
	Illegitimate Fertility Rates			
15–19	10.30	.17	135.40	20.97
20–24	31.59	1.45	247.99	61.57
25–29	51.80	6.45	228.68	90.53
30–34	44.05	8.29	162.72	91.38
35–39	24.73	4.04	99.67	61.37
40–44	7.35	1.05	30.23	24.41
15–44 total	20.20	1.64	168.24	49.12

Approximate probability of an unmarried woman 15–44 giving birth:

	1/50	1/610	1/6	1/20

		Legitimate Fertility Rates		
15–19	469.64	271.15	544.73	630.48
20–24	287.24	337.02	387.48	454.02
25–29	210.50	240.07	301.14	343.44
30–34	115.31	92.68	223.93	260.89
35–39	53.30	21.06	155.56	176.55
40–44	13.93	3.67	57.39	78.98
15–44 total	107.61	119.87	202.15	277.15

Approximate probability of a married woman aged 15–44 giving birth:

	1/10	1/9	1/5	1/4
Crude birth rates	18.4	18.6	39.4	32.8

SOURCE: Hartley (1970a).

1. There is a great variation in rates by age of mother. For England and Wales in 1964 an unmarried woman aged 25 to 29 was five times more likely to produce a birth out of wedlock than an unmarried girl aged 15 to 19. These data destroy the simplistic notion that illegitimacy is basically a problem for the very young or innocent. As we attempt to understand this or any social phenomenon the forces at work increase in complexity.[14]

---

[14] In future chapters we will examine the differential probabilities of marriage following conception, by age of the mother. The possibility of married women contribut-

Peaks in the probability of producing a child out of wedlock vary within nations. The highest age-specific illegitimacy rates occur for the age category 30 to 34 in Japan and Chile, for 25 to 29 year olds in England and Wales, and for 20 to 24 year olds in Jamaica. (Age-specific rates for the United States in 1964 were similar to those for England and Wales.)

2. The most extreme contrast is between the rates for Japan, which has very low levels of illegitimacy, and those of Jamaica where there are very high levels of illegitimacy. The general illegitimacy rate for all women 15 to 44 years of age is 100 times higher in Jamaica than in Japan. Yet at the years indicated, the 15 to 19 year olds in Jamaica were 800 times more likely to give birth to a child out of wedlock than the same age category in Japan.[15] At every age the probability of producing an illegitimate child was very low in Japan: even the age group with the highest rate produced only eight children out of wedlock for each thousand unmarried women in 1964. At the higher Jamaican rates, the women aged 20 to 24 would have produced about a thousand children for each thousand women unmarried over a four-year period. Over all ages, about 2 percent of the unmarried women in England and Wales and about 5 percent of those in Chile produced a child out of wedlock each year.

3. For England and Wales (in 1964) and for Chile (in 1960), unmarried women aged 15 to 44 were one-fifth as likely to produce a child as married women within the same age range. For Japan (in 1964), unmarried women in the childbearing years were only about one-seventieth as likely to produce a child as a married woman of the childbearing ages. In Jamaica in 1957, however, the unmarried woman in the childbearing years was almost as likely to produce a child as her married counterpart.

4. Finally, the nations listed in table 9 have widely different fertility overall. Jamaica and Chile are high fertility nations (though not the highest in the world), while England and Wales and Japan have relatively low fertility for the world as a whole, Japan being the only nonwestern country to have gone through the "demographic transition" in this century.

---

ing to births registered as illegitimate may also be examined as it varies by age of the mother (Hartley, 1969b).

[15] More recent data by age groups are not available for Jamaica.

Several years ago, using the age-specific legitimate and illegitimate fertility rates in table 9, I played around with a series of "what ifs," giving special attention to nations that report little or no information on illegitimacy. I was able to determine what the percentage of births out of wedlock would have been *if* the married and unmarried women of any given country were to have the age-specific fertility rates of England and Wales, Jamaica, Japan, or Chile. (The procedure, called standardization, is typically used to plot "standard" age-specific death rates against a variety of age structures for different countries; see Barclay, 1958.) With four standard sets of fertility rates, it was possible to say that the age and marital structure of India in 1961 would have produced 0.2 percent of all births out of wedlock if the rates were as in Japan, or up to 7 percent of births out of wedlock if the illegitimacy rates were as high as in Jamaica. It was also possible to determine that in spite of the fact that Venezuela has an illegitimacy ratio 20 percentage points lower than Jamaica, the age-specific illegitimate fertility rates must be almost identical. On the other hand, even though Jamaica has a very high proportion of women unmarried, if they had the age-specific illegitimate and legitimate fertility rates of Japan they would have had only 8 percent instead of over 70 percent of all births out of wedlock. The standardization procedure was interesting in a number of ways, not the least of which was the establishment of some upper and lower limits on illegitimacy ratios, given the age and marital structures reported by 68 nations (see Hartley, 1970a). It demonstrates the overwhelming importance of the differential propensity of unmarried women to produce children (indicated by illegitimacy rates).

The great mass of statistical data presented in this chapter is offered at the beginning of our study to indicate that the data are not ends in themselves, but rather a means of aiding in the ongoing study of births out of wedlock. Reservations on the accuracy, the consistency, the availability, and the comparability of data and definitions need not prevent the study, but should imply a realistic recognition of the limits of purely statistical analysis. Nevertheless, the vast array of data that are available will be useful in a review of the previous suggestions regarding causes of illegitimacy as well as in formulating a multidimensional scheme for the analysis of illegitimacy as a societal phenomenon.

3. *Previous Theories or Propositions*

As IS true of most social phenomena, there are a variety of suggested reasons for illegitimacy. Some of the explanations proposed are the facile "off the top of the head" variety, others have come from long years of research related to the phenomenon. Each of us, however, is limited in the extent of the world we are able to comprehend, and many of our explanations have come from "particularistic" experience: the study of one society, or one segment of society, or even from a few personal acquaintances. My own study began with a look at illegitimacy in England and Wales and a curiosity about the rising levels of births out of wedlock in that "advanced" civilization. The initial research stimulated a whole series of questions about illegitimacy in similar "westernized" societies and about contrasting situations in countries where levels were very high, very low, or declining. To what extent could illegitimacy be the result of poverty? Or the sex drive? Or race? Or youth and naiveté? A lack of sex education?

Let us examine a variety of the explanations that have arisen, in light of the international data presented in chapter 2, before we go on to present in the next chapter a more complex scheme of analysis that will incorporate some aspects of these prior insights. The review of previous theories is organized under four general headings: physical factors, psychological explanations, social structural, and cultural explanations. I will deal critically with each of these in order to clarify the inadequacies in the singular approaches and the need for a multidimensional approach to the study of births out of wedlock.

PHYSICAL FEATURES

HUMAN PHYSIOLOGY

Probably one of the most immediate comments on the cause of births out of wedlock is human sexuality. In our post-Freudian age some consider sex as the main motivating factor in human behavior. The sexual "instinct" is often viewed as a force so powerful that it propels human beings toward sexual intercourse with any convenient object. Childbirth outside of marriage would be seen as merely the unintended outcome of this acting out.

In contrast, we must note that, whether the sexual capacity is viewed as an "instinct" that must be acted on or a "drive" that orients individuals without compelling particular action, it is a human universal and cannot be used to explain a variable, illegitimacy. The more societies one studies, the more impressive are the myriad ways in which human groups organize to take care of their needs. *The Material Culture and Social Institutions of the Simpler Peoples* by Hobhouse, Wheeler, and Ginsberg (1915:167) and *The History of Human Marriage* by Westermark (1925) pointed out hundreds of different patterns of social organization relating to sexual intercourse and the care and rearing of children. These varied patterns cannot be explained by the sex drive alone.

The continual rather than only periodic capacity of the female to be sexually receptive is one physiological distinction between the human and lower species. That capacity facilitates the long-term pairing of human beings. In addition the very long period of childhood dependence gives some advantages, if not direct encouragement, to stable unions.

The need to prove one's physiological capacity to bear children is offered as another distinct reason for childbirth out of wedlock. It has been suggested that for some societies now, and for others in earlier times, the most important contribution of a woman to the union is her ability to produce children. In these societies pregnancy is an immediate cause for marriage, often no ceremony is needed, pregnancy being sufficient for the social recognition of the union. The possibility of a male backing out of such a marriage about equalled the probability of illegitimate birth. The penalties included severe beatings, lifelong disgrace, fines, and even death. It is not surprising that the prevalence of illegitimacy among primitives varied inversely with the severity of the penalty (Westermark, 1925:152-57).

The aim of demonstrating fecundity may backfire where women have sexual relations with many men and medical control of venereal disease is inadequate. Sterility as a result of venereal disease may be rather widespread in some countries where births out of wedlock have been frequent (UNESCO, 1956:619). For instance, in the 1960 Jamaican census almost 20 percent of women aged 30 to 54 reported that they had never had a child even though yearly about one-fourth of all unmarried women 20 to 24 years old bore a child. With rates of illegitimacy as high as they have been in Jamaica, it is improbable that 20 percent of the women were exempt from sexual relations. Evidence indicates that the very early and promiscuous mating patterns have led to high rates of venereal disease and consequent sterility (see Tekse, 1968).

The physical strength of the male may be thought to allow them to force sexual intercourse on the weaker of the species. Most social groups organize to protect the young and weak from the physical attack of the older or stronger. Thus societies have incest taboos as well as the ideal of legitimacy. Most groups have laws and related sanctions for the violation of these, but to the extent that the society or social group is less well organized, they are inadequate to demand conformance or impose penalties. Thus, in Jamaica, Judith Blake (1961:89) noted that family disorganization means that young women and girls are unprotected in several ways:

> One of the most important and effective ways of protecting young girls from sexual exploitation is for male relatives to be ready and able to retaliate if such exploitation occurs. Whether this condition prevails depends heavily on the organization of the family.... Among lower-class Jamaicans, however, a father is as likely as not to be absent from the family picture. Brothers may be merely half-brothers, or living elsewhere.... The sexual exploitation of young girls therefore both results from family disorganization and contributes to it. Men are provided with a far wider range of sexual partners than they would be if girls were protected. Thus, there are fewer pressures on the man to form a permanent liaison. Moreover, once a woman has a child or two, her desirability can always be weighted by men against that of the childless young girl. Thus, because young girls are in many ways unprotected from male advances, older women are unprotected from the competition of young girls.

Some members of the new women's liberation movement suggest that rape is a "political" or power phenomenon rather than the result of the physiological sex drive. The fact that rape does not seem to decline even if prostitution is available or legalized implies that more than physiology is involved.

Related to the actual physical strength of the male is the idea of *machismo*—that a man demonstrates his strength and virility via feminine conquests involving both sexual intercourse and the production of children, in or out of wedlock. The "false conception of masculinity" was cited by both Uganda and Venezuela as a factor leading to births out of wedlock (U.N. Sub-Commission, 1967:12). The *machismo* theme is especially prominent in Latin America, but it is not without influence in other parts of the world (see Rivera, 1971:51). Criticism of the theme is implicit in the historical and structural analyses of the Billingsleys (1966) and Johnson and Cutright (1973).

RACE

Those who have examined the data on illegitimacy in the United States or have read of the high levels of births out of wedlock in the Caribbean are likely to suggest that there may be a connection between race and illegitimacy.

Although it is clear from tables 10 and 11 that within the United States the rates, ratios, and even numbers of illegitimate births are far greater for the nonwhite than for the white category, it is clear that the increases have been less rapid in most cases for the nonwhite than for the white. Age-specific rates for nonwhites even declined for the three categories age 20 to 34 between 1960 and 1968 (see table 10).[1] Therefore, the rise in ratios and in numbers of births out of wedlock can only be due to a nonwhite decline in the proportions who were married (see for instance, Gendell and Van der Tak, 1973). In chapter 5, we will examine some of the social forces that influence proportions married.

The blacks in the United States (about 90 percent of the nonwhite category) like those of the Caribbean and Latin America have been torn from their historical patterns of social organization by the forced migration of slavery. While white racists tend to emphasize the nonwhite nations and sub-groups that have high levels of illegitimacy, their arguments do not hold up. International data on illegitimacy

---

[1] See also Cutright (1973a) for estimates that take account both of underregistration of births and census undercounts of unmarried women over time.

clearly indicate that within black Africa, Nigeria stands out as a nation reporting (1957 through 1961) only 0.1 percent of all births as illegitimate. Most nations of the Middle and Far East are at the bottom of our rank ordering of nations. There is no reason to suppose any hereditary racial proclivity to giving birth out of wedlock.

Table 10. Illegitimate Birth Estimates for Unmarried
Women 15–44 by Color and Age, United States

Color and Age	Rate per 1,000 Unmarried Women				
	1940	1950	1960	1965	1968
White					
15–19	3.3	5.1	6.7	7.9	9.9
20–24	5.7	10.0	18.6	22.2	22.6
25–29	4.0	8.7	17.6	24.3	21.5
30–34	2.5	5.9	10.6	16.6	14.9
35–39	1.7	3.2	{ 3.9	4.9	4.7
40–44[1]	0.7	0.9			
15–44 total[2]	3.6	6.1	9.3	11.6	13.0
Nonwhite					
15–19	42.5	68.5	78.8	75.9	86.5
20–24	46.1	105.4	160.7	152.6	109.0
25–29	32.5	94.2	169.0	164.7	96.6
30–34	23.4	63.5	104.9	137.8	75.1
35–39	1.7	3.2	{ 3.9	4.9	24.2
40–44[1]	0.7	0.9			
15–44 total[2]	35.6	71.2	98.8	97.7	83.0
Total					
15–19	7.4	12.6	15.7	16.7	19.8
20–24	9.5	21.3	40.3	38.8	36.1
25–29	7.2	19.9	42.0	50.4	39.4
30–34	5.1	13.3	27.5	37.1	27.6
35–39	3.4	7.2	13.9	17.0	14.6
40–44[1]	1.2	2.0	3.6	4.4	3.7
15–44 total[2]	7.1	14.1	21.8	23.4	24.1

SOURCES: U.S., H.E.W. (1968a: 4). The 1968 total rates are from U.S., *Vital Statistics* (1968); the 1968 white and nonwhite categories are from Cutright (1973: 384).

[1]Rates computed by relating births to mothers aged 40 and over to women aged 40–44.

[2]Rates computed by relating total births, regardless of age of mother, to women 15–44.

Table 11. Number and Ratio of Illegitimate Births by Color, United States

Category and Color	1940	1950	1960[1]	1965[1]	1968
Ratio of illegitimate births per 1,000 births					
White	19.5	17.5	22.9	39.6	53.3
Nonwhite	168.3	179.6	215.8	263.2	312.0
Total ratio	37.9	39.8	52.7	77.4	96.9
Number of illegitimate births					
White	40,300	53,500	82,500	123,700	155,200
Nonwhite	49,200	88,100	141,800	167,500	183,900
Total number	89,500	141,600	224,300	291,200	339,200

SOURCES: U.S., H.E.W. (1968a: 8) and calculations therefrom. The 1968 data are from U.S., *Vital Statistics* (1968).

[1]Based on a 50 percent sample of births.

CLIMATE OR GEOGRAPHY

We have already pointed out that the international data are patterned in geographic regions. To what extent do the physical attributes of a geographical area influence the production of births out of wedlock?

Those who have studied illegitimacy have been initially interested in the phenomenon where it looms large, at least proportionately. Thus, in examining illegitimacy in the Caribbean or in Central America, researchers have wondered if the hot weather, the humidity, or the balmy nights might have some influence on the prevalence of sexual relations and therefore on illegitimacy. Aside from the fact that sexual intercourse outside of marriage is a necessary but not sufficient condition for births out of wedlock, we have again an easy refutation of the climatic theory in the international data. Among the countries both high and low on measures of illegitimacy are the hottest and most humid nations of the world. Similarly one may find high or low levels of our measures in cold, mountainous regions and at desert and sea level. There is little basis in geography or climate for suspecting a causal relationship with illegitimacy.

PSYCHOLOGICAL EXPLANATIONS

It is not surprising to find that psychologists tend to offer psychological explanations for births out of wedlock. There are now innumerable studies of mothers out of wedlock that focus on personality factors that may have predisposed them to premarital pregnancy. Whether by way of short- or long-term clinical observations and interviews, or by way of psychometric, or personality, testing, the unwed mother has been found to exhibit a variety of personal disorders.

PERSONALITY PROBLEMS OF UNWED MOTHERS

The array of generalizations about unmarried mothers would lead almost anyone to a state of depression. Labels applied to explain these mothers out of wedlock include "hysterical disassociation" (Kasanin and Handschin, 1941:83), "inner conflicts" (Terkelsen, 1964:19), "serious personality or behavioral inadequacy" (Pearson and Amacher, 1956:19), "depressive reactions" and "overt psychopathology" (Loesch and Greenberg, 1962:627), "pervading personality disturbance" (Trout, 1956:21), either objective or neurotic "anxiety" (May, 1950), "severe emotional deprivation" (Nielsen and Motto, 1963), and "moderate to severe character disorders ranging from the sociopathic to the schizoid" (Khlentzos and Pagliaro, 1965:782). Some researchers needed several categories adequately to "diagnose" unwed mothers. Of 54 unwed pregnant women awaiting delivery in a maternity home in New York City, Cattell (1966:66) classified 30 as having "character disorders," 17 as "schizophrenics," and the remainder as having "neurotic reactions." The incredible fact in most of these studies is that *none* of the mothers was found to be "normal," and pregnant simply as an unintended consequence of having had sexual intercourse. Since the latter possibility was ignored, all of these diagnostic studies must be seriously questioned.

Research procedures do become more sophisticated over time, however, and there have been recent studies in which women pregnant out of wedlock were matched with nonpregnant women of similar age, socioeconomic background, education, and so on (Vincent, 1961). Personalities of women in the two categories were diagnosed by psychologists who had no knowledge of pregnancy status. Although the items of the California Personality Inventory consistently indicated less positive personality profiles for the unwed mothers than for the matched group, the differences were smaller than might have been anticipated.

An even more crucial research paper was produced by Pauker (1969) who was able to obtain the Minnesota Multiphasic Personality Inventory administered in the ninth grade throughout Minnesota, in order to compare scores of girls who later became pregnant out of wedlock with others matched by school, age and socioeconomic status. The 117 pairs showed very few differences on 10 scales developed from 566 statements. For this group, personality problems could not have been a causal factor in pregnancy.

Anxiety following pregnancy is another matter altogether. It may then be related very closely to the objective situation. Whatever worries married mothers exhibit are likely to be exaggerated for the unmarried: concern about money, a job, housing, care of the infant, and in addition, lack of the emotional security of a husband and father for the child. As already noted, one study of the personality attributes of unwed mothers and plans for the child indicated that those who wanted to keep the child were less secure, more excitable and emotional, less intelligent and mature, and more submissive than the mothers who planned to allow adoption of the child (Jones, Meyer and Borgatta, 1966:227).

UNCONSCIOUS BUT PURPOSIVE BEHAVIOR

A number of psychologists, especially those of the Freudian persuasion, have suggested that pregnancy out of wedlock can best be understood by psychoanalysis. Khlentzos and Pagliaro (1965:780) claim that "chance pregnancy is improbable." Concluding analysis of more than 100 unwed mothers, they suggest:

> The unwed neurotically seeks from the alleged father gratifications desired but not received from love objects within her family group. She becomes pregnant in a desperate attempt to satisfy oral dependency needs. She usually is not seeking erotic gratification. She is searching for nurturance from a mother figure symbolized in the sexual act as a forbidden kind of eroticized nurturing provided by the alleged father.

A more detailed psychoanalytic explanation is offered by Leontine Young (1954) in her book, *Out of Wedlock*. In reviewing case studies of unmarried mothers, Young was initially puzzled by the large number of unwed mothers who met the father in an unconventional fashion. Not only did the mothers show little feeling for the man, but also they often had trouble describing him as a person. "These

girls 'rarely' ever considered contraceptive devices even though knowing that sexual intercourse might result in pregnancy. Typically the
girl reports that she 'doesn't know" why she hadn't thought of
contraception." Young's portrait of the unwed mother is of a girl
who usually denies any sexual wish and acts without conscious
awareness. She ignores the question of participation in and responsibility for sexual activity. Furthermore, these girls did not desire
abortion even though they evidenced no fear or moral scruples about
it (p. 21-59). (Nor would those who really desired an abortion be
found among unwed mothers.)

According to Young, Freud proved that human behavior is purposive, even if the purpose is unconscious. Unwed mothers, she suggests,
have an unconscious desire to have a birth out of wedlock.

Young sees these cases as either mother-ridden or father-ridden.
On the one hand, the "mother-ridden" girls express an infantile
dependence on or intense hatred of their own mothers who they
picture as dominant in the home. In such cases the girl appears to
have a powerful drive to give the baby to her mother as a sort of
punishment for both the mother and herself. The "father-ridden"
girls are very aware of their fathers, whom they describe as dominat-
ing, rejecting, tyrannical, and cruel. As fathers for their own babies,
these girls seem to choose men who are either casual contacts or
continuing sexual partners and who are inconsiderate and sadistic
in nature. Such mothers rarely consider taking the baby home, but
they may want to keep it as a weapon against its father. These
"psychotics" usually will not surrender legal custody of the child
but leave it in a boarding home where it is likely to grow into an
unhappy, insecure, rejected adolescent (ibid.).

Yet dominant or domineering parents have obviously been on the
decline (in this country and probably in many others), and permissive
child rearing has been the order of the day for at least a third of
a century (see Miller and Swanson, 1958; Bronfenbrenner, 1964). Thus
we can hardly use the dominant parent theory to explain the
tremendous rise in all measures of illegitimacy. Nor do the Freudians
pretend to take a random or representative sample of all unwed
mothers. Those who go for counseling are not necessarily like all
the others. Young neglects the possibility that more than one goal,
conscious or unconscious, may be involved in human behavior. It
would be difficult to square the psychoanalytic model with the

international data on illegitimacy. It is too much to imagine that women in the Caribbean countries are even more eager than women elsewhere to produce children out of wedlock in order to make life even more difficult for their mothers and themselves! In fact, countries of the Orient and Middle East, where parents have been totally dominant and domineering, have the lowest illegitimacy levels in the world. Surely there are more adequate explanations that do not employ the forever unknown unconscious.

UNSOCIALIZED PERSONALITIES

Any of the psychological problems of unwed mothers discussed above may in turn be ascribed to faulty socialization. Psychologists often look beyond personality or behavioral analysis to the process and problems of growing up. Thus the manifest or unconscious personality patterns of the unwed mother may be viewed as resulting from impaired socialization,—that is, from various impediments to interaction, communication, and learning. The obstructions may be intellectual, attitudinal, social, or psychological in nature (McClosky and Schaar, 1965:15).

Even when young people have quite adequate patterns of human relationships, it is often the case that different agents of socialization: the family, peer group, mass media, and schools, may be offering conflicting values and role models. Indeed, Clarke Vincent found that the unwed mothers studied, in contrast to nonpregnant girls of similar age and status, were less likely to have a clear set of secure values or goals toward which they felt capable of planning. We do not know whether the "principle of legitimacy" was not clearly communicated, whether a conflict in values left the girls unable to choose, or whether they consciously chose pregnancy.

In a 1941 study of 350 unwed mothers in Switzerland, D. Hans Binder found that the largest group, those who had had frequent sexual relations in one or more love affairs, tended to have an exaggerated hunger for affection as a result of having been either starved for affection or spoilt in their own homes. Professor Binder found that only 10 percent had had a normal relationship with their parents.[2]

---

[2] As many as 55 percent had received too little affection, while 10 percent had too much affection of an exaggerated kind. The other 25 percent had had a thoroughly

Harrison Gough's well-known socialization scale (1961) has been used on a wide variety of groups. Unwed mothers scored very low on the series of items making up the socialization scale in comparison to all other groups of women. Only women in prison were ranked lower on the average.

In another study in the United States, unwed mothers were found to be social isolates with few or no friends and no groups to which they belonged or in which they participated (Reeder, 1965). Yet, other studies have found nearly normal relationships continuing even after the baby's birth (Bowerman et al., 1966).

How is it possible to resolve the inconsistencies in the data? Most authors readily admit that they do not presume to generalize for all unmarried mothers from their own limited samples. Yet the conclusions often leave one with the feeling that the generalizations are there. It is easy to put off the inconsistencies by suggesting that different explanations hold for distinct groups. But, in that case, these studies do not lead to increased understanding or predictability, much less to control of the phenomenon.

Psychological studies have tended to begin with the assumption that something must be "wrong" with the unwed mother. They usually go on to find that something and label it. The fault may be found in the "personality" of the mother, in presumed unconscious drives or in the prior socialization patterns of the woman that lead to specific personality problems or the unconscious "set." These studies have not considered that it is possible simply that some portion of women are unmarried, that some participate in sexual intercourse, that some of those conceive and are either unable or do not wish to marry the father and either do not believe in, or want, or know how to obtain an abortion and thus produce a child while unmarried. That there are a series of factors related to each of these is undeniable. That the woman's personality may be relevant to one or more of these possibilities is also undeniable. But that personality differences could explain the differences in tendency to produce children out of wedlock for the many countries of the world seems absurd on the face of it.

---

inconsistent upbringing—too much affection one day, too little another (Wimperis, 1960:103). In 62 percent of these homes, domestic conflict was serious and frequent; in another 18 percent, there was hidden conflict. Young people have difficulty becoming socialized to stable affective relationships in these surroundings.

STRUCTURAL EXPLANATIONS

The most general explanation of illegitimacy ties the phenomenon directly to the social structure (Davis, 1939a). Although we must understand the norms against illegitimacy, we must also recognize that the norms themselves are tied to the patterning of human group life. The social definition of "the family" implicitly, if not explicitly, defines the nonfamily.

LEGALISTIC APPROACH

There has been a nearly universal rule that the illegitimate child does not acquire full membership in the family. In patriarchal, patrilineal societies he cannot continue the family line, because he is attached to the parent that is not lineally significant (Davis, 1939a:227). Attempts to redefine the social structure through law have not been successful. In France following the revolution and in 1920 in Russia, all legal distinctions between legitimate and illegitimate children were abolished. The revolutionary idealists supposed that "by the simple expedient of abolishing a word, the Convention had all the satisfactions of abolishing a condition, and not nearly so many of the inconveniences" (Brinton, 1936:33). Yet in both France and Russia, the actual experience produced a worsened position for mothers and children. In Russia the "magnificent slogans of the liberation of sex and the emancipation of women proved to have worked in favor of the strong and reckless, and against the weak and shy . . . millions of children had never known parental homes" (Timasheff, 1960:58; see also Coser, 1964). This is certainly one of the reasons that human groups have organized to provide socially sanctioned family units for the care of the young. When adults refuse the rights and responsibilities with regard to their offspring, the children are in a disadvantaged structural position. The experiments in abolishing the family in France and Russia were followed by strict legislation relating to both the mother and her illegitimate child. Visions of equality cannot make up for the long-term commitment of a responsible father and mother.[3]

---

[3] Utopians and idealists have the continuing opportunity to demonstrate that alternative family forms really are advantageous over time. Even the very intelligent, well-organized, and highly motivated system of the Kibbutz appears to be returning

There is, therefore, a complementarity between marriage and bastardy. Rules (such as that of legitimacy) and the relevant sanctions are formulated by social groups, not because perfect conformity is expected (then the rule would be unnecessary), but to limit the extent of deviations. In the application of negative sanctions, society not only punishes the deviate, but also, and most importantly, reinforces the norm that was violated.[4] So, too, in examining illegitimacy we will be interested in the strength of sanctions against illegitimate childbirth as one clue to the strength of the principle of legitimacy.

POVERTY

If poverty is a cause (or *the* cause) of illegitimacy, as is often suggested (U.N. Sub-Commission, 1967:11) then evidence should be clearly available from the international data to demonstrate at least a relationship between the two. The question of relationship, however, is complicated by the fact that there are two relevant aspects of poverty to be considered: absolute poverty and relative poverty. Keeping this distinction in mind, there are a number of available economic measures that may be compared to levels of illegitimacy.

Absolute Poverty

If we examine evidence on absolute poverty, we can use the widely available information on gross national product per capita. And just as we have measures for illegitimacy at single points in time and measures of change over time, we have G.N.P. measures for specific years and measures of change over time.

Table 12 displays the raw data that will concern us in the following discussion. With nations listed in rank order of their illegitimacy ratios, it becomes possible to search for an ordering among the other variables listed. Looking down column 3 we find a nearly random distribution of per capita gross national product according to ordered illegitimacy ratios (reflected in a low Pearsonian correlation of − .24).

---

to more traditional family forms. The many interesting communes rarely remain stable enough to provide data on long-run results for children.

[4] Durkheim (1949:chapter 2) noted that crime is normal to all societies and that it performs a service to the society, but *only* when it is punished.

Table 12 Rank Order of Illegitimacy Ratios of Countries and Economic Variables

(1) Year and Country	(2) Percentage of Births Illegitimate	(3) 1963 GNP per capita in (U.S.) $	(4) Average Annual Growth in Real GNP per capita 1960-67	(5) Percentage of Labor Force Unemployed, 1965	(6) Average Persons per Room	(7) Percentage of All Females Economically Active*
1964 Jamaica	74.1	$ 446	2.7%		1.9 (1960)	30.3
1967 Panama	70.0	472	1.6 (1950–58)	7.6	2.4 (1960)	14.5
1965 Guatemala	67.4	299	2.2		2.6 (1964)	7.9
1968 El Salvador	67.2	247	1.8 (1953–59)		2.2 (1961)	11.3
1957 Honduras	64.5	211	2.0		2.4 (1961)	7.7
1968 Dominican Republic	61.8		-0.7		2.0 (1960)	5.9
1967 Nicaragua	53.4	304	4.5		2.8 (1963)	12.3
1967 Venezuela	53.2	768	4.4 (1950–60)		1.6 (1961)	11.4
1969 Peru	48.9	236	2.9		2.3 (1961)	13.6
1968 Paraguay	43.0	199	1.3		–	14.4
1967 Trinidad and Tobago	41.1	653	6.0 (1952–60)	14.0	1.8 (1966)	17.9
1966 Mozambique	34.3	71	–		1.0 (1950)	5.1
1963 Angola	32.6	71	–		–	4.7
1966 Ecuador	32.2	186	1.0		2.5 (1962)	10.5
1967 Iceland	30.0	1719	2.5		1.0	21.5
1966 Argentina	26.4	564	1.3	5.3	1.4 (1960)	16.4
1967 Costa Rica	25.8	370	–		1.5 (1963)	9.6
1967 Colombia	23.4	266	1.5		1.9 (1964)	11.6

1965 Puerto Rico	23.2	982	6.5	12.0	1.1 (1960)	12.2
1968 Mexico	22.5	386	2.3 (1948–59)		2.9 (1960)	11.6
1963 Uruguay	20.0	607	-0.3		—	19.3
1967 Chile	17.7	324	2.3	5.4	1.7 (1960)	14.2
1958 Bolivia	17.2	117	2.8		—	42.2
1967 Sweden	15.1	2230	3.8	1.1	0.8	29.8
1968 New Zealand	13.0	1756	2.1		0.7	21.0
1960 Brazil	12.9	268	1.1		1.3 (1960)	13.1
1968 Austria	12.0	1087	3.6	2.7	0.9 (1961)	36.0
1967 East Germany	10.7	600 (1957)			1.2	39.8
1966 Denmark	10.2	1689	3.6	2.4	0.7	31.8
1968 United States	9.7	3166	3.6	4.5	0.7	30.2
1968 Bulgaria	9.6	365 (1957)	6.5 (1953–60)		1.2 (1965)	45.7
1968 England and Wales	8.5	1603	2.3	1.5	0.7	32.6
1967 Yugoslavia	8.3	265 (1957)	7.2 (1953–60)	6.1	1.6	31.1
1967 Canada	8.3	2121	3.7	3.9	0.7	19.7
1967 Australia	7.7	1811	3.0	1.3	0.7	25.0
1968 Portugal	7.4	343	5.1		1.1	13.1
1956 Congo, Democratic Republic (Zaire)	6.7	178	2.7 (1950–59)			49.6
1967 France	6.1	1745	4.3		1.0	28.0
1968 Norway	5.6	1564	4.3	1.2	0.8	17.8
1967 Czechoslovakia	5.4	680 (1957)	6.0 (1952–60)		1.3 (1961)	37.8
1967 Finland	5.1	1408	3.7	1.4	1.3	34.8
1968 Hungary	5.0	490 (1957)	4.8 (1952–60)		1.5	32.8
1968 Poland	4.9	475 (1957)	5.8 (1953–60)		1.7	40.1
1968 West Germany	4.8	1666	3.2	0.6	0.9	33.2
1968 Switzerland	3.8	1996	2.3		0.7	27.4
1956 Morocco (So.)	3.8	187	-1.9 (1952–60)		2.2 (1960)	—

Table 12   Rank Order of Illegitimacy Ratios of Countries
and Economic Variables

(1) Year and Country	(2) Percentage of Births Illegitimate	(3) 1963 GNP per capita in (U.S.) $	(4) Average Annual Growth in Real GNP per capita 1960–67	(5) Percentage of Labor Force Unemployed, 1965	(6) Average Persons per Room	(7) Percentage of All Females Economically Active*
1968 Ireland (Eire)	2.6	811	3.0	5.6	0.9	20.1
1967 Belgium	2.5	1498	3.8	2.4	0.8	19.9
1967 Philippines	2.5	254	1.1	7.1	1.1	16.3
1967 Italy	2.0	988	4.2	3.6	0.8	19.5
1968 Netherlands	2.0	1220	3.8	0.7		16.1
1968 Taiwan	1.6	186	7.1	3.4	1.9 (1966)	16.1
1968 Spain	1.4	517	5.7		1.1	13.5
1964 Albania	1.4	175 (1957)				36.3
1968 Greece	1.1	555	6.4	5.2	1.5	27.8
1967 Japan	0.9	709	9.1	0.8	1.2 (1963)	39.1
1968 Israel	0.6	1093	4.3		1.6 (1966)	18.3
1965 Tunisia (Moslem)	0.3	218	1.6			3.0
1968 Mauritius	0.3	303			1.9 (1962)	9.8
1968 Algeria (Moslem)	0.2	284	5.6 (1950–58)			1.8
1961 Nigeria (Lagos)	0.1	75	1.2 (1953–57)		3.0 (1961)	16.0
1967 United Arab Republic (Egypt)	0.0	155	—	(1964) 1.9	1.6 (1960)	4.8
1955 Syria	0.0	188	−2.2 (1954–60)	7.4	2.3 (1962)	5.4

SOURCES: Column (2), per figure 1; (3) UNESCO, *Yearbook* (1970) and Russett (1964); (4) UNESCO, *Yearbook* (1969: table 179) and Russett (1964); (5) UNESCO, *Yearbook* (1969: table 22); (6) UNESCO, *Yearbook* (1969: table 199); (7) International Labor Office (1972: table 1).
*Economically active includes self-employed, employed, and working in a family business or farm, at most recent census date (1950–70).

Per capita G.N.P.s for Jamaica and Japan, at opposite ends of the ranking of illegitimacy ratios, were almost identical in 1950, but by 1963 the Japanese had improved their position more than the Jamaicans. Guatemala, El Salvador, and Honduras, with about 65 percent of all births out of wedlock, had per capita G.N.P.s in 1963 similar to those for Algeria, Tunisia, and Taiwan, which reported 1 percent or fewer illegitimate births. Industrialized countries with gross national products greater than one thousand dollars per year per person tend to fall in the middle area of this rank ordering (with the United States, highest in per capita G.N.P., about midpoint) although one cannot say they "cluster" there, for, in fact, the distribution is very broad and a relatively full range of per capita G.N.P.s is found in the middle section of rank-ordered illegitimacy ratios.

Average Annual Change in G.N.P. Per Capita

Davis (1963) has noted that the Japanese controlled their fertility in order to take advantage of new opportunities for increasing their standard of living. Perhaps it is to be expected, therefore, that illegitimate fertility should also decline with increases in opportunities for material advance within a given society. Indeed, if we examine countries whose illegitimate fertility ratios have declined from relatively low levels (chapter 2), we find a rather large average annual percentage change in per capita G.N.P: 4.3, 3.7 and 9.1 (1960-67) for Norway, Finland, and Japan, respectively (see table 12, column 4). However, we also find a 4.5 percent average annual increase in G.N.P per capita for Nicaragua whose illegitimacy ratios remained at very high levels over the same time period. In Jamaica G.N.P. per capita increased at 7 percent per year from 1953-60 (dropping to a 2.7 percent average for 1960-67), while its illegitimacy ratios, already the highest in the world, continued to rise. (For all countries listed in columns (2) and (4) the Pearsonian $r = -.26$, still not statistically significant at the .05 level.)

In examining data for 23 developed countries, Cutright (1971b:39) found a very strong negative relationship between changes in per capita G.N.P. and changes in illegitimacy rates for 1950 to 1960. Yet, with the addition of two marital fertility measures to the analysis, as indicators of the increasing availability of birth control, the explanatory power of the initial relationship dropped to 6 and 11 percent for early vs. late marriage nations, respectively. From these data, therefore, we cannot assume that illegitimacy will decline with decreases in absolute levels of poverty and opportunities for increasing material living conditions.

Relative Poverty

We know that G.N.P. is not equally divided among members of any nation. Perhaps high levels of illegitimacy are more closely related to relative poverty internally than to absolute poverty. However, large differences in per worker productivity, one measure of inequality within nations (Cutright, 1967), are found in nations with low, medium, and high levels of illegitimacy.

The Gini index of inequality (Russett, 1964:247), a measure of internal differences in income distribution after taxes indicates that there is little relation to illegitimacy ratios. (Very few countries provided data for both measures, however.)

Wherever detailed studies within nations have been produced (Vergara, 1965 (Chile); Clarke, 1966 (Jamaica); Leffingwell, 1892 and Hartley, 1969a (England); and Goldstein and Mayer, 1965 (U.S.)) the expected correlations[5] between poverty and status levels and illegitimacy rates or ratios were *not* found. Although data within the United States indicate very high levels of illegitimacy among poor blacks, the same is not true for equally poor Orientals. Most convincing overall is the fact that, even though large proportions of the poor in Central and South American countries produce children out of wedlock, a very small proportion of the poor masses in India, the Orient, and the Middle East do so. Therefore poverty cannot be considered the cause of illegitimacy, but perhaps it is some of the concomitants of poverty that affect the level of illegitimacy. We will examine some of these briefly.

---

[5] Caution must be used in the interpretation of these "ecological" correlations (the relations between statistical properties of groups). Robinson (1950) has pointed out that correlations between such group data must not be used to infer correlations between properties of individuals. That is clearly not the goal here. We do claim that *if* poverty were the cause of illegitimacy, then at the very least one would expect that the poorest local communities within nations and the poorest nations of the world would have high levels of births out of wedlock; most do not.

Percentage of Labor Force Unemployed[6]

Unemployment or underemployment could affect the level of births outside of marriage by magnifying the instability of family life. In particular, husbands and fathers who are unemployed are not able to fulfill one of their functions for the family unit. The male may, consequently, be less willing to obligate himself through matrimony or may leave a situation in which he feels degraded. In spite of the plausibility of this reasoning, available international data on unemployment,reported in column 5 of table 12, contain too much variation for us to regard this factor as causal. High levels of unemployment—over 7 percent of the labor force--are reported for both Panama and Syria, at the top and bottom of the rank ordering by illegitimacy ratios. There are too many intermediate variables for any consistent relationship between working and avoidance of births out of wedlock.

Living Conditions

Scarcity of housing or crowded living conditions may be cited as leading to postponement of marriage (Sweden) or increased opportunity for nonmarital sexual relations. One index of crowding, the average density of persons per room as of the 1960 round of census reports is listed in column 6 of table 12. Although the available data produce a Pearsonian correlation of $+$ .47, which is statistically significant, we cannot view the high average number of persons per room as causing high ratios of illegitimacy. The correlation is, in part, a function of the inclusion of large numbers of Central American nations and a lack of data for nations of the Orient and the Middle East. Syria, Morocco, and Nigeria among the most crowded of countries in terms of the number of persons per room, report very low illegitimacy ratios. These societies have very effective social controls surrounding social and sexual intercourse outside marriage.

Proportions of Women in Work Force

As women in the less-developed countries free themselves from family controls by increased employment in the whole process of

---

[6] Reports of the percentage unemployed should be used with caution, as these data have varied sources and the term itself is not uniformly defined worldwide.

industrialization, it is sometimes assumed (e.g., Goode, 1961, 1963; U.N. Sub-Commission, 1967) that illegitimacy is bound to increase. Yet, if we examine column 7 of table 12, it is clear that the percentage of women economically active is only minimally related to illegitimacy. Overall the correlation (r = −.33) indicates that the greater the proportion of women in the labor force the lower the proportions of births that are out of wedlock. Variation over all countries listed is great, however.

Theoretically, an increase in the proportion of women in the labor force could have any of several possible effects on the level of illegitimacy:

1. Working could lead to the postponement of marriage while saving for marriage, or the income from female employment may make it possible for a young couple to be financially independent and marry at younger ages. Illegitimacy could increase *or* decrease as a result.

2. The increased mixing of the sexes in the commercial world could lead to increased extramarital sexual activity and increased illegitimacy.

3. Participation in the labor force may make for the increased independence of women in relation to the male and result in lower illegitimacy, e.g., in Jamaica.[7] On the other hand, the increased independence of women in relation to their own families could lead to higher levels of illegitimacy, as Goode (1963) predicts will be the case for the Arab countries in the future.

4. Control of the young may be transferred from the family to the work place. In Japan, for instance, it is still not uncommon for fathers to contract their daughters to factory work for 7 to 10 years and then to marriage. Factories often have dormitories with familial type supervision and separation of the sexes (Abegglen, 1970). Such a system may work to lower or maintain low levels of illegitimacy.

Differential Importance of "Status Placement"

Goode (1960b) and Scott (1972) argue for the modification of Malinowski's "principle of legitimacy" claiming that the importance

---

[7] Not merely *participation* in the labor force but also equalization of salary is an important factor here—about which little is known. It is said that in Jamaica while

of the father is not so much a matter of paternal protecti
is a question of status placement (see also Coser and Coser, 1970).
They suggest that the lower classes are less concerned about status
placement for their offspring and therefore feel free to violate the
norm of legitimacy. However, if we look at the international data,
we must ask why the lower classes in some countries, e.g., Egypt,
Japan, Greece, and Spain, apparently consider status placement
within recognized family units very important. One could argue that
it is at least as important, if not more so, for lower-class children
to be *located* in the social structure as it is for children of
other classes. Precisely because of other handicaps, it may
be most important for the lower-class child to know who he is
and where and how he is expected to participate in social life.
True, the question of who is to inherit wealth poses few problems
when there is little wealth, but families transmit more than physical
property. They transmit succession to political, occupational, and
religious statuses as well as class status; they transmit membership
in wider social groups; and they transmit a general cultural heritage
as well as the family's idiosyncratic culture (Davis, 1948:405). Since
the neonate becomes fully human only by way of social transmission,
one cannot declare the process less important to one class than to
another. In a relatively open class society, the adequacy of cultural
transmission may determine the extent to which the young are able
to take advantage of opportunities for advancement or personal
growth. In a closed class system such social transmission may be
necessary for physical survival.

Neither poverty nor its concomitants are a direct cause of illegitimacy. Many more studies are needed before assumptions about
lower-class illegitimacy may be confirmed or rejected. It seems most
accurate to conclude not that lower class status as such leads to
high levels of illegitimacy, but that a lack of a stable family structure,
which may or may not be found among the lower classes, is likely
to lead to high levels of illegitimacy. Because the family is the primary
unit of socialization, children in unstable units are likely to become
adults who repeat the pattern of instability.

---

unskilled men may earn $20 per day, most women work as domestic servants for $5
to $10 per week. They often must support themselves and several children on that
income. Independence cannot be real under these circumstances.

Perhaps rather than poverty causing illegitimacy, illegitimacy perpetuates poverty in that the young of disorganized families are repeatedly at a disadvantage in preparation for whatever opportunities for progress present themselves. Davis (1965:311) indicates the extent to which families in the United States would *not* have been classified as impoverished if they had fewer children to care for on a given income. Overall the largest category of persons below the poverty level (excepting the aged) are those in "fatherless families."

CONSENSUAL UNIONS AS THE STRUCTURAL AND FUNCTIONAL EQUIVALENT OF MARRIAGE

Closely related to the idea that the poor need not be as concerned about status placement as the middle classes or that they can less well afford marriage is the view that consensual unions are for the lower classes either the "functional equivalent" or a "transitional" stage en route to marriage. Henriques (1952), for instance, argues that in Jamaica concubinage or the consensual union is the social equivalent of legal marriage for the lower classes. Roberts (1957) suggests that "the basic characteristic of the common law type of union is its transient nature," that is, it is transitional between the single and married states. These authors argue that for lack of money for a wedding celebration, proper housing, etc., a couple live together for some time, bear children, and only later complete the legal or religious ceremonies.[8]

Yet, available research indicates that these unions are neither structurally equivalent nor transitional to marriage. The following evidence is pertinent:

1. Roberts and Braithwaite (1961) reported research in Trinidad indicating tht common law unions are more likely to end in the single than in the married state.

2. In Venezuela dissolution of consensual unions (by other than death) is estimated to be eight times more frequent than dissolution of marriages (Arriaga, 1968).

---

[8] In this reasoning after the fact, several questions are overlooked:Why should the marital commitment take second place to the expensive celebration? How is it that the poor of India, Africa, and the Middle East manage both? Why are housing requirements different for consensual unions?

3. Stycos and Back (1964:132) report that of the 560 common law relationships reported by Jamaican women aged thirty to forty, only one in five had resulted in marriage.[9]

4. Blake's (1961) respondents reported a median duration in consensual unions of only 3.6 years, and 35 percent of her male respondents reported more than fifteen unions.[10]

5. Data from the 1960 Jamaican census indicate that 67 percent of *mothers* in the 15- to 19-year-old age group reported that they had "*never* lived with a partner" (emphasis added) (Francis, 1963).

Although some consensual unions do end in marriage, these data cannot lead one to conclude that such unions are functionally equivalent or transitional to the married state. Children born out of wedlock seldom have the advantages of a stable father figure and an intact family unit. Illegitimacy in countries with relatively high proportions of the population in consensual unions cannot, therefore, be considered only a nominal distinction for it is descriptive of very real differences in the conditions of birth and life.

SEX RATIO

It has been suggested that one structural or demographic factor contributing to the probability of consensual unions and thus to the level of illegitimacy is an imbalance of the sex ratio, or ratio of males to females. Keith Otterbein (1965:66-79) concludes a secondary analysis of twenty community studies within the Caribbean area by stating that "economic-demographic factors—in particular, opportunities to earn and save money and the sex ratio—are the major determinants of Caribbean family systems." Those family systems,

---

[9] The Styckos and Back survey has resulted in some overestimation of the union types, since they omitted potential respondents who were single or between partners at the time of the survey.

[10] The attitude involved in so many unions was expressed in an analogy drawn by a respondent in Trinidad. Rodman (1971:71) had been "asking an informant the same series of questions about each of the five women he had lived with. One question was on the reasons for separation. "When I asked him about the third woman he changed his tone of voice in order to see whether he could finally explain matters to me: 'Look, na. A woman today, jus' as a bus. Oh, the bus gone, man! Well, don' get frighten, you catch the nex' one!'" (If one wanted to carry analogy a step further, marriage might be likened to the commitment one makes in buying a car, new or used.)

e.g., consensual unions, contribute to high illegitimacy. Otterbein's argument is confused, but we do have a clear opportunity to test for a relationship between the sex ratio and the percentage of births out of wedlock.

Among 50 countries of the world for which it was possible to compute data, no relationship was found between the ratio of males to females (the sex ratio) and the ratio of illegitimaate to all births.[11] If we examine the data for Jamaica over time there is no relationship between reported sex ratio and percentage of births illegitimate. Otterbein does not test the relationship directly although 12 of the 20 studies he examined did report information on both variables. Again these 12 communities in the Caribbean show no relationship between sex ratio (he reverses the demographer's male to female ratio) and the illegitimacy ratio (which he calls rate).

SOCIAL DISORGANIZATION

One of the main propositions of William Goode's (1961) theory of illegitimacy is that societal disruptions (which occur when a foreign power takes over a country or when migrants enter a new country or newly expanding urban areas) lead to a breakdown in family organization and thus to high rates of illegitimacy. Any alteration in traditional patterns of human relations may nullify traditional mechanisms of social control. Lack of assimilation into the new or imposed systems of sanctions may facilitate deviant patterns. As cultural and structural assimilation occurs, social controls are reestablished and illegitimacy decreases.

Goode attaches significance not only to disorganized family structure, but also to the level of integration or disintegration of the whole community. He finds communities that measure low in cultural integration to be those with high levels of illegitimacy. He suggests that

it is the *community*, not the individual or the family, that maintains conformity to or deviation from the norm of legitimacy. The community defines and confers legitimacy. The individual decision, his or her role bargain, determines whether illegitimacy will be risked, and both family and individual may lose standing if illegitimacy results, but there is little stigma if the community itself gives almost as much respect for nonconformity as for conformity. Lacking integration, the community

---

[11] The Spearman rank order correlation = .07.

cannot easily punish the deviant. In any population, the maintenance of a high individual or family commitment to a given norm or conformity to the norm, is dependent on *both* the commitment of the community to the *cultural* norm and the strength of its *social* controls (Goode, 1961:917; see also Bock, 1964).

The problem we face in assessing the strength of commitment of the community or the individual to the norm of legitimacy, as one of the determinants of conformity to it, is that it is difficult to measure strength of commitment independently of extent of community controls or actual violations of the norm—in this case illegitimacy. Both of these are structural features, indicators of the degree of commitment to a cultural norm. Yet, as we will see, measures of behavior are influenced by factors other than acceptance or rejection of the norm.

Goode suggests that assimilation into new systems of sanctions occurs in phases such that illegitimacy rates (sic) increase in urban areas more than in rural areas in early phases of urbanization and industrialization, but that eventually urban illegitimacy "rates" (he uses ratios) should be lower than rural rates in Latin America even with disturbances caused by continuing urbanization. The available data for South America are contradictory in their implications for Goode's proposition. To prove his hypothesis, he would need data for both urban and rural areas over time. The Caribbean rural-urban differences show illegitimacy slightly higher in urban than in rural areas, even after heavy urbanization, but Goode suggests that they are in a different situation than the continent and will take more time to reverse differentials. (When measuring national integration in terms of percentage of national population living in major metropolitan areas, Goode obtains a Spearman-Brown coefficient of correlation of .50 with rank order of illegitimacy ratios.) Internal village social and cultural systems rated as highly integrated were found to have low rates of *social* illegitimacy (public marriage had been according to village standards but lacked legal registration). Yet, in studying the data for Chile, Vergara (1965) found illegitimacy highest in both the large urban areas and in the most sparsely settled rural areas. Johnson and Cutright (1973:400) argue convincingly that Latin American illegitimacy may be better explained by the "unusually high degree of sexual exploitation of women established by the

˙˙nquistadors and continued by their descendents . . . than the more remote and unmeasured changes in feelings of national integration."

Although we may feel some sense of logic in the relationship suggested by Goode, as we examine international data over time, problems in the integration-nonintegration hypothesis appear. The highest percentage of illegitimate births within nations typically occur during wartime, yet esprit de corps (integration?) is consistently assumed to be higher during wartime mobilization. If nonintegration is correlated with illegitimacy, are we to assume that illegitimacy is an available indicator of disintegration? Social scientists might delight in the use of so ready a measure if its utility could actually be demonstrated. However, much as some analysts might accept the recent rapid rise of all measures of illegitimacy in the United States and Great Britain as a sign of social disintegration, if a decline in births out of wedlock accompanies legalization of abortion, do we assume a healing of social disorganization? Could we really say that Nigeria, with its tremendous internal problems, is more integrated than Sweden? We need a much more detailed analysis of the ways in which community integration affects each of the series of variables to be discussed in the remaining chapters.

INDIVIDUALISM AND WELFARE STATE IN COMBINATION

In my own early study of "The Amazing Rise of Illegitimacy in Great Britain" (Hartley, 1966), I wondered whether the "welfare state" might remove, to some degree at least, the necessity to plan ahead (as via birth control) and to take the responsibility for one's actions. Long ago Durkheim (1949) had noted with concern the rise in individual consciousness at the expense of "collective consciousness." This transformation can become complete only when the state provides cradle to grave security. If the rise of the state frees the individual from the oppression of the primary group, the family, does it free the individual to a state of anomie and irresponsibility, or may reponsibility accompany the increase in individualism and the rise of the welfare state? Although the question seemed appropriate to the English case study, when tested on the relevant data for other welfare states, the hypothesis had to be discarded.

The economic underpinning provided by the welfare state does not necessarily free individuals for counternormative behaviors (including the production of children outside family units), but it may build into the larger social system some of the same motivational structures and sanctions that smaller primary groups are able to handle less formally. The case of Norway and the manner in which the state establishes parental responsibility there will be contrasted to the English situation in chapter 7.

It is clear that the welfare state cannot by itself be considered a deterrent to reductions of births out of wedlock (see also Cutright, 1973b). The question broadens to require an examination of the specific ways in which the primary group or the whole social system can most directly affect the factors involved in the production of births out of wedlock and the summary data on these national statistics.

CULTURAL EXPLANATIONS

CULTURAL RELATIVISM

Different group patterns of beliefs or attitudes have been used to account for different ratios of illegitimacy or, more frequently, to account for different behavior with regard to premarital sexual relations. In an excellent series of papers, Harold Christensen (1953, 1958, 1960) discusses the different premarital sex norms of three cultures as these relate to (1) differential rates of childbirth within the first six and nine months of marriage, (2) ratios of illegitimacy, and (3) differential probabilities of divorce. Cultural relativism—distinct patterns of beliefs and behavior—was evident.

Christensen's study is an advance over all those that examine only one or two variables, since he examines attitudes and values as well as a series of behavioral measures. But we have yet to explain the vast difference in societies that agree on premarital sexual permissiveness—Denmark and Jamaica, for instance—but produce very different levels of illegitimacy. Christensen's work leads very well into our concatenated scheme of analysis, which includes more variables in the total analysis.

Cultural relativism is often used by the unsophisticated student in a tautological manner to explain any and every difference found

among the cultures of nations and of subgroups. To suggest that
a subculture has different attitudes, values, beliefs, behavior, etc.,
because it has different attitudes, values, beliefs, etc., is not an
explanation. A superior, multidimensional analysis by the Billingsleys
(1966) has related the subcultural differences of the Negro family
in America to six major social transitions.

> (1) from Africa to America, (2) from slavery to emancipation, (3) from
> rural to urban areas, (4) from the South to the North and West,
> (5) from negative to positive social status, and (6) from negative to
> positive self-image. Each of these transitions represents a major crisis
> in Negro family life.
>   The first two of these transitions are securely in the Negroes' past.
> Transitions 3 and 4 have passed the halfway mark. And the latter
> two have barely begun. (Billingsley and Billingsley, 1966:134)

Since the Negro man was not allowed to serve as protector of a
legitimate family unit during slavery, the Negro woman became the
central, responsible focal member of the family. The disruption of
emancipation and later rural to urban migration accentuated the
development of female headed households and illegitimacy.

VALUE STRETCH

One of the most recent "theories" of illegitimacy is that proposed
by Hyman Rodman in two articles purporting to explain illegitimacy
in the Caribbean as a result of lower-class willingness to stretch
generally held values to fit their own life circumstances. He suggests:

> By the value stretch I mean that the lower-class person, without
> abandoning the general values of the society, develops an alternative
> set of values. Without abandoning the values of marriage and legitimate
> childbirth he stretches these values so that a nonlegal union and legally
> illegitimate children are also desirable. The result is that the members
> of the lower class, in many areas, have a wider range of values than
> others within the society. They share the general values of the society
> with members of other classes, but in addition they have stretched
> their values, or developed alternative values which help them to adjust
> to their deprived circumstances. (Rodman, 1966:679; see also Rodman,
> 1963)

Recognizing that human beings do often alter values to fit life's
circumstances, that humans simultaneously hold many values and

motives, that these are often in conflict, and that it is often more appropriate to think of norms as encompassing a range of expected, acceptable behavior than a single position, how do we discriminate between situations in which values will or will not be "stretched"? Why do the lower-classes of the Middle and Far East not "adjust to their deprived circumstances" and produce a majority of children out of wedlock?

Although Rodman declines to make any formal distinction between values, norms, aspirations, and goals, he seems to use the term *normative* at different times to mean desired, ideal, accepted, expected, and common or usual. In presenting his own research, however, he makes a pointed distinction between preference questions and normative questions. Preference questions indicate what is "better" or more desirable, that is, values. The results of his interviews with 676 persons in Trinidad are most interesting. Of those who prefer marriage on all three or on two of the three preference questions, we find the following percentages:

	Upper-Lower Class	Lower-Lower Class
Prefer Marriage to "living"	94% of females	82% of females
	79% of males	51% of males

These data support rather than contradict the Blake and Goode analyses that Rodman purports to modify. Respondents overwhelmingly prefer marriage to living arrangements or consensual unions. The exception of lower-lower class males implies that they are less likely to prefer marriage, not that they have a wider range of values.

On the other hand, questions, which Rodman calls "normative," that suggest that "living" is "all right," "not sinful," or "also good" suggest not desirability but permissibility. Responses that accept "living" on all three or two of the three relevant "normative" questions are as follows:

	Upper-Lower Class	Lower-Lower Class
	24% of females	45% of females
Permit "living"	(little stretch)	(moderate stretch)
	62% of males	60% of males
		(little stretch)

Rodman's data certainly indicate that there is a real difference between preferred and permitted: especially interesting are the differences between the two divisions of the lower class and the different responses of men and women. We will want to examine the implications of this position as we analyze the data for other areas of the world. If Professor Rodman really offers the "theory of the lower-class value stretch" as a general sociological theory, as he seems inclined to do—the stretch being attributed to the conditions of lower-class life (Rodman, 1963:214)—the theory must be affirmed by data beyond Trinidad. A number of questions pose themselves as we seek to evaluate this contribution to the literature:

1. Is the theory generally applicable to the lower-classes with reference to births out of wedlock? If so, why don't the lower classes worldwide respond in a similar fashion?

2. Do questions regarding the acceptability of "living" indicate the acceptance of "illegitimacy in the Caribbean"? Apparently respondents were not asked to evaluate births out of wedlock. One may accept nonmarital sex without approving of births out of wedlock.

3. Do the data presented by Rodman necessarily indicate an inverse relationship between social class and value stretch?[12]

4. Is it possible that a large part of the argument about illegitimacy in the Caribbean is due to different definitions of the terms *value* and *normative*?

Closely related to the idea that the lower classes stretch their values to include the acceptability of "living" as an alternative to marriage is the view that consensual unions are, for the lower classes, either the functional equivalent or a stage of transition to marriage. The actual patterns of family organization are a part of the social structure. The attitudes, beliefs, expectations, values, and so on, that people have about the pattern are a part of the cultural system of the group or society. We must try to maintain a distinction between the pattern (structure) and ideas about the pattern (culture). We

---

[12] The greatest area of overlap or "stretch" is found among *upper*-lower class males. Only 21 percent do not claim to "prefer marriage to living" while 62 percent permit living, a 41-percentage-point overlap. Among lower-lower class males there is only an 11 percent overlap; because they have a lower preference for marriage to begin with, they show the least value stretch of the four categories. The responses of females were quite different and deserve greater attention.

have just seen that a group may agree that they prefer marriage while actually avoiding it. Why should this be so?

In the cultural realm persons have values not only regarding marriage and legitimacy, but also regarding premarital sex, contraceptives, abortion, and so forth. Granting that values may be "stretched" in one way or another, or that values regarding one aspect of life may be in conflict with other sets of attitudes, values, and beliefs, we still have not *explained* why one or another should take precedence in determining human behavior. Is the low marriage rate of the Caribbean really "explained" by suggesting that if the couple cannot afford the wedding celebration they will forgo the wedding altogether? Does one's rationalization after the fact explain behavior? Probably "a more satisfactory use of 'values' in sociological analysis is to abandon them as causal agents" (Blake and Davis, 1964:461).

The more complex the society, the more likely a cultural disjunction in specific components. Although the legitimacy ideal is supported in the United States by both state and church, advertising and various types of entertainment keep up a ceaseless sex bombardment.[13] The development of contraceptive technology may have taken away much of the risk of nonmarital sexual intercourse, yet both church and state have been ambivalent about approving the distribution of contraceptive information especially to unmarried persons. In the United States, for instance, the Protestant churches are almost unanimous in recent years in recognizing the need for family planning, with the Catholics assenting to the use of the "rhythm method," but Protestants have been inconsistent and Catholics absolutely opposed to the distribution of contraceptive information to the unwed—and especially to unwed mothers! They apparently fear the threat to the family as a social institution.

RELIGION

The decline or absence of religion, or of a particular type of religion, has been another source of blame in the production of births out

---

[13] See Clark Vincent for a discussion of cultural inconsistencies in the United States. These become personal problems for the unwed mother, e.g., an inability to identify independently with a given value-system *or* behavior pattern, and subsequent disinclination to assume any individual responsibility for sexual behavior (Vincent, 1961:260).

of wedlock (see Tomasson, 1971). If religion is viewed as an integral part of the culture complex (beliefs, values, and norms) of each social group, it may be studied in the same way one would study any belief pattern that might influence levels of illegitimacy.

It is not enough to say that Spain is a Catholic country, and therefore it has low levels of illegitimacy. Our international review indicates that most of the Catholic countries of Latin America have very high levels of illegitimacy. One needs to know whether religious beliefs and the patterning of behavior influences the group level of illegitimacy specifically by promoting universal and early marriage, as seems to be true for the Moslems and Hindus or, perhaps, by restricting premarital sexual relations. On the other hand, religious beliefs may inflate the possibility of childbirth out of wedlock by effectively prohibiting the use of contraception or abortion. Exactly how would the religious group influence these variables: by personal rewards for conformity, shunning the nonconformists, promising supernatural sanctions, or promoting formal laws and related punishments for violation of specific standards? Is it the religious beliefs or the related sanctions, rewards and punishments, that produce behavioral results? These questions have almost endless research possibilities.

The cultural components may reinforce structural arrangements, or they may conflict with one another or with the patterning of human group behavior, as is the case in many countries of Latin America and the Carribean

GENERAL EDUCATION

Still another area of cultural confusion, if not outright contradiction, is the dichotomy between the importance placed on general education and strict limits on sex education. Let's look first at education in general and then move on to examine the relevance of sex education.

One of the more widely accepted factors used to explain high levels of illegitimacy is ignorance, especially in women. There are a number of relevant aspects that may affect births out of wedlock:

1. A low level of education and, therefore, a lack of general information or mental retardation may mean that persons are unable to assimilate any information that is available. Those who were actively involved in the early distribution of the means of family

planning learned of the creative misuse to which the means of avoiding conception might be put.

2. There may be widespread ignorance of the direct cause of conception and childbirth. Indeed, Judith Blake (1961:52-56) found that in Jamaica her respondents claimed that, at least in their very early sexual unions, they did not know "how babies happened." Most respondents were shielded from parental intercourse and even restricted from contact with other children, so that sex knowledge came neither from peers nor from the parents.

3. One may have misinformation on the high probability of conception. A widely used college text in the United States erred in reported probability of conception by a factor of 365 (days in the year).

4. There may be a lack of knowledge or a restriction of knowledge regarding the means of contraception. In fact, the assumption underlying the worldwide family-planning movement is that with contraceptive knowledge unwanted births will be virtually eliminated.

5. The lack of education on the part of young women may mean that there are few alternatives to motherhood for the woman. Both Blake and Goode point out the low bargaining position of women in the Caribbean, especially once pregnancy occurs. The female respondents in Blake's Jamaican study (1961) claimed that, in twelve cases out of fifteen, the first common-law union was precipitated by pregnancy. Later unions were also entered into because of the need for help. A forced bargain was drawn as a result of female dependency.

If we again examine figures 1 and 2, with these five aspects of ignorance in mind, we cannot conclude that this factor alone would offer itself as *the* cause of illegitimacy. Surely neither the general population nor the women of childbearing years in Egypt, Syria, Nigeria, or Tunisia, or even Greece are much better educated than those of Central America and the Caribbean. If we examine the percentage of populations aged 5 to 19 attending primary and secondary schools, as reported by UNESCO Yearbooks, we find that those countries reporting the lowest proportion of all births out of wedlock also report the lowest proportions (less than 33 percent) of school-aged youth in school. Furthermore, the five nations with the very highest proportions of school-aged youth in school—the United States, Canada, Australia, New Zealand, and England and Wales—have all reported rapidly increasing illegitimacy rates and ratios.

SEX EDUCATION

If education itself bears no relationship to illegitimacy, one might suppose that more specific sex education might be relevant in minimizing illegitimacy. What can be learned from the available data on this score?

The logic of providing information to those who know little or nothing about conception and contraception is very appealing. Yet history indicates that all social groups have had some means of controlling conception (Himes, 1936). The more accurate and complete the information, the more one would expect that births out of wedlock would be prevented.

Unfortunately, our expectations are not always well founded. There seems to be more emotionalism than knowledge in the arguments about the advisability of sex education. The only country that has instituted compulsory sex education for all youth is Sweden. Comparing the time of introduction of that program with the later reports of births out of wedlock (chapter 7 and table 21) we find that as women who have been exposed to the very detailed and moralistic sex education enter the childbearing years, the age-specific rates of illegitimacy have generally increased instead of decreased. Thus, the information itself cannot be said to be advantageous in reducing births out of wedlock. On the other hand, we cannot know what the illegitimacy rates would have been in the absence of the compulsory program. Without programs of sex education, some countries have reported similar increases, while other countries have had declines. As in so many areas, we need more controlled and comparable research.

SINGLE VERSUS MULTIPLE CAUSATION

Although the proponents of most of the theories or propositions about the causes of illegitimacy have not specifically claimed their proposals would apply universally, the discussions have tended to imply the validity of generalizing from the study of a particular case to all societies. While each explanation has some plausibility, we have shown that none is universally adequate.

Part of the problem is that most of the causal factors previously suggested are what David Yaukey (1969:101) refers to as "class A" variables: that is, they relate to the physical environment, the social structure, or the cultural norms (see figure 14) without delineating how these factors work through the series of intermediate, or "class B" variables inventoried by Davis and Blake in 1956. Just as the class C variable, fertility, can be understood as a direct result of the intermediate variables, an explanation of societal levels of illegitimate fertility requires an explanation of *how* the social structural and cultural variables influence those intermediate variables appropriate to births out of wedlock. The concatenated or interdependent series of variables outlined in the next chapter will be viewed as determining illegitimacy directly, yet each one is influenced by environmental, structural, and cultural forces. We may see, then, to what extent the previous theories may be contributory, if not sufficient in themselves, to an explanation of illegitimate fertility.

One of the intriguing, if frustrating, aspects of sociological analysis is that whenever we find one or more independent variables that we believe cause some other social factor or "dependent variable," we are never finished. It is always possible to go farther back in the causal chain to search for the factors on which the independent variable depends. As we examine variations in societal levels of marriage, nonmarital sexual intercourse, contraception, abortion, and marriage during pregnancy as these lead to societal levels of illegitimacy, we will want to begin the search for the social forces that produce societal differences in proportions married, extent of sexual intercourse outside marriage, the knowledge and availability of contraception and abortion, and the push toward marriage once pregnant. These factors may in turn be influenced by societal levels of illegitimacy. Thus no variable may truly be described as "independent"; all social variables are interdependent and reflexive (Davis, 1963). For example, a change in one variable—the rise of illegitimacy in England and Wales—may cause a reaction among the population that leads to changes in other variables—such as the legalization of abortion or a greater push toward marriage following pregnancy, which then reflects on (and reduces) the initial variable, illegitimacy. Illegitimacy as a social phenomenon may be studied as a cause or as a result.

My argument, although presented with the societal level in mind, should not be misunderstood to suggest that society "causes" illegiti-

Figure 14. Three Classes of Variables Related to the Study of Illegitimacy

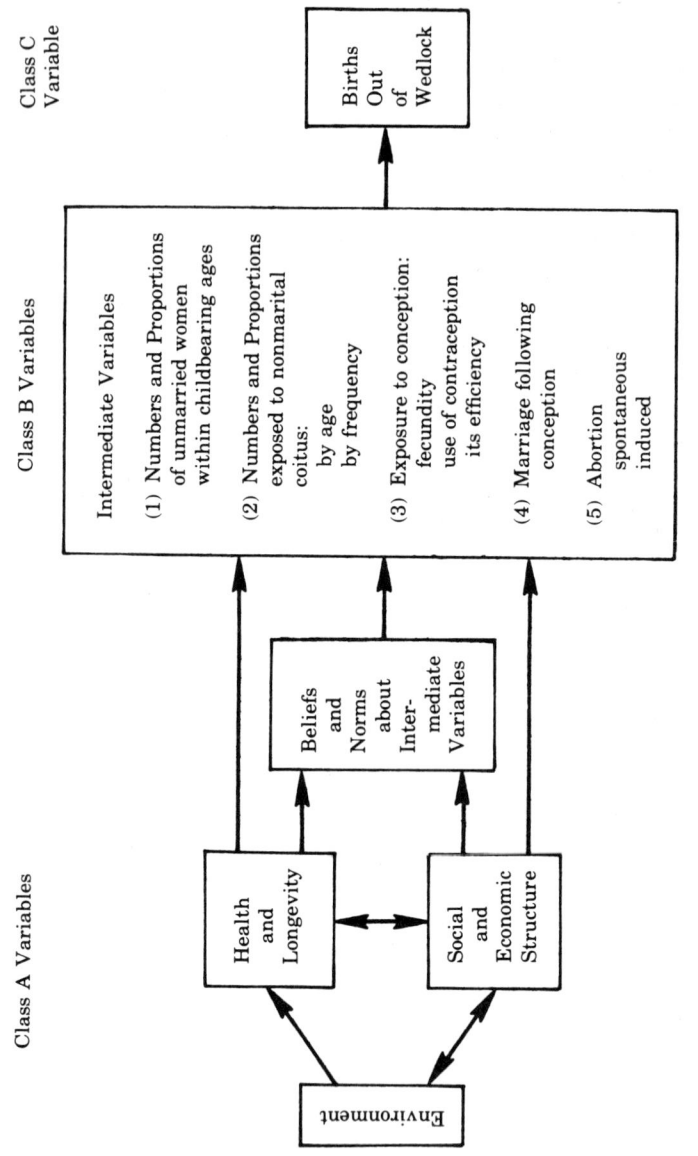

Class A Variables   Class B Variables   Class C
                                                      Variable

Intermediate Variables

(1) Numbers and Proportions
    of unmarried women
    within childbearing ages

(2) Numbers and Proportions
    exposed to nonmarital
    coitus:
      by age
      by frequency

(3) Exposure to conception:
      fecundity
      use of contraception
      its efficiency

(4) Marriage following
    conception

(5) Abortion
      spontaneous
      induced

Births
Out
of
Wedlock

Beliefs
and
Norms
about
Inter-
mediate
Variables

Health
and
Longevity

Social
and
Economic
Structure

Environment

SOURCE: Adapted from the discussions of general fertility theory by Yaukey (1969: 101) and Davis and Blake (1956).
See also Yaukey (1973: 13–16, 33–36, 46–48).

macy, except in the sense that society *is* human beings in interaction. Individual persons make decisions that may lead toward or away from the possibility of children being born out of wedlock. Those individuals, however, do not act in a vacuum, but construct their behavior as they perceive and define stimuli, consider possibilities and potential consequences. Individuals who perceive catastrophic results should they conceive and bear a child out of wedlock are likely to behave differently from those who do not know that sexual intercourse may lead to conception and childbirth or those who do not care. The perceptions of individuals are the result of their interaction with others over time, the interpretations and influence of significant others, and the attitudes and behavior of persons in one's membership and reference groups.

How then do the various patterns of human group life lead to the great differences we have noted in levels of illegitimacy? The concatenated scheme of analysis detailed in the next chapter should help us to understand, explain, predict, and possibly control births out of wedlock.

4. The Concatenated Theory of Illegitimacy

ILLEGITIMACY may be studied as the result of a process of interdependent events, which may be avoided at any one of several stages. At each stage in the chain of events, social factors influence the outcome. Rather than thinking in terms of individual (or paired) pathology, we will examine intimate (small) group and larger (societal) pressures and the conflict, imbalance, or disjunction they frequently create. Individual decision making occurs against a backdrop of social learning and is influenced by "significant others" and the values of various groups to which the individual belongs. The myriad considerations involved in the production of births out of wedlock influence at least five concatenated factors in a sort of funneling process that narrows the range of alternatives to registration of a birth as illegitimate. The sum of illegitimate births in a given society during a given period determines the societal level of illegitimacy in relation to all births (the ratio) and to the population of unmarried women at risk (the rate). We have already seen that ratios and rates are not random but are patterned according to time and place: a "social fact" par excellence.

THE CONCATENATED THEORY

We know that each society has certain marital patterns. One result of these patterns is that rather stable proportions of the female population of childbearing ages are unmarried, and, therefore, demographically "at risk" of contributing to illegitimacy. We recognize, however, that not all these females are really "at risk," because during any particular period only some of the available unmarried women of childbearing ages engage in nonmarital sexual intercourse. Of those who do, only some of them become pregnant. For those who become pregnant out of wedlock there are two alternatives to illegitimate birth: (1) marriage of the partners in conception before the birth of the child, and (2) spontaneous or induced abortion of the fetus. We are left, finally, with certain numbers of births recorded as illegitimate in the given time period. At each stage in the chain of events resulting in illegitimate births, positive and negative social controls lead to specific persons producing illegitimate children, to different patterns of illegitimacy among subcultures, and to national levels of illegitimacy that are patterned over time. Let us turn to an examination of each of the factors mentioned above (proportions unmarried, sexual intercourse, conception, marriage during pregnancy, and abortion) in terms of the forces that influence societal differences in each, referring from time to time to the diagramatic presentation of these factors in Figure 15. The factors will be briefly discussed here. Social variations will be detailed in succeeding chapters.

The formal aspects of the concatenated theory are related to the value-added theory of collective behavior developed by Neil Smelser (1963). Both theories require multivariate analysis, both treat the phenomenon as the result of a process, both point to various stages during the time sequence, both are clearly sociological rather than psychological in mode of analysis, and both examine each major variable in terms of the probability of increasing or decreasing the likelihood of the end phenomenon, whether it be collective behavior or illegitimacy. While Smelser emphasized the additive aspects of the variables considered, I have concentrated on the alternative outcomes available over time in various societies.

PROPORTIONS UNMARRIED

Since only women can conceive and bear children, our analysis begins with the recognition that the proportions of women in the various childbearing ages (generally 15 to 44) may vary at different times and in different societies. Societies that have experienced very rapid population growth in the last 20 to 30 years will have about twice as many women in the youngest group (15 to 19) as in the oldest (40 to 44) of the childbearing years. Because both illegitimate and legitimate fertility rates vary greatly by age, these differences

Figure 15. Diagrammatic Representation of the Concatenated Theory of Illegitimacy

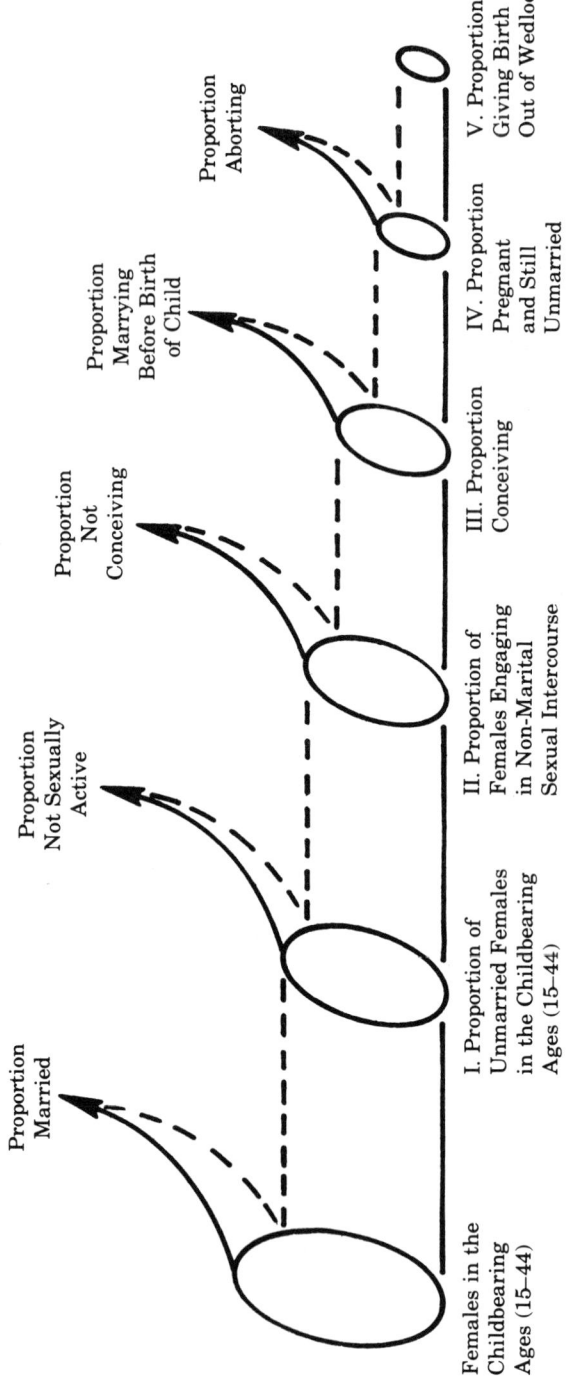

in the proportions of women at specific ages will influence both the general illegitimate fertility rate and the percentage of all births that are illegitimate (see Kumar, 1969; Hartley, 1969a and 1970a).

Societal factors influence the proportions of unmarrieds at specific ages through the childbearing years. Young people show the greatest variation in proportions married cross-nationally. While 99 percent of all 15-to 19-year-old females in Jamaica and Japan were unmarried at the 1960 census, only 30 percent of the 15- to 19-year-old women in India were unmarried. Moreover, although Jamaica and Japan have had identical proportions of unmarried females in the early age group, in the later childbearing years (35 to 44) 48 percent were still single in Jamaica but only 6 percent were still single in Japan (1960, 1965 censuses). These data imply that such disparities are not caused by industrialization or urbanization but by the very real differences in the structure of social relationships.

The state of being unmarried, or of a society's having a large proportion of unmarried females, is a necessary but not sufficient condition for very high social levels of illegitimacy. We have just noted the very high but similar proportions of 15- to 19-year-old unmarried females in Jamaica and Japan. Yet relative to their numbers the Jamaicans of that age group contribute 800 times as many births out of wedlock as do their Japanese counterparts (see table 9). Obviously illegitimacy is not merely the result of differential proportions of the population at risk, but also a matter of the channeling of behavior by and for those capable of bearing children out of wedlock.

SEXUAL INTERCOURSE

In any given society or subculture the pattern of human relationships may favor or limit the possibilities for nonmarital social and sexual intercourse. The old chaperonage system and the custom—still fairly prevalent in the Middle East (Berger, 1962:99)—of separating the sexes from puberty until marriage may be contrasted with the "modern" permissive society, which encourages mobility and freedom for individuals to meet others without any external social controls. The more individualistic the society the greater the "structural conduciveness" (Smelser, 1963) or freedom of individuals to meet whomever they wish, wherever they wish, for whatever purposes.

Similarly, the culture of society—in its knowledge, belief, and normative system—may encourage or discourage miscellaneous sexual alliances. Beliefs and norms are powerful motivators of human behavior when they are implemented by a system of rewards and punishments. For example, in some societies the violation of a woman is the gravest kind of misbehavior and is severely punished. Some social groups believe that nonsanctioned sexual relations lead to permanent contamination. This belief usually involves a double standard, which is expressed by a respondent in Trinidad as "fame for the man" is "shame for the woman" (Rodman, 1971:60). Other (mainly Western) societies have adopted the Freudian mystique of antifrustrative sexual release. Even when frustration is viewed as the greatest of all evils, however, there usually is some channeling of sexual behavior (Foote, 1954). Most societies fall between these extremes; it is typically a matter not of one or the other but of varying emphases.

The numbers and proportions of persons engaging in nonmarital sexual intercourse are not actually known for any particular period, and the illegitimacy outcome does not necessarily reflect the extent of nonmarital intercourse. The responses of interviewees to questions of a sexual nature tell us how many are willing to say that they have *ever* in their whole lives engaged in any specific activity, not the extent to which such activities were repeated over time.

CONCEPTION

Although fecundity, or the ability to conceive, depends in part on nonsocial factors such as age of partners, the general level of nutrition and health care in a social group will influence involuntary as well as voluntary sterility, etc. (see chapter 7).

The probability of conception is influenced by the extent of repetition of nonmarital sexual intercourse and by the use or lack of contraception. Henry (1961) has estimated a 50 percent probability of bearing a child in a given year for women aged 20 to 25 in populations with uninhibited sexual practices and no attempt to prevent conception. When contraceptives are used, the probability of conception varies greatly according to the method employed (Garcia, 1963:63).

Societies may promote or restrict knowledge of conception and contraception. Knowledge of conception need not be specific and complete but it must include the recognition that conception is a possible result of sexual intercourse.

Knowledge about contraception varies from one society to another. What is believed to be known may be more or less accurate and may involved more or less efficient methods of avoiding conception. Primitive social groups may "know" that unseen spirits cause conception and, therefore, devise rituals and taboos to prevent or, more likely, to encourage the "powers" of procreation. Contemporary scientists, on the other hand, recognize that they do not know as much about contraception as they would like. While the primitive may be sure he knows about contraception, he is not likely to control that phase of life as well as the contemporary scientist, who, recognizing that more detailed knowledge is desirable, may nevertheless be able to control conception very well with the knowledge already available.

Although we still search for "ideal" contraceptives, there are already enough means for the effective control of conception if it is desired. Between the two extremes of primitive beliefs and scientific knowledge lie the vast majority of social systems. If we wish to encourage rational behavior by individuals, it seems advantageous for social groups to disseminate specific and detailed information in this area. We know, however, that in many countries political and religious leaders work to suppress contraceptive information. Evidence indicates that while some information is widespread anyway, it is not always the most accurate or pertinent.

Not only knowledge but also availability of the tools of contraception may be facilitated or limited by societies. Family planning groups, social workers, and public health nurses may be forbidden or encouraged to offer knowledge and tools of contraception to unmarried persons. National governments have not been particularly successful in completely controlling population, but family planning programs in India and Taiwan have demonstrated that fertility reductions are at least possible with programs distributing information and tools of contraception.

On the other hand, knowledge and availability are mediated by both positive and negative motivations to use the known and available means of contraception when engaging in sexual intercourse out of wedlock. For example, even when knowledge and techniques were available, many unwed mothers have said they rejected the use of contraceptives because prior planning seemed to imply, to themselves if not to the partner in conception, an image of immorality. The female "cannot maintain her self-image as a 'nice girl' through rationally planning possibly 'not to be one'" (Bowerman et al., 1966:391). Therefore she typically relies on the male to use contraceptives, an obviously unfounded reliance in the case of unmarried mothers.

Positive motivations for use of contraceptives may operate simultaneously with motivation for nonuse, and societies may inflate or reduce the relative strengths of a variety of mixed motives. Some societies, for example, by providing state support for unmarried mothers and their children, may reduce the motivation to prevent illegitimate births, especially when the risk is moderated by the possibility of keeping the partner or of obtaining a husband through pregnancy.

MARRIAGE DURING PREGNANCY

Once conception out of wedlock occurs one of the alternatives to a birth out of wedlock is, clearly, the marriage of the partners in conception before the birth of the child.

Many nations of northern Europe have had historically institutionalized patterns of premarital sexual relations. In peasant populations such patterns provided a guarantee of fertility in prospective marriages. Where fathers relied on their children to maintain the land by work and legal inheritance, and children were the only possible old-age insurance, a woman's most important contribution to the family was her ability to bear children. Probably one-third to one-half of all marriages occurred after the girl was pregnant (Hair, 1966). In some societies it appears to have been the peer group that exerted the social pressure toward marriage when the young man hesitated. Some villages still follow this pre-Christian tradition today (Wikman, 1937; also Myrdal, 1945).

Some estimates on postconception marriages are available for white and nonwhite categories in the United States. With the greater detail available for England and Wales, it is possible to compute age-specific probabilities of premarital conceptions being legitimated by marriage before the birth of the infant. The probability of legitimation of a premaritally conceived child has been much higher in the younger age group (15 to 19 years) than in the older groups. For all age groups the English evidence indicates a decline over time in the probability that a premarital conception would be legitimated by marriage of the parents before birth. With a high proportion of the young pregnancies leading to marriage before birth, we may conclude that social forces favor this alternative to that of an illegitimate birth. Moreover, in the younger age group there is a greater likelihood that both partners in conception will be free to marry.

Without the sizable proportions of legitimations by marriage before birth, the levels of illegitimacy in many countries would be a great deal higher than is presently the case. Without such postconception marriages, we know that the illegitimacy ratio and rate for England and Wales would be about twice its recorded level. However, not all societies exhibit the same preference for marriage as an alternative to illegitimacy. Each society will offer different combinations of influence—by peers; family; and economic, legal, and religious institutions—that motivate individuals toward or away from marriage as an alternative to childbirth out of wedlock. Outside the advanced industrialized nations, data on births according to the months of marriage are seldom available. From the detailed data collected for Jamaica and Japan, however, we may infer that marriages occurring after conception but before birth are relatively rare in those particular societies.

ABORTION

Of all pregnancies out of wedlock not all end in childbirth. As is the case for conceptions within wedlock, there are an unknown number of spontaneous or induced abortions.

Spontaneous abortions are only slightly related to social factors such as the general level of health of the population, the quality of prenatal care, and so forth. Induced abortions, however, are very much subject to social controls. While no society or social group could hope for complete control, there are great differences in the extent of control depending on whether societies formally and informally facilitate or restrict the opportunities for safe, inexpensive induced abortions. It is difficult to measure the extent of variation, however, since few countries permit the abortion rate to be reasonably well known.

It is often assumed that the Scandinavian countries have legalized abortion, but their abortion laws have actually been rather restrictive. In Sweden, for instance, special consulting officers have been set up to discourage women from applying for abortions, and of those who persisted in applying in 1964, 1,200 of the 4,500 official applications were refused (Lader, 1966:118). In the same year it was estimated that about one-third of all abortions were granted to unmarried women. Therefore, approximately 1,100 illegitimate births were prevented by legal abortions. Had those been added to the 16,117 registered illegitimate births (U.N. *Demographic Yearbook*, 1965:528) the percentage of illegitimate births would have risen from 13.1 to 13.9. The effect on illegitimacy, then, would not have been very great. Because abortion was not completely free for the asking, however, we might expect that illegal abortions continued to be performed.[1] Estimates range as high as 12,000 illegal abortions per year in Denmark, more than twice the number of legal abortions (Lader, 1966:120).

The Japanese Diet, a democratically elected parliament, passed a Eugenic Protection Law in May of 1948 that legalized abortions only for women whose health might be impaired from "the physical or economic viewpoint." Two amendments in the next few years provided for virtually unlimited abortion at the woman's request. The measures were aimed to relieve a national population crisis. While successful in rapidly lowering the crude birth rate, it also facilitated the most rapid reduction in illegitmate fertility ever recorded.

The attitude toward abortion in Western Europe may have been much more tolerant between 1900 and 1935 than it is today.

There is indirect and approximate evidence that in the late nineteenth and early twentieth centuries in Western Europe abortion played a

---

[1] Ironically, controls had been so tight in Sweden in past years that student tourists' trips to Poland to secure abortions were ended when the Swedish government announced that participants were liable to prosecution (Lader, 1966:119). The 1971 report of a Swedish committee to study abortion recommended liberalization of the grounds for abortion, but it specifically rejected the termination of pregnancy "on demand" (Tietze, 1972).

great role. David Glass, who in 1940 summarized the findings of eight northwest European countries, cited the records of women under a German sickness benefit fund which show a gradual climb in abortions from 38 per 100 births in 1908 to 113 per 100 in 1932. In Belgium there were many books explaining how to induce abortion and any woman could buy, for 60 centimes, a uterine syringe and use this to induce an abortion. In both France and Germany advertisements by abortionists were freely published (Davis, 1963:345, 346).

Abortion is not a *new* response, then, to population or birth control, nor is it peculiarly Japanese. "It is not an outgrowth of tradition in Tokugawa times; not an outgrowth of the absence of Christian ideology. It is a response to social and economic conditions arising in country after country at a particular time in the process of modernization" (Davis, 1963).

The reports of increasing use of abortion after it was legalized in the communist bloc nations of Eastern Europe are similar to the record for Japan. Bulgaria, Hungary, and Poland followed the Soviet Union's lead[2] by legalizing abortion in 1956, and Rumania did so in 1957 (reversing themselves in 1966). Czechoslovakia started with unrestricted abortions but began to tighten its controls in 1962. Yugoslavia, outside the bloc, established a similar system of modified controls in 1960.

These countries, together with the Scandinavian nations and Japan, predominate among those countries that have reported declining levels of illegitimacy. All four nations with declining *rates* of illegitimcy—Hungary, Norway, Finland, and Japan—legally allow some induced abortions. The details of the decline in rates and ratios of illegitimacy in Japan indicate the extent to which abortion has affected illegitimacy there. Illegitimacy among young women in Japan has been virtually eliminated. In 1964 unmarried women aged 20 to 24 produced one-tenth as many births per thousand as that age group in 1940, or somewhat more than one birth out of wedlock for each thousand unmarried women. Meanwhile, in England and Wales

---

[2] The Soviet Union first legalized abortion in November 1920 but reversed itself in 1936. New laws legalizing abortion in 1955 were followed by the people's republics in Eastern Europe. Atlhough the Soviets have never released abortion statistics, all evidence indicates that their abortion rate may be as high as any in the world. Dr. Tietze estimates a minimum of two million annually, while David M. Heer arrived at a figure of 5,829,000 for a recent year (see Lader, 1966:120 ff.).

almost 32 births out of wedlock were registered in 1964 for each thousand unmarried women aged 20 to 24. In Jamaica in 1957, 248 births out of wedlock were registered by the same age group for each thousand women. It will take some time to judge the effect of the recent changes in English and American abortion laws on their levels of illegitimacy.

ILLEGITIMATE REGISTRATIONS

We are left with certain numbers of births recorded as illegitimate to mothers at specific ages, which allow us to calculate age-specific illegitimacy rates, general illegitimacy *rates*, and *ratios* or percentages of births out of wedlock. At each stage in the above positive and negative social and/or subcultural controls lead to specific persons producing illegitimate children and to social levels of illegitimacy that are patterned over time.

PROPOSITIONS TO BE TESTED

From this general discussion of the stages in the production of societal levels of illegitimacy and the ways in which societies differ in their patterning and value orientation with regard to each of the stages, we may move on to the development of some specific hypotheses to be tested in the following chapters. The numbers of derived propositions could be inflated almost without end. We shall begin with the most basic statements and derive numerous others from them.

The most general proposition to be developed from the preceding is: WHENEVER A SOCIETY OR SOCIAL GROUP, IN THE PATTERNING OF SOCIAL RELATIONSHIPS (SOCIAL STRUCTURE) AND ITS CULTURAL ADJUNCTS (CULTURAL SYSTEM), PROMOTES ONE OR SEVERAL OF THE ALTERNATIVES TO CHILDBEARING OUT OF WEDLOCK, THE LEVELS OF ILLEGITIMACY WILL BE LOW.

From our review of the stages or intermediate variables directly influencing societal levels of illegitimacy, we obtain the following specific propositions:

1. When a large proportion of women within the childbearing ages

are married, the social group or society will record a low percentage of births out of wedlock.

a. A large percentage of women unmarried does not *necessarily* lead to a large proportion of births out of wedlock.

b. Societies in which the structural and cultural systems promote universal and early marriage will be those in which the greatest proportions of women in the childbearing ages are married.

c. Social sanctions are a powerful influence on individual marital decisions within the societal framework.

2. When a large proportion of unmarried women avoid or refuse sexual intercourse, there will be low rates (and ratios) of illegitimacy.

a. It is not necessarily true, however, that high involvement in nonmarital sexual intercourse will lead to high levels of illegitimacy.

b. The greater the structural and cultural impediments to sexual intercourse outside of wedlock, the lower the levels of illegitimacy.

c. The strength of social sanctions against nonmarital sexual relations will influence the extent to which individuals participate.

3. When a large proportion of those unmarried women who do engage in sexual intercourse use highly effective contraceptives, low levels of illegitimacy are maintained.

a. Nonuse of contraceptives, however, does not guarantee high levels of illegitimacy.

b. The greater the (1) knowledge about, (2) availability of, and (3) motivation to use effective contraceptives, the lower the conceptions out of wedlock.

c. Social sanctions promoting or reducing knowledge about, availability of, and motivation to use contraceptives will affect their use by individuals within societies.

4. When a large proportion of those who conceive out of wedlock are married before childbirth, illegitimacy levels will be low.

a. Nonmarriage following conception does not necessarily produce high levels of illegitimacy.

b. The greater the structural and cultural push to marry following conception, the lower the illegitimacy levels.

c. Social sanctions, rewards and punishments, may push or prevent marriage by the couple conceiving out of wedlock. Those social sanctions may be directed by the families of the couple, by the peer group, by religious organizations, or by the state.

5. When a large proportion of those who conceive out of wedlock abort the fetus, illegitimacy levels will be low.

   a. Freely available, safe abortion does not guarantee low levels of illegitimacy.

   b. Restriction of the availability of abortion does not necessarily lead to high levels of illegitimacy.

   c. Societies that facilitate (in structural opportunity and cultural beliefs) abortion as an alternative to childbearing outside of wedlock, will tend to have low levels of illegitimacy.

   d. The greater the economic and emotional burden of illegitimate children on the mother and father, and the fewer the potential rewards of such childbirth, the lower the levels of illegitimacy.

In sum, then, social groups that reject or reduce the possibilities for all alternatives to illegitimacy will report high levels of births out of wedlock. All societies confirm the "principle of legitimacy" as an ideal. They differ, however, in the structural patterning and cultural motivations that lead to high conformance with ideals, preferences, or values. Illegitimacy rates and ratios are indicators of behavioral conformity or nonconformity with the principle of legitimacy. According to our hypotheses, social groups have not one but a number of ways in which they may attempt to channel behavior to avoid illegitimacy. Different societies stress different alternatives. Where cultural elements are inconsistent, or where group values disavow the alternatives as well as illegitimacy, it will be difficult to maintain low levels of illegitimacy. At the same time, even in those societies with cultural "fit" or consistency, the patterning of behavior must be organized so as to allow and encourage the production of children within wedlock. Social groups that are unable to channel behavior to achieve their stated goals are called disorganized. Individuals within societies conform to the principle of legitimacy to the extent that they have the ability, the knowledge, and the motivation to do so.

To the extent that it is possible, these propositions will be tested in the following chapters. No individual sociologist could hope to complete the job. Many more researchers will want to test these with the detailed data from specific societies or subcultural groups.

With something over 130 nations or states in the world, no one person would claim to grasp the details of all, even when concentrating on a single phenomenon such as illegitimacy.

Perhaps this is the point at which to indicate my view of the relationship between theory and empirical data. I consider neither one more important than the other; both are tools to increase our understanding of any phenomenon we study. Often we carry ideas in our heads without specifically formulating them as "theories." Similarly, we think we know something about observable reality. The purpose of science is to specify our ideas or theories, so that they can be tested by evidence specifically collected for that purpose. The data gathered are or become part of public knowledge. It is not merely one individual's subjective interpretation of what he thinks is reality, for the data require agreement, or what scientists call "intersubjectively defined empirical information." The observable data may help to initiate theory, to recast or refocus theory, or to clarify the concepts used in theory construction (Merton, 1957:chapter 3).

The advantage of theory in scientific enterprise is that it provides a focus for research, defines the level of causal analysis (Allport, 1950), so coordinates research that separate findings support each other, and indicates what relationships are well established and which ones need further research (Zetterberg, 1965; see also Selvin, 1958; Smelser, 1968, 1971; Stinchcombe, 1968).

Neither theory nor research, then, can be considered an end in itself (although, regrettably they are taught separately in our universities). They are truly complementary: the scientist may begin with either. This study, fo example, began with research on illegitimacy in England and Wales; that initial study led to a number of hypotheses, further research, more questions about relationships, more data collection, and finally the series of interrelated propositions presented here for further testing. The process may be likened to a spiral beginning at base with a few crude ideas about what is and why. Gathering data brings us to a new level, a new series of questions and relationships to test with more data. Each increase in the amount of information and its detail leads to greater acceptance, rejection, or refinement or reformulation of theory. Reasoning and research are never-ending reciprocal processes (Batten, 1971).

CONCEPTS DEFINED, OPERATIONALIZED

An illegitimate birth has been defined as one that has been produced outside a socially sanctioned union. For most nations of the world this means a birth outside a legally registered marital union. In theory, a birth by a village or tribally recognized union, not registered with national authorities, would be considered legitimate; in practice, the birth, like the union, is unlikely to be registered and may or may not be included in the national estimates of illegitimacy.

Although we are concerned about all births out of wedlock, we cannot speculate about those that are not registered. Operationally, therefore, illegitimate births are taken to be those reported by national authorities. We recognize that a woman giving birth out of wedlock may be more or less motivated to avoid registration of the birth as illegitimate. The greater the stigma on mother, child and family, the more likely is underregistration. More permissive societies will vary in the opportunity to fake legitimacy. In some hospitals the mother is allowed to fill out birth forms as though the child is legitimate; marriage licenses are not generally necessary for the registration of a child as legitimate. Yet in some advanced countries that keep current population registries of all citizens, it becomes more difficult to falsify birth forms. All we are able to conclude from the above is that records may be biased in a downward direction relative to actual illegitimate births.

The operational definitions of other variables also depend on the records available. Age and marital statuses are reported by the nations of the world at their various census dates. Yet census reports are only as reliable as individual reports to the census taker and the tabulation of the reports. Another problem I have encountered in my detailed analyses is a variation in the reporting of women who are legally married but separated from their husbands. Some nations report these as a distinct category; others include them with the married; still others with the widowed and divorced. It is clear that such women are demographically "at risk" of bearing illegitimate children. Whenever census reports allow it, separated women will be included with those who report themselves as single, widowed, or divorced. The variations among countries both allow and require the detailed analysis of interested researchers around the world.

The data on proportions engaging in, and frequency of, nonmarital sexual intercourse and the use or nonuse of different types of contraceptives must come from what people have said on questionnaires or in interviews. Respondents are not likely to be representative of all persons in the population under study. Yet, when respondents are subdivided by age or year of marriage, we may obtain some idea of the relative difference by age. The few studies conducted cross-nationally may give us some clues about national variation. Single nation studies will be included only as points of reference. In all cases our recognition of the inadequacies of present research reports should help lead the way to more complete cross-national studies in the future.

Like the reports on other variables, the estimates of illegal abortions are wide ranging. I have often wondered why we bother to repeat such estimates, but we have nothing better with which to work. Even presumably legal abortions may be hidden by other surgical labels. Furthermore, in countries such as Japan where legal abortions are easily obtained and inexpensive, there are still supposed to be significant proportions of additional abortions that are obtained illegally or simply not reported. It will be interesting to compare data on changes in legal abortions, operationalized as those that are reported, to changing illegitimacy levels.

Only when births within the first eight months of marriage are reported and recorded in national records, is it possible to compute the extent of marriage following conception. Very few of even the most advanced countries make the necessary data available. Yet, because the data are available in some places, certain clues may lead us to suspect similar patterns elsewhere. Furthermore, recent surveys in the United States validate prevalence of marriage during pregnancy here. Details of these and other measures will follow as we examine each of these major factors one by one to try to capture the extent of variation from one nation to another. Although the next chapters will attempt to draw together the available international data on these variables, there is no way to finalize a worldwide study of illegitimacy at this time. Thus, while we have a great deal of good data for some variables for some countries, others are more elusive and will require more detailed investigation in the future. Much of the data that is available is illustrative only and not conclusive. It is most important, therefore, to focus on the multidimensional scheme of analysis to judge its utility for the study of illegitimacy as a societal phenomenon.

5. Marriage as a Social Phenomenon

IT IS common for family sociologists to define the family in terms of the social recognition and accountability given by and to the larger society. The United Nations, in its *Principles for a Vital Statistics System*, suggests that "marriage refers to 'the legal union of persons of opposite sex. The legality of the union may be established by civil, religious, or other means as recognized by the laws of each country'" (Shryock and Siegel, 1973). No matter which of many forms the family may take among various societies (see Davis 1948:397-424), it is the group itself that defines the procedures for entry, recognition, and dissolution of the marriage.

PROPOSITIONS TO BE EXAMINED

As a part of the larger scheme of analysis we have suggested a basic proposition and several derivations relating the extent of marriage or nonmarriage to levels of illegitimacy.

1. When a large proportion of women within the childbearing ages are married, the social group or society will record a low percentage of births out of wedlock.

   a. A large percentage of women unmarried does not *necessarily* lead to a large proportion of births out of wedlock.

   b. Those societies in which the structural and cultural systems promote universal and early marriage will be those in which the greatest proportions of women in the childbearing ages are married.

   c. Social sanctions are a powerful influence on individual marital decisions within the societal framework.

As was the case in our general overview of illegitimacy, we must rely on the reports of the nations of the world for information on marriage. Marriage rates have been said to be inversely related to illegitimacy. Three different *rates* may be used to test that notion: (1) the marriage rate per thousand population, (2) the rate per thousand persons aged 15 to 44, or (3) the rate per thousand unmarried persons over age 15. All these have as the numerator the numbers of marriages registered in a given year. Information is often available so that these rates may be computed yearly.

The proportions of women of childbearing ages who are married is generally available only as reported on census dates, usually every tenth year. Because we depend on summary data as reported by nations on the basis of individual responses to census takers, we must operationalize the variable proportion married in terms of the proportion who claim they are married or who are reported by others as married at the time of the census. A basic problem is that, because a marriage license need not be shown to the census taker, a woman reporting a man or child in the household may find it easier to say she is married than to make obvious a "living" only arrangement.

In some countries (i.e., Japan) women who are "married but separated" are categorized in such a way that they may be included in our group of women "at risk" of contributing to births out of wedlock. As already indicated when possible I have included these with the single, widowed, or divorced for the total group at risk of illegitimacy, if not strictly unmarried.

We have already noted that only because we have the status of legal marriage within which offspring are described as legitimate, do we also have the alternative category of children born outside legal marital unions. If an entire population were married through the childbearing years and there was no possibility for sexual intercourse outside marriage, there would be no illegitimate registrations. It follows that the greater proportion of the population married during the childbearing years, the lower the portion "at risk" of bearing children out of wedlock. The relationship, however, is far from being as simple as might be supposed. Let us look at the available indicators of the extent of marriage within nations to see what can be learned about a possible relationship to illegitimacy.

MARRIAGE RATES AND ILLEGITIMACY

CRUDE MARRIAGE RATES

When the number of registered marriages per thousand persons in a population—the crude marriage rate—is compared to the illegitimacy ratio, we find considerable inconsistency in the cross-national results. It has often been noted that the nations with the highest percentage of illegitimate births (in the Caribbean or Central America) have the lowest marriage rates, and of course they do. It *requires* a large unmarried population in the childbearing years to produce 60 to 70 percent of all births out of wedlock. On the other hand, low marriage rates do not necessarily lead to high proportions of births out of wedlock. At two different points in time I computed Pearsonian correlations on available data. In the mid-1960s a correlation of $-.16$ was obtained for 63 countries reporting both crude marriage rates and illegitimacy ratios. In 1973 the same variables at the most recent date (figure 1) for 65 countries produced an $r = -.59$. The latter, but not the former, indicates statistical significance if not a perfect negative relationship between the two variables.

Examining the same variables over time, 1950 through the mid-1960s, we find that only 11 countries out of 51 with available data gave evidence of simultaneous movement in the expected (opposite) directions. For 7 of the 51 countries (see table 13) marital rates were decreasing, while illegitimacy ratios were increasing. Only 4 countries reported marital rates that were increasing slightly while illegitimacy ratios were decreasing. Twelve countries reported an unexpected relationship: while marital rates declined, so did the percentage of births out of wedlock.

However, crude marriage rates based on the entire population are not the best measure. What do other indicators of the incidence of marriage in a population contribute to our analysis?

RATES PER THOUSAND 15 TO 44 YEAR OLDS

Comparing the numbers of marriages per thousand persons aged 15 to 44 (Russett et al., 1964:228-30) does not improve the relationship. Ireland with 14.1 and Jamaica with 12.8 marriages per thousand persons aged 15 to 44 report 2 percent versus 74 percent of all births illegitimate. Finland and Trinidad (and Tobago) have almost identical rates at 17.6 and 17.0 marriages per thousand 15 to 44 year olds, yet Trinidad reports 42 percent and Finland 4 percent of all births as out of wedlock. Finally, Japan and Iceland with 19.4 and 19.2 marriages per thousand persons aged 15 to 44, report 1 percent and 27 percent of all births illegitimate, respectively.

Table 13. Trends in Marital Rates and Illegitimacy Ratios, 1949–66

Direction of Illegitimacy Ratios, 1949–64	Direction of Crude Marriage Rates, 1950–66		
	Down	Relatively Stable	Up
Down	Poland		
	Norway		
	France		Venezuela
	East Germany	Chile	Portugal
	West Germany	Finland	Japan
	Hungary		Philippines
	Bolivia	Italy	
	Paraguay		
	Austria		
	Belgium		
	Taiwan		
	Czechoslovakia		
Relatively Stable	Honduras		
	Ecuador		
	Mozambique	Mexico	Netherlands
	Colombia	Nicaragua	Angola
	Iceland	Peru	Panama
	Costa Rica	Uruguay	Greece
	Argentina	Switzerland	Syria
	Spain	Ireland	
	Israel		
	Egypt		
Up	Jamaica		
	El Salvador	Guatemala	
	Canada	Denmark	
	Australia	Sweden	
	New Zealand	England and Wales	
	United States		
	Bulgaria		

SOURCES: For illegitimacy ratios, U.N., *Demographic Yearbook* (1959; 1965: table 20); for marital rates (registered marriages per 1,000 population), UNESCO, *Yearbook* (1960: table 20; 1966: table 24).

RATES PER THOUSAND UNMARRIED

Even when I tried relating the number of marriages to those "at risk" of marriage—the numbers of unmarried persons aged fifteen or over—there was little improvement in the relationship between marriage rates and illegitimacy.[1] These data indicate, then, that low rates of marriage may be necessary but cannot be considered a sufficient condition for high levels of illegitimacy. If we shift our focus from yearly marriage rates to census reports on the proportions of women in the childbearing years who are married and unmarried perhaps there will be a more definitive relationship.

PROPORTIONS OF WOMEN AGED 15 TO 44 WHO ARE UNMARRIED

The 1962, 1963, and 1964 United Nations *Demographic Yearbooks* reported the latest available census data, which went back as far as 1947, but most countries reported results from the 1960-61 round of censuses. Including in the unmarried category all women who were reported as single, widowed, divorced, or separated, there seemed to be a division of nations into those in which 40 percent or more of the women were unmarried and those in which less than 40 percent were unmarried.

Nations in which most women of childbearing ages are married (usually only one-quarter to one-third unmarried) reported illegitimacy ratios varying from 0.1 to a high of 11.3 (see table 14). Most of these nations reported from 2 to 7 percent of births out of wedlock, relatively low on the world scene. For the countries listed in table 14 the Pearsonian correlation is .80, indicating a strong and statistically significant relationship between the proportions of women unmarried and the illegitimacy ratio. These data support our first proposition that when a large proportion of women are married there tends to be a low illegitimacy ratio. In addition, we know that countries, such as India and Pakistan, that do not report illegitimacy

---

[1] In most cases where comparison became possible, the direction of change was the same as for crude rates. Only two countries now appeared in an expected relationship to the trend in illegitimacy ratios that had not done so in the initial comparison. With marriages related only to the marriageable population, Denmark exhibited a decrease in marriage rates during a period of increasing illegitimacy ratios. At the same time, Poland exhibited an increase in marriage rates while reporting a decrease in the percentage of illegitimate births. Although these two nations have moved into expected situations, the new calculations would also remove the Philippines and Jamaica from their previous relationships, and we are left with no improvement in the relationship over time between marriage and the percentage of children born out of wedlock.

Table 14. Percentage of Unmarried Women (aged 15–44) and Illegitimates by Country

High Proportion Unmarried (>40 Percent)				Low Proportion Unmarried (<40 Percent)			
Country	Date	Percentage Unmarried	Percentage Illegitimate	Country	Date	Percentage Unmarried	Percentage Illegitimate
Jamaica	1960	74.3	72.4	Sweden	1960	38.9	11.3
Panama	1960	70.5	66.5	Bulgaria	1965	24.6	9.4
Honduras	1961	69.5	64.5 (1957)	Yugoslavia	1961	32.2	8.4
El Salvador	1961	71.8	64.1	Denmark	1960	37.4	7.8
Venezuela	1961	65.6	54.2	Guinea	1955	8.6	7.2
Peru	1961	57.8	42.6	Congo, Democratic Republic	1955–57	21.4	6.7
Ecuador	1962	55.0	32.5	England and Wales	1961	32.2	6.0
Argentina	1947	40.3	26.4	France	1962	37.1	5.9
Peurto Rico	1960	50.9	25.4	Germany Federal Republic	1961	38.4	5.8
Iceland	1960	42.3	25.3	New Zealand	1961	32.7	5.8
Mexico	1960	48.5	25.0	Hungary	1960	30.5	5.5
Colombia	1964	44.9	22.6	United States	1960	30.8	5.3
Chile	1960	51.7	15.9	Australia	1961	32.8	5.1
Brazil	1950	44.7	13.8 (part)	Canada	1961	32.3	4.5
Austria	1961	42.7	12.6	Czechoslovakia	1961	31.0	4.5
Portugal	1960	45.5	10.0	Poland	1960	31.1	4.5
Finland	1960	42.2	4.0	Morocco	1960	17.7	3.8
Switzerland	1960	44.2	3.8	Norway	1960	35.8	3.7
Ryukyu Islands	1960	47.0	3.6	Taiwan	1966	34.6	2.7
Italy	1961	42.7	2.4	Belgium	1961	31.5	2.0
Spain	1960	45.2	2.3	Netherlands	1960	38.6	1.3
Ireland	1961	53.2	1.6	Mauritius	1962	37.9	0.7
Greece	1961	42.9	1.2	Albania	1955	29.0	0.5
Japan	1964	42.5	1.0	Israel	1961	29.8	0.3
Philippines	1960	40.9	0.7	Egypt	1960	25.2	0.1
Macau	1960	40.2	0.2				

SOURCES: Calculations on unmarried from U.N., *Demographic Yearbooks* (1962, 1963, 1964, 1970); illegitimates per chapter 2.

figures must have low proportions of births out of wedlock, because large proportions of women are married there (for details see Hartley, 1970a). Although a large proportion of married women allows only low ratios of illegitimacy, does a large proportion unmarried lead to high ratios?

Examining table 14 we see that among the 26 countries with 40 percent or more of their women aged 15 to 44 unmarried, only six have 40 percent or more births out of wedlock. Indeed, an equal number of nations in that category have 2 percent or fewer births out of wedlock. Ten report 4 percent or fewer illegitimate births. Proposition 1(a) is also confirmed; a large percentage of women unmarried does not necessarily lead to large proportions of births out of wedlock.

That proposition looks even better when age-specific data are examined. Comparing Japan and Jamaica as exemplary of low and high illegitimacy countries, respectively, we find that both have about 99 percent of their 15 to 19 year olds unmarried. Yet we have seen in table 9 that for women in that age group the Jamaican illegitimacy rate was 800 times that of the Japanese. Clearly, the reason for such divergence and for the firm acceptance of proposition 1a is that even with large proportions of women unmarried, the *rates* of illegitimacy may be high or low. It is not simply a matter of proportions unmarried; a more important factor is the behavior of the unmarrieds in relation to the production of births out of wedlock.

Nevertheless, because a large proportion married is predictive of low illegitimacy, we are interested in the social and cultural patterning that leads to that end. How is it possible that some societies are able to channel the young into marriage at a very early age, while other social groups cannot, even though its members claim to "prefer marriage"?

SOCIAL STRUCTURING OF MARRIAGE

Although this is not the place to review the marriage customs of all the societies of the world (see Nimkoff, 1965; Queen, 1967; Goode, 1963), we may review some commonly mentioned features of marriage and compare these with the proportions of young women married where those data are available.

Of the eight traditional forms of marriage in India in none did the bride or groom have anything to say (Goode, 1963). Marriage was and has continued to be a religious and social duty in India. Only a legal son could perform the sraddha ceremony for the transmigration of the soul and reincarnation. Marriage was the first step in obtaining male offspring. Although the average age at marriage has risen from 12.5 for girls and 19 for boys in 1890 to 15.2 for girls and 20 for males in 1951, the averages are still very low internationally. In 1961, 70 percent of the 15- to 19-year-old females were already married. Even as late as 1921, 39 percent of all girls were married before their tenth birthday. Only morons and cripples remained single.

Both China and Japan have moved from an historical situation of partnerships completely arranged by parents or their agents toward free choice of a marriage partner and a higher age at marriage. These historical structural and cultural systems forced early and universal marriage. Both societies have had historically legal concubinage and from this a category of illegitimate children who could be legally recognized by the father even though not the equal of legitimate offspring.

In China concubinage was opposed by Sun Yat-sen. A survey of 38,256 rural families in the 1930s found only one concubine to every 81 wives. Yet, among 1,700 college and high school students, 11 percent reported a concubine in the home. The Communists officially oppose bigamy and concubinage, but unless one of the females complains apparently no legal action is taken (Goode, 1963:284).

In Japan the Meiji Restoration of 1868 began degrading concubinage, but it was not totally outlawed until 1946. This source of registered births out of legal wedlock, therefore, has disappeared.[2] Simultaneously we have witnessed—not merely since the legalization of abortion in 1949-50, but as far back as 1900—a long decline in the numbers, the ratio, and the rate of Japanese illegitimacy.

In the Islamic countries of the Middle East, marriage was also ideally a family decision, the groom was not allowed to see the bride before the wedding and there was great emphasis on her virginity (see Davis, 1955; Hamady, 1960). By the 1920s in the more educated, modern sectors the young man would be allowed to see the girl and

---

[2] For the relative weights of the two types of illegitimate births, see Taeuber (1958) or Hartley (1969a).

to express his opinion, but strictly speaking he had no right to choose. The girl had no right even to an opinion. The Koran allows polygamous unions of up to four wives, if they are all treated equally. Nevertheless, because of a relatively equal sex distribution, most men could not obtain more than one wife at a time. Census data from the various Moslem nations indicate that no more than 2 to 11 percent of married males have reported more than one wife. Age at marriage has also risen over time. In 1850 girls were reported to have been married at an average age of 12 or 13. By 1959 the legal minimum was was 15 or 16 years of age for girls and 16 to 18 for males, depending on the specific country (Berger, 1962). The 1960 census for Egypt, most populous of the Arabic group, recorded 32 percent of the 15- to 19-year-old women as married. In Iran about 40 percent of the same age group were married, while in Moslem Pakistan 73 percent of the 15- to 19-year-old girls were already married.

Table 15. Women 15 to 19 Reported Married by Country

Country	Year	Percentage Married
Pakistan	1961	73.0
India	1961	69.6
Iran	1956	40.0
Turkey	1960	32.4
Egypt	1960	31.6
Mexico	1960	16.4
Romania (14–19)	1956	15.2
United States	1960	15.1
Soviet Union	1959	15.0
Brazil	1950	14.8
Venezuela	1961	11.6
Taiwan	1956	11.4
Canada	1961	8.7
Chile	1960	8.2
Denmark	1960	4.9
Norway	1960	4.7
Italy	1961	3.8
France	1962	3.3
Sweden	1960	2.7
Jamaica	1960	1.3
Japan	1960	1.2
Ireland	1961	1.1

SOURCE: Computations from U.N., *Demographic Yearbook* (1962, 1963: 718 ff.).

In Africa south of the Sahara there are a great variety of marriage customs, differing not merely by nation, but also according to different tribal customs. In all, however, the social or group definitions prevail. Changes have taken place in the cities largely because the conditions of life are different and tribal sanctions have little power. Although only about 20 percent of Africans live in urban areas (U.N. Bureau 1969:73), the young, often unmarried male is overrepresented. Those who are married seldom want to bring their wives to the city, either because of financial and housing problems, or because they believe the woman will be less susceptible to seduction or prostitution within the tribal society. Being without wives, however, the drifting male often contributes to the prostitution and rising illegitimacy of the urban areas (UNESCO, 1956). Urban marriages that do occur are typically established by the young persons independently of parental or tribal sanctions. The bride price generally continues to be a necessary validation of the marriage, but its meaning has changed.

In those countries where nonlegal sexual unions predominate, a variety of solid evidence indicates that consensual unions are not the functional equivalent of marriage (see chapter 3). Shryock and Siegel (1973:550) point out that "even if the definition of marriage were to include consensual unions there remains a problem of obtaining statistics on these." The common law union is still a legal marital form in some states of the United States and should not be confused with consensual or "living" unions. To be a valid common-law union, its partners must "have presently consented to be husband and wife," the marriage must have been consummated, and the spouses must have "publicly held out each other as such" (Krause, 1971:17). Where valid, such a union produces legitimate children; the rights and obligations of the partners as parents is the same as for any other recognized union. However, the public verbal commitment must be unambiguously pronounced and is not to be assumed merely because persons have engaged in sexual relations or are living together. The trend toward abolition of the institution of informal or common-law marriage may result in increases in illegitimacy or increases in legal marital forms. In some countries of Latin America local or national governments are providing mass weddings, formalizing by ceremony and registering partners in consensual unions. Reports of hundreds and even thousands of happy participants with their children are relayed by the news media. Those who decline to be happy participants are, of course, not among the statistics.

In Westernized countries the decisions relating to marriage have increasingly been left to the decision of the young themselves. There is no doubt that parents influence the choice of their offspring, in the process of socialization and in exposure and opportunity to meet others, but the final decisions are less and less a matter of parental control. In some of these countries the age at marriage has increased slightly, in others it has decreased slightly. Young men are more easily able to afford a wife, but the standards of life—expectations in general and educational levels in particular—have risen and these contradictory forces may offset one another. Increased sexual freedom further removes an impetus to early marriage. Yet the proportion ever married remains at about 90 percent over the last 60 years or more in the United States. There has not been the recent marriage explosion anticipated as the baby boom babies of the 1950s have reached marriageable age. It remains to be seen whether we are witnessing a postponement of marriage or its partial rejection. In fact, as new opportunities become available to women in higher education and top level occupations, we might expect a decline in desirability of marriage or, at least, its inevitability (Dixon, 1971). Overall, however, it is clear that as indicated in proposition 1b in those societies where universal and early marriage is encouraged there are greater proportions of women within the childbearing ages who are married.

SOCIAL SANCTIONS

It has already been suggested that social sanctions may be more or less powerful in influencing individual decisions within the societal framework. We have hypothesized that the more powerful and uniformly applied the sanctions promoting marriage, the more frequent the phenomenon. While we have no way to test for all societies of the world, it is hoped that those who specialize in the study of specific societies or culture areas will contribute relevant data. We must resort to a selection of examples for which information is available, trying to include any negative evidence as well as evidence that seems to confirm the hypothesis.

We have already touched on one indicator of the very great social power forcing early entrance and maintenance within the marital relation historically in China and Japan. In both cases the burden of adjustment to the arranged marriage was on the wife. The only and final escape was suicide, and the suicide rate in these countries was among the highest in the world for women in the early married years.

In India supernatural sanctions were brought to bear by the claim that fathers committed a sin by not marrying off a daughter before puberty. The extent of early marriage may be taken in turn as a sign of the effectiveness of that belief, together with others requiring sons for the performance of religious rites and so on.

In the Arab world "marriage is chiefly a joining of two families rather than of two individuals. Family life is shaped by the older generation for the younger, and by the desires and values of the men imposed upon those of the women" (Berger, 1962:99; see also Hamady, 1960; Leoy, 1965). The adult control of marriage and of female chastity before marriage has led to the very low illegitimacy ratios reported in chapter 2.

In *contrast*:

> The mass of Jamaicans inherited from slavery an unusually disorganized family system. . . . There is an unusual hiatus between what Jamaicans want and what they actually get in the way of family ties: their expectations of what a daughter should do, of what a mate should do, of what a father should do, are frustrated to an amazing degree. Underlying and explaining this frustration is the more impersonal aspect of disorganization: the fact that the institutional *system does not enforce* a consistent and functionally adequate set of family norms. The man who seduces a young girl, or who abandons a mate who has borne him children, is not penalized. Because so many mothers and children are abandoned by men, young girls are often brought up in families without fathers and hence without male protection. They are thus easy marks for seduction, despite (or because of) the unrealistically strict upbringing attempted by their mothers and grandmothers (Blake, 1961:246-47). (Emphasis added.)

Writing in 1927, Briffault found a similar phenomenon operating in Uganda as males moved to urban areas and factory jobs. Although the phenomenon has presented a worry or at least a puzzle to many,

Briffault suggests that as men earned more money they could afford to do without marriage. As long as sexual relations are freely available or available at small cost, men may do without wives. Since the social sanctions of tribe and parental family are not within the immediate scope of activity and new societal norms have not yet developed, men are not forced into unions unless the woman and partnership become an end in themselves. Although there are other alternatives than births out of wedlock, these are less likely to be widely available in nonmodern societies.

Even in Germany during the nineteenth century birth control and abortion were not used to an extent that would have prevented a direct relationship between marriage patterns and illegitimacy. Knodel (1967) found that during the 1830s restrictive marriage laws were instituted in many southern and middle German states. As general illegitimate fertility rates became available in the 1860s, those states with restrictive laws, i.e., high minimum ages at marriage, tended to have higher rates of illegitimacy than states with few marriage restrictions. As states repealed their restrictive marriage laws a decrease in illegitimacy was recorded while rates remained stable in states without changed legislation. Knodel concluded that raising minimum age at marriage has little necessary effect in reducing fertility. Only forcible separation of the sexes (i.e., conscription) was offered as a possible solution to overall fertility control.

On the other hand, late marriage does not necessarily lead to nonmarital coitus and births out of wedlock. Studies in historical demography in England have led Peter Laslett to conclude that "when the parishoners of pre-industrial England married early, illegitimacy amongst them was high, and when they married late, the number of bastards went down. This we believe falsifies any argument which supposes a necessary positive connection between sexual deprivation and the procreation of children outside marriage" (Laslett, 1973).

Although social sanctions are indeed a powerful influence on individual marital decisions as indicated in proposition 1c, it must be clear from the variety of examples above that (1) a very rigid social structure and the strict sanctions which accompany it is not necessarily a positive good. There are trade-offs to be made in any society that is so highly organized that little or no deviance occurs.

But also (2) early and universal marriage is not the only way to prevent or reduce births out of wedlock, (3) nor does it prevent adulterous forms of illegitimacy.

ADULTEROUS ILLEGITIMACY

I do not know of any nation that would, as a general policy, challenge the legitimacy of a child born to a married woman. Since social groups seem to prefer legitimate childbearing, there is little reason to challenge the appearance of births within wedlock. We therefore tend to assume that all illegitimate births are produced by unmarried persons. Yet there is evidence that (1) some births registered as legitimate could not have been fathered by the legal husband of the mother, and (2) some births registered as illegitimate are produced by women who claim to be married on their census forms (Hartley, 1969b).

The first possibility has been investigated by geneticists (Schacht and Gershowitz, 1963) studying the blood types of mother, child and the mother's husband.

A study made in the early 1960s in the Detroit area showed that 1.41% of a sample of 1417 white children, though not admitted by their mothers to be illegitimate, were demonstrably not the children of their mother's husbands. The detection was done with the use of blood group systems, and the proportion is certainly an understatement of the true figure. In the case of the 523 negroes tested 8.89% were detected as extra-marital. (Laslett, 1967:29)

If these percentages were applied nationwide and were added to the illegitimacy ratios for 1965, they would have increased the proportion of births out of wedlock for white in the United States from 3.96 to 5.37 percent and for nonwhites from 26.32 to 35.41 percent. It is interesting that for each category there is the same proportional relationship between adulterous illegitimacies discovered by blood differences and the nominal proportion of births out of wedlock. For both whites and nonwhites adulterous illegitimacies were about one-third of the estimated percentages of births out of wedlock.

In my own detailed study of England and Wales I found data that allowed estimates of the extent to which married women contribute to illegitimate births. By matching three of every ten births registered as illegitimate (in the same month that the census was being taken) with the marital status reported by mothers to the census taker, it appeared that about 26 percent of births registered as out of wedlock were to women who claimed to be married. These tended to be cases in which the births were registered on the joint information of the mother and the natural father. We do not know whether the mother was still legally married to someone else, was separated and living with the natural father, or merely lied to the census taker. There are indications that all three factors may be at work, but to what extent each prevails we cannot tell. The data do indicate that women in the married-but-separated category should be included with the single, widowed, and divorced women demographically "at risk" of producing a child out of wedlock.[3]

In chapter 3 we referred briefly to the three types of adulterous illegitimacy:

1. One-sided adultery where the woman is married.
2. One-sided adultery where the male is married.
3. Symmetrical adultery where both are married to other persons.

In the 1950s Virginia Wimperis found that in one city in England 57 percent of the parents of illegitimate children would have been unable to legitimate the nonmarital conception even if they had been desirous of doing so because one or both parents were already married (Wimperis, 1960:66). These studies raise additional questions. Why were these births to relatively mature individuals not prevented? Why was there no recourse to divorce, remarriage, and legitimation of the child?

AVAILABILITY OF DIVORCE AND ILLEGITIMACY

At least one author has suggested that about 40 percent of the births registered as illegitimate in England are so designated because of stringent divorce laws (Johnston, 1968:379). But if the difficulty

---

[3] In a recent study of illegitimacy in Washington, D.C., Gendell and Van der Tak (1973) computed two sets of illegitimate fertility rates. When the women who were married but separated from husbands were included with the unmarrieds "at risk" of pregnancy out of wedlock, the general illegitimacy rate was about 15 percent lower than when the separated women were included with those married. There was wide variation in rates by age and racial categories (differences being greatest in the older ages where proportions of women separated were large).

of obtaining a divorce is a cause of children being labeled illegitimate, we would expect that where divorce is relatively easy illegitimacy levels would be low, and that as divorce becomes easier over time births out of wedlock would decline.

The underlying assumption that persons would marry and produce legitimate children if they were free to do so needs to be examined. In Jamaica parents of children born out of wedlock are overwhelmingly free to marry, yet they do not. Why should we assume that English persons who were not satisfied in one legal marriage would necessarily want to make a new legal commitment? These questions aside, the demographic data simply do not indicate that stringent divorce laws influence illegitimacy.

While it is true that many of the countries of the Caribbean have very low crude rates of divorce and very high illegitimacy ratios, we also find that countries with the most stringent divorce laws of all, i.e., Italy, Spain, and Ireland have the lowest levels of illegitimacy. Furthermore, the most rapid increases in crude divorce rates have occurred in Bulgaria and England and Wales,[4] both of which have experienced a rapid rise in the percentage of births registered as illegitimate. But, again, we may object that crude rates are not the best measure of the extent of divorce. After all, the Caribbean nations may have low crude divorce rates at least in part because they have so small a portion of the population "at risk" of divorce, i.e., married.

A more adequate indicator of the extent of divorce within a society is the divorce rate among the married population. The United Nations *Demographic Yearbook* for 1958 has reported the average annual number of divorces for census years per thousand married couples. Wherever possible I computed the rates for the more recent census period.

These rates are highest (as were crude rates) in Egypt and the United States. Egypt has had very high rates of divorce and very low illegitimacy ratios reported over time. The United States has had high, fluctuating, but generally increasing divorce rates at the

---

[4] From 1958 to 1965 for Bulgaria and from 1959 to 1964 for England and Wales the increase in crude divorce rates, or divorces per thousand persons in the population was over 30 percent. In the longer period from 1938 to 1964, the divorces granted per thousand married women aged 20 to 49 in England and Wales increased fivefold: from .97 to 4.70. See Great Britain, General Register Office (1963: pt. 3, p. 57; 1964: pt. 2).

same time that illegitimacy was rising rapidly. The lowest divorce rates are found among the Central American and Caribbean countries. In almost all of these countries the number of divorces per thousand marriages has been increasing with little change in the percentage of births out of wedlock. We need to remind ourselves (since they are not included on divorce tables) that Spain and Italy which have no legal provisions for divorce have reported decreasing percentages of births as illegitimate.

Trends in the two variables over time and across countries also imply a lack of correlation. Of those European countries with significant increases in divorce rates, Czechoslovakia, Finland, Hungary and Austria also report decreasing levels of illegitimacy, while Denmark, Sweden, England and Wales report increasing proportions of illegitimate children. It happens less often that evidence of a significant decline in divorce rates is reported. The three countries where this evidence appears to be consistent (rather than fluctuating) are the Netherlands, Norway, and Japan: all have also reported decreases in the proportions of children born out of wedlock.

Therefore we conclude that none of the statistical data indicate a relationship between the ease or difficulty of obtaining a divorce, as reflected in divorces granted, and the levels of illegitimacy. This is not to suggest that there would not be some individual cases of divorce and remarriage if divorce were made more easily obtainable. Some illegitimate birth registrations might thereby be prevented. But we should not assume any significant decrease in illegitimacy would result from easier divorce laws alone.

6. *Variations in the Extent of Pre- or Nonmarital Sexual Intercourse*

WE HAVE already suggested a number of propositions related to the question of nonmarital coitus. These hypotheses lead us to an examination of research findings on the extent of pre- and nonmarital sexual intercourse across countries and over time as these relate to levels of illegitimacy. We will then discuss the structural and cultural factors which are at work to influence levels of coitus outside of marriage. Finally, the social sanctions involved will be reviewed.

PROPOSITIONS TO BE EXAMINED

2. When a large proportion of unmarried women avoid or refuse sexual intercourse, there will be low rates (and ratios) of illegitimacy.

a. It is not necessarily true, however, that high involvement in nonmarital sexual intercourse will lead to high levels of illegitimacy.

b. The greater the structural and cultural impediments to sexual intercourse outside of wedlock, the lower the levels of illegitimacy.

c. The strength of social sanctions against nonmarital sexual relations will influence the extent to which individuals participate.

PREMARITAL SEXUAL EXPERIENCE

Data on pre- or nonmarital coitus are based on the reported behavior of persons who are willing to cooperate in social research. Unfortunately there are few studies that are comparable across nations and over time. Because the research depends on individuals who are willing to answer questions related to a very personal aspect of their lives, there is no way to obtain a random or representative sample of any population. College students are often questioned in lieu of a wider sampling. In the absence of more adequate data, many observers have been content to use the rise and fall of illegitimacy rates and ratios as an indicator of the prevalence of nonmarital sexual intimacy. We have already recognized the inadequacy of such an indicator. In countries where marriage may intercede between conception and birth and where contraceptives and abortions may be used, births out of wedlock may be a very small proportion of all births even though premarital coitus is widespread.

Questionnaire and interview reports of premarital coitus are available for both males and females. Because only the female is able to become pregnant and bear a child, we are most interested in whether large or small proportions of women say that they have engaged in sexual intercourse outside of marriage. Where the double standard has predominated (with sexual freedom allowed males but forbidden females) large proportions of men were presumably limited to a small proportion of women who were prostitutes or "fallen women," and only those women were "at risk" of conception. A review of both male and female responses, however, indicates that changes over time in the proportion of men involved in premarital coitus are small, while females have reported increasing experience.

Caution should be used in interpreting the results of the many studies of premarital coitus included in table 16. Respondents were selected by a variety of sampling methods; they vary by age, education, proportion of total sample who have answered, and year of study. These studies are reported for reference only and are not representative of women in the nations indicated nor truly comparable across nations.

CROSS-NATIONAL STUDIES

There are two recent cross-national comparative studies that have questioned university women only. Of those who were asked and were willing to complete the questionnaires, we can compare the proportions who say that they have experienced coitus.

Table 16. Percentage of Women Reporting Premarital Coitus

Publication Author and Date Sampling	Country	Number of Respondents	Percentage Reporting Premarital Coitus		Specific Characteristics
Kantner and Zelnik (1972)	United States	4,240 never-marrieds	*Black*	*White*	Age:
National probability sample of women 15–19 interviewed in 1971.			32.3	10.8	15
			46.4	17.5	16
			57.0	21.7	17
			60.4	33.5	18
			80.8	40.4	19
Bell and Chaskes (1970:83)	United States		*1958 sample*	*1968 sample*	Coitus during:
Volunteers in 45 college classes. Similar samples on age, university attendance, religious makeup, and occupational status of fathers taken at two dates			10	23	dating
			15	23	going steady
			31	39	engagement
Christensen and Gregg (1970:621)	United States Midwestern University	142 / 238	1958 / 1968	25 / 32	Women in college
Questionnaire administered mostly in social science classes.	United States Intermountain University (Mormon)	74 / 105	1958 / 1968	10 / 32	
	Denmark University	86 / 61	1958 / 1968	60 / 97	
Packard (1968:510)	Canada	85	35.3		Juniors and seniors in college, 19–22 years old
Handout samples, voluntary returns.	England	86	62.8		
	Germany	96	59.4		
	Norway	56	53.6		
	United States	688	43.2		

Study	Country	N			Age / notes
Burgess and Wallin (1953)	United States				Age:
Response to questionnaires in *Seventeen* magazine		604	15.0		13–19
			25.0		18–19
Kinsey (1953:339)	United States		Of those still unmarried by age:		Who were born:
			20	25	
Interviews with volunteers, all social classes and ages		5,800	8	14	before 1900
			18	36	1900–1909
			23	39	1910–19
			21	37	1920 on
Schofield (1965)	England				Age:
Teenagers		475	6		15–17
		464	16		17–19
French Institute of Public Opinion (1961)	France				Age:
		1,050	37		21–24 Had coitus
			15		45–49 with husbands before marriage
Chesser (1956)	England		married	single	Born:
Questionnaires filled out by patients of general practitioners		6,034	19	18	before 1904
			36	32	1904–14
			39	30	1914–24
			43	30	1924–34
				21	1934 on (under 21 at time of response)

In the mid-1960s Vance Packard had questionnaires distributed at colleges and universities in five countries (see item 4, table 16). Although he had 688 female respondents in the United States (which allowed detailed analysis of differences for regions of the country and so on), there were fewer than a hundred returned questionnaires from women in each of the other countries. For women respondents in the junior or senior year of college, 63 percent in England, but only 35 percent in Canada, said they had experienced premarital coitus. Respondents from the United States were second to the Canadians in low proportions reporting sexual experience. Yet, of these five countries, Norway, not Canada or the United States, has had the lowest levels of illegitimacy. Reported incidence of premarital coitus by these selected respondents parallel neither the ratios nor the rates of illegitimacy for these countries. Therefore, even though these figures are not necessarily representative for the nations and do not indicate frequency of premarital coitus, they do force caution in using births out of wedlock as an indication of the extent of premarital coitus.

Christensen and Gregg (1970) were able to compare cross-cultural data collected in 1968 to similar research carried out by the senior author 10 years earlier (see item 3, table 16). There were significant increases in the proportions of university women in each cultural setting responding that they had experienced premarital sexual intercourse, but Danish women were much more likely than the Americans sampled to report sexual experience (see also Croog, 1951; Christensen and Carpenter, 1962; and Tomasson, 1971). While Vance Packard had found great differences in the responses of university women at specific campuses and for different regions of the United States in 1968, the midwestern and intermountain university women responding to Christensen's questionnaire appeared more alike in 1968 than had the 1958 respondents. Nevertheless, in the United States less than a third of Christensen's respondents indicated sexual experience in contrast to 43 percent for Packard's slightly older (on the average) respondents.

From these reports, however, we are having some difficulty locating groups of unmarried women who overwhelmingly avoid or refuse sexual intercourse. For the most part the more reserved women of the middle and far eastern nations have not been polled. Nevertheless, we may be able to learn something from the patterning of responses for different groups and over time.

Although we do not have historical surveys of individuals' sexual lives, we do have evidence that when Puritanism was at its height in England, illegitimacy levels were at an historical low: about 1 percent of recorded baptisms (Laslett, 1967). We will examine some of the ways in which societies have organized themselves to limit nonmarital sexual contacts. First, however, we have some direct evidence on changes over time from the statements of real persons, rather than from inference alone.

The lowest percentage reporting coitus for those in the cross-national comparisons (table 16) is the 1958 Utah sample. Although we cannot take the sample to be exactly representative even of all the women on that campus, much less representative of all unmarried women in the state, we may for purposes of discussion assume that proportions coitally active would be low there relative to women in other states of the United States. Examining illegitimacy data, by reporting states (U.S., H.E.W. 1968a:42) we find that the ratios of illegitimate births for white women in Utah is lower than for any other of the thirty-five reporting states from 1940 to 1964. Furthermore, there is an increase over time from about 0.5 percent to 1.8 percent of white births occurring out of wedlock for the years indicated. Although these two variables need not change together, increases in premarital sexual intercourse are often accompanied by increases in illegitimacy. The experience levels are very different for Denmark, but there, too, illegitimacy has increased from under 7 to over 10 percent of births over the time of increased premarital experience reported by Christensen's investigation.

The variety of studies reporting on respondents in the United States (and England with fewer data) are consistent in that the more recently the data were collected, the higher the proportion of respondents saying that they had participated in premarital sexual intercourse. Reports also consistently indicate the progressive nature of premarital experience. It seems not merely that some women are likely and others unlikely to engage in premarital coitus, but that the probabilities increase as the unmarrieds age and as commitment of the partners moves toward engagement and marriage (see especially Bell and Chaskes, 1970 item 2, table 16). At least for the countries listed, as young women become older opportunities for nonmarital coitus probably increase while inhibitions decrease or are worn down.

It took Kinsey, a zoologist, to begin asking those questions that social scientists had assumed to be too personal to ask. Interviewing 5,000 women volunteers in the late 1940s, Kinsey could subdivide the responses by age in order to study cohort patterns in premarital sexual intercourse. The most significant changes were found for those born before and after 1900 who turned 20 before and after 1920. If we can take responses as of at least relative significance in the breakdown by age, those who were born before 1900 experienced different socialization influences from those born after the turn of the century. People have hypothesized that the First World War may have made a difference, or the "Roaring Twenties" or urbanization, or industrialization; whatever the cause, the proportions of Kinsey's respondents reporting experience are twice as high for those born after 1900 than for those born before, with only slight variation for later birth cohorts (see item 6, table 16).

The incidence of reported premarital coitus for those born before 1900 was low in relation to all others. Was there a significantly lower level of illegitimacy during the early childbearing years of these women? For the United States, our earliest information on illegitimacy is for the period 1916 to 1920. The disruptions and typical increase in illegitimacy during wartime periods would already have had an influence on earlier trends. Nevertheless a relatively low 2.2 percent illegitimate is recorded (see table 5). There is an apparently gradual rather than sharp rise of 41 percent within the following 10 year period. By 1938 about 4 percent of all births were out of wedlock, with little change (except during World War II) until the mid-1950s rise to approximately 10 percent. National fertility surveys conducted by the Bureau of the Census (see table 27) have found only slight variations in the percentage of white women first married over the years 1900 to 1945 whose first child was born prior to or within the first eight months of marriage. From these bits of data it is possible to conclude that while the earliest records indicate that very low proportions of unmarried women engaged in premarital sexual intercourse, recorded ratios of illegitimacy were also very low: evidence in support of proposition 2.

RACIAL DIFFERENCES

Another relative comparison that may be made is between the white and black respondents of the Kinsey group. The percentage of women who reported premarital coitus by the time they were 20 was much higher for Negroes than for white respondents (table 17). See also the teen-aged responses reported by Kantner and Zelnik (1972), in item 1, table 16. There is a significant difference, however, in the pattern for the college-educated Negro woman; she is either socialized differently or protected to a greater extent (or both) than her less well educated counterpart. (We will examine some of the aspects of socialization into sexual experience for the ghetto child in later sections.)

Table 17. Negro Women with Premarital Coitus and Conception, by Educational Level

	All Negro Women			Negro Women with Premarital Coitus		
	Educational level			*Educational level*		
Age	*0–8*	*9–12*	*13+*	*0–8*	*9–12*	*13+*
	Percentage with coitus			Years of coitus per 100 women		
15	62.2	48.2	7.8	242	228	
20	81.5	81.7	48.8	351	324	340
25	80.6	81.2	70.8	395	441	487
30	78.2	80.0	75.4	410	580	586
	Percentage with premarital conception experience					
15	22.8	9.5	0.4	36.7	19.8	
20	38.3	34.8	8.7	46.6	42.6	17.9
25	41.9	40.6	19.8	52.0	50.0	28.0
30	41.0	38.0	21.1	52.5	47.5	27.9
	Number of respondents					
15	127	199	230	79	96	
20	107	115	172	88	94	84
25	93	69	106	75	56	75
30	78	50	57	61	40	43

SOURCE: Gebhard et al. (1958:157).

From 1940 to 1960 unmarried white women, with much lower proportions engaging in nonmarital sexual intercourse, had general illegitimacy rates (per thousand unmarried) about one-tenth those of black women. Through the 1950s even the ratios were about 10 times higher for blacks than whites. Since then, however, note that the illegitimacy rates have actually declined for blacks while continuing to rise for whites. Between 1957 and 1965 the percentage of births out of wedlock increased by 100 percent for whites while rising by 27 percent for the blacks (U.S., H.E.W., 1968a).

The evidence reviewed offers support for proposition 2: groups in which large percentages of unmarried women avoid coitus do have low levels of illegitimacy. If data were available, we would expect more adequate proof from the middle eastern countries where structural patterns of "seclusion and exclusion" of women (Youssef, 1970), prohibit structural opportunities for the private meeting of unmarried persons of opposite sexes. Many societies have tried physically to separate young unmarrieds: school segregation by sex, seclusion of girls, sexual division of labor, and systems of chaperonage all reduce the possibility of sexual encounters among unmarried persons. Under these circumstances whatever premarital intercourse takes place is surely limited in terms of the proportions of women involved and the frequency of coitus. These very restrictive societies have apparently succeeded in limiting births out of wedlock.

POSTMARITAL SEXUAL EXPERIENCE

Although we have been referring to never-married women and premarital intercourse, because that is how the survey questions have generally been asked, we need to remind ourselves that separated, divorced, and widowed women are also capable of contributing to births out of wedlock (adulterous conceptions of married women being concealed from the records for the most part, as indicated in the last chapter). The only data I have found on postmarital coitus comes from the Kinsey volunteers and cannot be generalized to the entire population. For all divorced, separated, and widowed nonprison white female respondents (N = 754), the proportion (73 percent) engaging in, and average frequency of, coitus was much higher than for single respondents. Fourteen percent of these said they had been pregnant in the postmarital period, with 21 conceptions for every one hundred women (27 percent of those conceiving having conceived more than once). Surprisingly, the numbers of conceptions per hundred women increased with educational level. Gebhard (1958:144) noted that "whatever knowledge of contraception these women obtained while married was to a considerable degree offset by their greater (as compared to premarital) frequency of coitus. Some of the women attributed their pregnancies to carelessness."

Education and especially knowledge about the availability of contraceptives is clearly not enough to motivate persons to prevent conceptions out of wedlock. Since never-married women become very scarce in the older age groups, the high rates of illegitimacy reported at older ages at least in the United States and England may be heavily weighted by the postmarital group.

HIGH INVOLVEMENT

Proposition 2a suggests that it is not necessarily true that high involvement in nonmarital sexual intercourse will lead to high levels of illegitimacy. What evidence is appropriate here? An examination of nations or groups with high levels of nonmarital sexual intercourse must be undertaken to see if all also report high levels of illegitimacy.

Although I have not been able to find a survey that asked Jamaican women about their nonmarital sexual behavior, we know from the high illegitimate fertility rates there that activity levels must be very great. The high illegitimacy rates (exhibited in table 9) for unmarried women in Jamaica were even higher by 1960, but age-specific rates were not available after 1957.[1]

But our proposition suggests that high coital activity outside marriages does not necessarily lead to high illegitimacy levels. We have evidence from a number of surveys that premarital sexual intercourse is taken for granted in much of Scandinavia. Yet, not 70 percent but 5 to 16 percent of all births are out of wedlock. What are the relevant differences in the Jamaican and the Scandinavian cases? One very important difference, discussed in the last chapter, is the variation in the proportions of women married. There simply are not, proportionally, as many unmarrieds available to produce children out of wedlock in the Scandinavian countries. But illegiti-

---

[1] We do know, however, that the Jamaicans have been conducting an energetic family planning campaign and that crude birth rates have declined in recent years after rising during the 1950s.

macy rates reveal that for each thousand unmarried women (aged 15-44) the Jamaicans produce about 10 times as many births out of wedlock as those in Scandinavian countries. In spite of almost universal premarital sexual experience, the Scandinavians produce far lower levels of illegitimacy than the Jamaicans. Recognizing that each of those paths of avoidance of illegitimacy to be examined in chapters below—contraception, marriage before childbirth, and abortion—are more likely to be used in Scandinavia than in Jamaica, it is clear why high involvement in nonmarital sexual intercourse does not necessairly lead to high levels of illegitimacy. We still do not know why the Jamaicans are so unlikely to employ any of the alternatives. Proposition 2a has found confirmation in actual cases; coitus outside of marriage is a necessary but not sufficient condition for the production of births out of wedlock.

STRUCTURAL AND CULTURAL IMPEDIMENTS TO NONMARITAL COITUS

Proposition 2b states that the greater the structural and cultural impediments to sexual intercourse outside of wedlock, the lower the levels of illegitimacy. Conversely, although we cannot predict that fewer structural and cultural impediments will always lead to high levels of illegitimacy, we do propose that increasing structural conduciveness and cultural acceptance will lead to higher levels of nonmarital coitus. What evidence is appropriate?

SOCIAL STRUCTURE

It is self-evident that if the social structure is so organized that unmarried persons of the opposite sex are separated, there is little or no opportunity for social or sexual intercourse. Although that kind of strict segregation seems unthinkable to most Americans, it has occurred historically and still operates in some parts of the world. At one time some of the Chinese communes operated on the military model with strict separation of the sexes, and there has been some speculation that control of births was one of the many goals of the program. The nunneries and monasteries of Europe were sexually segregated with rather strict limits on meetings between the sexes. The classic example of separation of the sexes is that of the Moslem countries of the Middle East. While some of the old patterns are beginning to break down in urban areas, traditional structure and cultural values still dominate the majority of the population, which is nonurban in way of life and in value orientation.

Morroe Berger, reporting on men, women, and families in *The Arab World Today*, details a familial organization that minimizes the possibility of nonmarital mating and illegitimacy.

> The most pervading feature of the Arab family is the strong code governing relations between the sexes. The highest value is placed upon premarital chastity in women and upon their marital fidelity. Young men and women are not free to meet one another as they please or to choose whom they will marry. Arrangements by which they come together are made largely by the parents, who take into account not only family needs and position but also the wishes of their sons and daughters. But marriage is chiefly a joining of two families rather than of two individuals. Family life is shaped by the older generation for the younger, and by the desires and values of the men imposed upon those of the women. The Arab Moslem family is rather like the Western family in that both are based upon similar attitudes towards sex, but the Arab attitudes are more rigid and more effective in practice. There are also important differences, which stem from male dominance among Moslems, such as polygamy and the greater ease with which men may divorce their wives.
>
> The high values placed upon female chastity before marriage and fidelity in it is enforced by largely confining women, after puberty, to their own company. Loss of chastity in a girl is still viewed, in all classes and communities, as the gravest kind of misbehavior, to be punished by her father and brothers: the penalty varies from severe disgrace to banishment and even to death in some traditional communities. (Berger, 1962:99-100).

It is not surprising, then, that we find Arab nations and Moslem nations outside the Arab world only at the very bottom of the table of rank ordering of illegitimacy ratios. Familial controls prevent the very first and necessary conditions of illegitimacy: the coming together of unmarried persons. At his writing, Professor Berger reported that even university students, who mingle freely on the campus, did not makes dates away from it.

In Iran the amount of dower paid by the groom to the bride is said to depend on four factors: the age of the girl, her virginity, her physical appearance, and her social class. Momeni (1972:548) suggests that:

the institution of the dower induces early marriage because of the high value placed on virginity. At this point it may be emphasized that the amount of the dower under discussion is for the virgin girls. The nonvirgin girls will be lucky enough if they can find a husband, let alone a large dower. Virginity, one of the transcendental Iranian values, constitutes an investment for girls and one of the main reasons for men to consider young girls for wives.

Although urbanization and industrialization are on the increase, the relations between men and women in the Arab world are still governed by old and strict codes for meeting, mating, and creating new families. The recent researches of Peter C. Dodd indicate that "one value complex, the valuation of the honor of the women, *il-'ird*, is central to the organization of Arab society and that this value complex presents strong resistance to the modernizing process" (1970:1).

> Although the essence of il-'ird is the protection of the chastity of the unmarried girl, it extends to the correct behavior of married women. It may be helpful to understand the modesty code as the maintenance of appropriate interpersonal distance between men and women. Some of the institutions maintain this distance ecologically: separate reception rooms for men and women, separate sections of places for public assembly, walls about the courtyard or garden. Other institutions maintain distance by dress and gesture. Still others have to do with the expression of distance in interaction: speech, tone of voice, avoidance of joking, topics of conversation. Throughout, the norms are maintained by the surveillance of other women, particularly by the older women, and by the presence of male relatives. (Ibid., p. 4)

Dodd and his colleague, Halim Barakat, interviewed Palestinian refugees of the war of June 1967. In addition to the explanations usually offered for the exodus: panic, terror, fear of bombing, deliberate eviction; 30 percent mentioned the "valuation of honor, either directly or indirectly, as a reason for leaving their homes. These were families who had left houses, lands, work and community: honor took precedence over these other considerations. The honor lost by fleeing, the ignoble status of refugee, is compensated for by the intact honor of the family" (Ibid., p. 5).

Because the social controls in the Arab societies are external to the individual and guaranteed by the social structure, or patterning of relationships, invasion and occupation could destroy the old structure and leave the males powerless to control their women and girls and helpless to punish violations of the norms. One respondent said, "In our village the women and the girls work in the fields while the men work in the town. Now the women could not go to work, nor could the men work in the fields, because then the women would be alone in the houses" (Ibid.). Another respondent said succinctly, "We ran away with our honor intact" (see also Dodd, 1973).

Some national and subcultural groups of Southern Europe and Latin America require chaperones during the semiprivate "dates" or get-togethers of young persons of the opposite sexes. The chaperones may keep a discreet distance, but they are there to ensure social and not sexual intercourse.

On the other hand, in Northern Europe the "ring engagement included rights to sexual intercourse and the obligation to marry if pregnancy resulted" (Croog, 1951; see also chapter 8; Tomasson, 1971; U.N. Sub-Commission, 1967:13). In these countries the structuring of human relationships could be conducive to premarital sex even though illegitimacy remained low because marriage followed conception.

In Japan an effective if unintentional system of separating the sexes before marriage is the practice of contracting young girls for 7 to 10 years of factory employment. The factories are typically located outside urban areas. The girls are provided dormitories and offered a range of educational or craft classes during evening hours. Whole industries, such as chinaware, transistor, camera, and television factories are staffed by young women whose male contacts are extremely limited. A significant proportion of their pay is sent to fathers who set something aside for a dowry. The girls have come from rural areas in the past, though the proportion of the population rural is fast declining. They have uniformly completed the required nine years of schooling but have not qualified for further education. The system offers the advantages of medical care, good food, continued education (mainly in the arts), and some saving for a dowry. However, the work itself is often tedious, ruinous to the eyesight, and highly restrictive in social and geographical mobility. Needless to say the unisex system of factory employment with adjacent dormitories limits the opportunities for premarital sexual encounters. As more young women are employed in urban areas with more opportunities to meet men, proportional opportunities for premarital sex will be altered.

Jamaica has a social structure that is conducive to sexual encounters outside of marital bonds. Historical records indicate that when the British took the island from the Spaniards in 1655, the native Indian population had already been annihilated. Repopulation was accomplished overwhelmingly with African slaves, who were the ancestors of the Jamaicans of today (96 percent being of African or mixed African descent; see Roberts, 1957). Slave owners found it to their advantage to encourage reproduction while discouraging permanent marital unions. Thus the pattern of childbirth out of wedlock has had a history of several hundred years. After emancipation, there was apparently no great motivation to register de facto sexual unions. The lack of stable family units has meant that young women have little protection from physically and economically advantaged males. The geographic mobility required of much of the male labor force provides an opportunity and excuse to leave one sex partner (and any children) for another. Women are forced into low-paying domestic labors in an attempt to support themselves and their children, but the children often lack supervision and are shifted from one household to another as necessity demands. Teenagers easily become involved in sexual relationships and are pregnant before they understand "how babies are made." "There is thus a viscious circle in which lack of control breeds lack of control, illegitimacy breeds illegitimacy, and frustration breeds frustration" (Blake, 1961:247).

The history of slavery and discrimination forced on blacks in the United States follows much the same pattern of familial disorganization as that of the Jamaicans. Here as there, however, there are great differences according to the levels of education. Sociological research has found repeatedly that in many aspects of both behavior and values, middle-class (well-educated) blacks "out-middle-class the middle-class whites." Gebhard (1958) indicates that Negro respondents who continued to college were only one-sixth as likely to have engaged in premarital coitus at an early age as those whose education ended earlier. A good part of these differences seems to be related to the structural and cultural patterns of the groups within which individuals questioned had been reared. Hammond and Ladner (1969) have painted a graphic picture of the way in which slum children are socialized into sexual behavior at an early age. They find the myth of Negro sexuality "absurd in all of its aspects . . . especially unfortunate [in] that a substantial number of lower-class Negroes have themselves absorbed much of this myth, making it a kind of 'self-fulfilling prophecy.'" (pp. 42-43).

> The destructive social and economic forces of the Negro ghetto often create a situation in which the young child is exposed to sex-socializing influences almost constantly. Beginning at about age five (and sometimes earlier), he begins to become aware of the area of sex to which he has often been blatantly exposed, and he absorbs as much of it as he is able to comprehend (p. 43).
>
> . . . . the gross lack of privacy forces into public and semipublic areas behavior which would normally be conducted in private. In the absence of more convenient facilities, stairways, halls, corridors, elevators, washrooms, parking lots, and lobbies, which are used to gain access to apartments, work areas, and recreational spaces, are also the main locations in which sexual activities of all kinds take place (p. 45).

Visibility, overheard conversations, and invitations expose children to sex "at such an early age that they have not had the opportunity to formulate convictions which would sustain them against sexual involvement. It was uncommon for children studied to reach the age of five or six without having acquired some knowledge of sexual intercourse" (p. 46). Furthermore, "the normal age barriers between the sexes, i.e., the laws governing statutory rape, are virtually inoperative here" (p. 49). Early behavior is imitative, but sex often becomes "a strategic game of survival" (p. 47). "Teenage girls, when asked to list the most serious problem of girls they knew, most often listed problems that were directly and indirectly related to teenage sexual involvement" (p. 47). Other studies (Rainwater, 1966: Komarovsky, 1962; Zelnik and Kantner, 1970) are consistent in finding that lower-class adults are not satisfied with their sex lives even when levels of "activity" are high.

CULTURAL SYSTEM

The culture, or subculture of any given group, in its knowledge, beliefs, normative and value systems, may be conducive to or retard miscellaneous sexual encounters with or without monetary or other rewards. Beliefs and norms when implemented by a system of positive and negative social sanctions are powerful motivators of human behavior.

In a national survey in Japan, three-fourths of the women and all the males interviewed said they preferred that the spouse be a virgin at marriage (Shinozaki, 1957:34). In some societies the sexual violation of a woman is believed to be the gravest kind of misbehavior, to be punished by her father or brothers, the penalty varying from severe disgrace to banishment and even death in some traditional communities (Issawi, 1947). Some social groups believe that nonsanctioned sexual relations lead to permanent contamination, damnation, etc. Jamaicans are reported to verbalize a contrasting belief: that sexual intercourse with a virgin will physically cure the male of gonorrhea (Clarke, 1966). Other, mainly westernized, societies or social groups, have adopted the Freudian mystique of nonfrustrative sexual release for males and females alike. Yet, even when frustration is viewed as the greatest of all evils, there are usually numerous rules regarding sexual behavior.

Clearly, most societies fall between these extremes with varying emphases of beliefs, values, and expectations and with various social sanctions to accompany them. In the United States, attitudes toward premarital sexual behavior differ greatly according to age of respondent and to religious devoutness and church attendance. In a series of studies (Reiss, 1964a, 1969: Heltsley and Broderick, 1969; Walsh and Bryant, 1971) college students who reported themselves religiously devout or faithful churchgoers were least likely to report sexually permissive attitudes. On the other hand, adult respondents to two recent Gallup polls indicate little attitudinal difference by religious affiliation, but great variation by age. Gallup surveys in 1969 and 1972 asked the following question: "There's a lot of discussion about the way morals and sex are changing in this country. Here's a question that is often discussed in women's magazines. What is your view on this—do you think it is wrong for a man and a woman to have sex relations before marriage, or not?" Blake's reports of the percentages who believe premarital relations are not wrong show that not only have the percentages increased for each category of respondent over time, but also the differences by age imply that premarital sex is becoming more acceptable (1973:711; see table 18). Still, in the latest 1972 survey only 30 percent overall thought premarital relations were not wrong.

Table 18. Percentage of Whites in Gallup Surveys Who Believe Premarital Coitus Not Wrong

	Men		Women	
	1969	*1972*	*1969*	*1972*
Religion				
Catholic	19	36	13	22
Non-Catholic	25	38	15	24
Age				
Under 30	48	65	27	42
30–44	26	45	13	29
45+	12	21	10	12
Total	23	37	14	23
Number of Respondents	653	708	680	724

SOURCE: Blake (1973:711).

Reiss suggests (1970:83n.) that we must distinguish between the

old and new basis of permissiveness . . . the old permissiveness was based in good measure upon the economic hardship of the lower classes and the resultant lack of advantage of the marital state over the other states. The new permissiveness is based more upon a rational, affection oriented, contraceptively informed, view of the psychic value of sexual intimacy. The clash of parent and child in these two types of permissive social settings will naturally differ.

Reiss leans toward the social and cultural support theory of deviance regarding premarital coitus. Studying group differences in premarital sexual attitudes, Reiss found:

. . . the importance of the basic setting of adult institutions, especially the family, and also the key importance of the autonomy of courtship groups. The courtship group has special characteristics which promote acceptance of premarital coitus, e.g., high exposure to temptation via privacy, dancing and drinking, youth culture approval of adventure and hedonism; and approval of youth culture for the importance of affections as a basis for sexual relationships. Thus, the degree to which a society or a group gives autonomy to such a courtship system is one important determinant of the level of sexual performance and belief. The second key determinant is the outside institutional setting of adults. Youth reflect this setting in a variety of ways. It is perhaps easiest to see that despite this very high degree of autonomy sexual intercourse is not a casual, randomized matter for most young people, particularly not for females. The parental values of love, responsibility and future orientation are obviously present. Because of special circumstances the courtship group will have more permissive standards than the parental groups but the relation of those standards to adult values is still clear. (Reiss, 1970:83).

In Reiss' (1967) study, approximately two-thirds of the students perceived their sex standards as similar to their parents. Of those who differed from their parents, the majority perceived themselves as being more permissive. He found that 77 percent felt their standards were similar to those of their peers and 89 percent felt their standards were basically similar to their very close friends.

I would take the social and cultural support theory to be a better explanation of lower-class subcultural differences (as well as of middle-class groups) than the oft-repeated idea that economic hardships lead to a "lack of advantage of the marital state over other states." That idea does not stand up to cross-cultural comparisons. Most of the wretchedly poor of the world in India, China, the Middle East, etc., have taken fierce pride in a close-knit family pattern that repudiates premarital sex, especially for the female. One could argue that because there is so little joy in life, the family is more important to lower than to middle- and upper-class groups. Safilios-Rothschild (1972) suggests that in the traditional culture of Mediterranean countries, "unless one is a member of the upper class or the power echelons of the society, social acceptance is not possible in the absence of unspoiled honor. . . . A man's social honor finally and irrevocably lies in the hands of his women. . . . A woman becomes dishonored when she behaves like a man, enjoying freedom, especially sexual freedom" (p. 84). The strength of the tradition continues (see Peristiany, 1965).

Not only does the traditional moral norm require that a girl be completely chaste at the time of marriage, but also it is *more* important for the poor than for the rich girl. The girl from a higher-class family can balance the lost chastity with a larger dowry; the worse the reputation, the larger the required dowry (Safilios-Rothschild, 1972: 92).

We have seen that the weight of evidence favors proposition 2b: the greater the structural and cultural impediments to sexual intercourse outside wedlock (such as those operating in Japan, the Middle East, etc.), the lower the levels of illegitimacy. Conversely, higher structural conduciveness and cultural acceptance of nonmarital intercourse (found among Jamaicans and lower-class blacks, and, increasingly, whites in the United States) leads to higher levels of nonmarital coitus and, without recourse to alternatives, correspondingly high levels of illegitimacy. Wherever old family traditions have been broken by slavery, urbanization, or migratory occupations, the disorganized pattern may itself be repeated for generations until reversed by social and cultural forces in the direction of stabilizing family organization. What are the social forces which have worked to minimize nonmarital coitus over time and space?

SOCIAL SANCTIONS

Proposition 2c states that the strength of social sanctions against nonmarital sexual relations will influence the extent to which individuals participate. Blake and Davis (1964:464) suggest that there are several aspects of social sanctions that are important to sociological analysis. (1) Are the sanctions maximal or minimal; (2) do they involve a reward or punishment; (3) if punishment, is it of the repressive or restitutive type; and (4) are the sanctions specific or diffuse?

> In most cases sanctions are informal—an approving or contemptuous glance, an encouraging or derisive laugh, a sympathetic or embarrassed silence. Such seemingly trivial but pervasive sanctions enable human beings to control informally a share of their own actions and reactions and the actions and reactions of others. However, it is also true that behavior is frequently controlled by formal sanctions as well—by a medal or a jail (p. 465).

We have seen that in some countries there is a strict physical separation of the sexes at puberty until, and sometimes even after, marriage. Negative sanctions have depended on the extent of violation. Punishment has been repressive, including shame, greater confinement, banishment, beatings, and sometimes even, in the case of premarital pregnancies, death. Even with a more conducive mixing of unmarried persons, *The Social Control of Sexual Expression* is rarely absent, as historically documented by Geoffrey May (1931). The methods of legal control varied widely over time, and laws were often not enforced very effectively, yet it is interesting to match the social controls discussed by May with the historical recording of births out of wedlock reported by Peter Laslett (1967:17). Registered illegitimacy ratios in fifteen parishes for which records were available from 1561 to 1837 indicate a decline and later rise of illegitimacy at the time of the rise and fall of Puritanism. After the execution of Charles I, Parliament legislated (in 1650) the penalty of death for adultery. Of course convictions were extremely difficult to obtain, yet in an historical period much less affected by contraceptives and abortion than the present, records of illegitimacy as low as 1 percent of all births from 1641 to 1660, may be taken as an indication of low levels of nonmarital sexual activity.[2] One can imagine that even the threat of maximum repressive sanctions combined with the high visibility of pregnancy would influence the behavior of many persons in avoiding prohibited outcomes. As such laws were not enforced over time, however (as many such laws in the United States are unenforceable, because they refer to behavior privately carried out), they no longer

---

[2] Caution in interpreting the data is always wise. In the case of the low point in illegitimacy in England in the 1650s

at the end of the fastest decline to be seen over the whole length of the four hundred year period. . . . We should have to know about the following factors before we could decide whether the trough in English illegitimacy figures in the 1650s was really due to the actions of the triumphant Puritans in reforming the manners of the people.

First would be the reliability of registration generally, for in that time of war and disorder English parish books were worse kept than before and survive in fewest numbers. Another would be the extent to which unmarried lovers became more careful at that time in practicing prevention, for we now believe that means of birth control must have been available to them, as they certainly seem to have been to married couples.

Another would be the number of guilty mothers-to-be who disposed of their babies before or during birth, or who concealed what was going on from the stern authorities in their own villages by moving elsewhere at the critical time (Laslett, 1973:258).

acted as sanctions and became useless. Laws are deterrent only when people believe they will be consistently and uniformly enforced.

We have noted the high value of "honour" in the Mediterranean countries. Social sanctions there have been so strong that restoration of honor can be accomplished only with blood.

> Women who feel ashamed because their unchastity or unfaithfulness is known can only resort to suicide if they have love of honor; they must not commit acts of violence. Male members of the family, on the contrary, must defend their honor and the family honor in an aggressive, violent manner by assaulting or killing the dishonored woman and/or those responsible for the dishonor. . . . In the light of traditional values, killing in defense of family honor was not considered to be a crime; it was, on the contrary, a socially expected and approved behavior (Safilios-Rothschild, 1972:84-85).

In light of the variety of norms and their related sanctions, the importance of adequate socialization—difficult to measure in itself— becomes clear. The learning, or internalization, of norms, values, and sanctions of the specific group is an important influence on the behavior of individuals. One indicator of differential patterns and content of socialization is religious affiliation and commitment. Because so much sexual behavior occurs in private and is, therefore, unrecognized, sanctions against illegitimacy, which is one of the few visible consequences, may be doubly severe. Yet social control is often most effective when it is least obvious, that is, when group standards are internalized: learned and accepted as one's own (Scott, 1971). The influence of the "moral community called the Church" (Durkheim, 1961) is evident in the variation in reported coital experience according to religious devoutness (Gebhard, 1958:72; see also table 19).

Table 19. White Women Reporting Premarital Coitus by Religious Devoutness

Age	Protestant						Jewish	
	Devout		Moderate		Inactive		Inactive	
	Percentage	N	Percentage	N	Percentage	N	Percentage	N
20	16.0	796	22.2	776	28.9	896	29.9	538
25	30.4	516	38.4	528	51.9	690	46.3	335
30	33.0	423	45.8	400	57.1	524	51.0	249
35	32.9	316	43.8	288	57.1	392	45.1	175
40	26.3	217	37.9	195	53.0	247	35.0	117

SOURCE: Gebhard et al. (1958:71).

Kantner and Zelnik recently studied (1972:15-16) 4611 women aged 15 to 19 in the United States. Among the 4,240 who had not yet married they found a strong negative relationship between both religious identification and church attendance and reported sexual intercourse. Variation in proportions who have had intercourse according to church affiliation is much greater for whites than for blacks. That is, whites who indicated membership in a religious group were only about half as likely to have had intercourse as whites with no religious affiliation. For both racial categories, the more regular church attendance was, the lower were the proportions sexually experienced.

In studying the illegitimacy patterns of the five Nordic countries, Tomasson (1971) found religion to be of overriding importance in explaining the variations both among and within each nation.

> Pietism and other forms of evangelical Protestantism were instrumental in subduing a certain Nordic "looseness" in relations between the sexes. Where these influences were minimal such as in Iceland, north Norway (particularly Finnmark), and in some of the more remote provinces of central Sweden, we find extremely high rates of out-of-wedlock illegitimacy. Where these influences have been strong, most notably in parts of western Norway and to a lesser extent in southern Sweden, we find relatively low rates of illegitimacy (p. 4).

Church membership, attendance, and expressed devoutness are indicators of a relationship to a "moral community" or subculture that both teaches specific standards regarding premarital sex and rewards the learning of and conformity to those standards by group acceptance. In addition, however, the church community has the advantage of invoking the supernatural sanctions of an omnipotent power.

The influence of group norms and sanctions is also indicated by the findings of Vance Packard. Within his sample of United States college women "colleges with liberal rules tend to have a somewhat larger-than-average proportion of coitally experienced students than do schools with conservative rules" (Packard, 1968:166). "The lowest incidence of coitus, less than 20 percent, was reported at Catholic University. At the Eastern womens college with liberal rules more than three-quarters reported coital experience" (p. 187). Causation may be circular with more liberal and sexually experienced girls choosing those schools with the most liberal rules, and the liberal rules and other sexually experienced students influencing those who might not otherwise have experienced coitus. In addition, men may be more likely to express different expectations of girls from the liberal campuses than of those from the more conservative campuses.

In addition, social groups and whole societies may promote values not necessarily related to sex that nevertheless have implications related to sexual behaviors. Contrast the tendency in the United States to commercialize sex, as discussed by Clark Vincent (1961), with the deemphasis on sex in some other countries.

Vincent's study of *Unmarried Mothers* led him to conclude that:

> . . . sources of favorable definitions of illicit coition are not only those individuals or groups who favor and engage in such behavior. Rather, favorable definitions of illicit sexual intercourse derive from a number of social practices and ideas which may be supported and promulgated as much by individuals who do not engage in illicit sexual intercourse as by those who do. These definitions may be accidental by-products of the commercialization of sex to promote box office, magazine and newspaper sales; of the publication of research data on sexual behavior; of the emphasis on premarital relationships in applying personal ideology for achievement of production quotas; and of the philosophy of fun morality in conventional areas like education and child rearing (p. 244).

7. Conception and Contraception

OF THOSE who participate in nonmarital sexual intercourse, not all become pregnant. Those who do not conceive (in any given time period under study) are channeled out of the chain of events that leads toward the possible outcome in births out of wedlock. The proportions who do become pregnant are influenced by factors such as the frequency of intercourse, the fecundity of the partners in intercourse, their knowledge of conception and contraception, the availability of the tools of contraception and their efficiency, the availability of voluntary sterilization, and the motivation of men and women to use available means of preventing conception.

FREQUENCY OF COITUS

The studies of nonmarital coitus reviewed in the last chapter have been more concerned with whether persons have ever engaged in nonmarital sexual experiences, not how frequently. The reports of Gebhard from the Kinsey group are especially interesting with regard to the question of frequency, because, although limited to the United States, they allow a comparison of frequency of coitus for white single women; separated, widowed, and divorced women, and Negro women with each group subdivided by age and often by education.

As might be expected, frequency of coitus for those who have ever participated in nonmarital sexual intercourse varies greatly. Female respondents of the Kinsey study who participated in premarital coitus "averaged about once in five or ten weeks among those under twenty. However, this coitus is ordinarily sporadic, occurring with some frequency for a period of time and then ceasing for weeks or months. During such a period of coital activity the frequency is usually high enough to make pregnancy likely were it not for contraception" (Gebhard, 1958:31).

For women who had been married but were separated, widowed, or divorced, at the time of the interview, 73 percent had had postmarital coitus, and the frequency was much higher on the average than for premarital coital experience. For females with postmarital coitus the average frequency was 1.4 times per week for the 21 to 25 year olds to 0.9 times per week for the 41 to 45 year olds. For those who conceived, the average frequency was 1.8 times per week for those aged 26 to 35 (Gebhard, 1958:145). The contrast with the young unmarrieds at 0.1 to 0.2 coital experiences on the average per week, indicates why conceptions are lower on the average for the young never marrieds than for the older ever marrieds. Yet, there are so many more young unmarrieds than separated, widowed, and divorced women that conceptions and births out of wedlock appear to predominate in the young: numerically they do, but in relation to numbers of unmarrieds they do not. Whatever knowledge of contraception the older, previously married women had gained during marriage was apparently offset by their greater frequency of nonmarital intercourse. Just as married women and their husbands may be careless in planning their children (with 17 to 35 percent of white and Negro married respondents claiming unwanted births (Bumpass and Westoff, 1970b)), unmarried women may "take a chance" without contraceptives or with inefficient ones.

Although education of the white ever marrieds did not make the expected differences in coital experience or conception, for the Negro respondents educational level made a great difference. A much smaller percentage of college-educated than noncollege-educated Negro females said they had had coitus. Of those who did engage in premarital coitus, a smaller percentage of college educated conceived out of wedlock (Gebhard, 1958:156-58). This may be due to lower frequencies of coitus for the college educated (though the number of years of exposure is little different than for the less educated): It may also be that (as is true of the white group) effective contraception and lower frequency combine to reduce conceptions for the better educated.

In England there has been one study of teenagers that has inquired about frequency of sexual intercourse. Schofield (1965:87) found that

60 percent of those teens who had experienced coitus said there had been 18 or fewer such experiences in the last year. Only 13 percent neared an average of once a week. Although we do not have information on subsequent pregnancies in this group as they might be related to frequency of intercourse, the Birmingham Pregnancy Advisory Service found that of 2814 girls applying for abortions,,1 in 20 said she became pregnant as the result of a *first* experience.

FECUNDITY

The physiological capacity for bearing children, fecundity, must be distinguished from the actual production of offspring, indicated by various measures of fertility. While there is no way to measure fecundity directly, it is clear that the potential for childbearing varies among the populations of the world according to varying ages at puberty (menarche for girls) and different levels of partial or complete sterility.

AGE AT MENARCHE

Relevant at least in passing is the knowledge that conception is possible at increasingly earlier ages in the more advanced countries. Frisch and Revelle (1969, 1970) suggest that it is an increase in the rate of physical growth, related to preadolescent nutritional and health care, that lowers the age of menarche. For girls the average age is estimated to have declined from 17 years a century or more ago to 12.5 to 13.2 years of age in the United States and northern and western European countries (Tanner, 1966:531-32). Although conception is not quite so likely in the early stage after puberty as in the years following, the potential age of conception has been lowered by several years.

At the same time, educational requirements and youth dependency have lengthened. That means that girls may be initiated into sexual intercourse and conceive children while they are themselves still children. At what age are individuals old enough to make independent decisions about bringing infants into the world and caring for them? Certainly most people of the advanced countries with educated populations do not choose to have children bearing children. Yet, nurses have reported 12- and 13-year-old girls crying for their mothers while delivering their own babies. It will be clear from the data on sex education in Sweden that the provision of information and contraceptive supplies is not enough, in itself, for the prevention of conception by the very young.[1] With increased sex education, illegitimacy rates in Sweden have risen especially fast for the youngest age groups (see table 21).

STERILITY OR LOWERED FECUNDITY

It is impossible to know the exact proportions of men or women in various societies who are not capable of conceiving children or have lowered fecundity or ability to conceive. The proportion of persons who have not had any children is only one indicator, since some may not have wanted to produce offspring.

However, when we find societies or subcultures that have low acceptance of contraception or abortion but very nearly free and promiscuous sexual relations, one may expect that childlessness is related to lowered fecundity. In Jamaica, in spite of very high fertility rates, both within and outside of wedlock, almost 20 percent of women completing the childbearing years reported to census takers (in 1943 and 1960) that they had never had a child. Such large proportions childless have led to the speculation that sterility caused by venereal disease had been prevalent in the population. There is clear evidence of an inverse relationship between birth rates and syphilitic deaths. Interestingly, crude birth rates rose from 30 to over 40 per thousand inhabitants from the early 1940s to late 1950s while there was a decline in percentage of deaths due to venereal infections (Tekse, 1968:figure 3). I have shown elsewhere (Hartley, 1969a:165) that the entire rise in crude birth rates was accounted for by the increase in age-specific illegitimate fertility that occurred between 1948 and 1957.[2] The rapid rise in already high age-specific illegitimacy rates

---

[1] New evidence suggests that IUDs can be used with success in the nulliparous, although they have traditionally been used only after a women has had at least one birth (Planned Parenthood, 1969:7). Medical examinations at puberty could, thus, include the insertion of an IUD to guarantee against conception in the very early years.

[2] The general illegitimacy rate (for unmarried women 15-44) continued to increase at least through 1960, but age-specific data were unavailable after the 1957 period.

corresponds to the decline in the percentage of younger women who were childless. As sterility due to venereal disease is brought under control, one would expect childlessness to decline, especially among the more promiscuous, who are most likely to produce births out of wedlock. The introduction and promotion of family planning in the mid-1960s may tend to reduce the number of children per mother, while the reduction of sterility increases the proportion of all women who are mothers.

A study of *Trends in Illegitimacy* in the United States also notes the possibility of a relationship between the rise in illegitimacy and the reduction of sterility associated with venereal disease.

> This cannot be demonstrated with certainty, but it appears to be a tenable hypothesis, particularly for the nonwhite population. We do know that among nonwhite married women, the prevalence of child-lessness was once quite high. Among ever-married nonwhite women 50-54 years of age enumerated in the 1960 Census, for example, 28 percent reported that they had never had any children. The proportion was much lower for younger women (14 percent for ever-married nonwhite women 25-29 years of age). It seems likely that this trend toward fewer childless women represents an increase in fecundity, probably due to the reduced prevalence of venereal disease.[3] If there has been an increase in the fecundity of the nonwhite population, it would affect the unmarried population as well as the married and raise the likelihood that premarital intercourse would lead to pregnancy and childbirth (U.S., H.E.W., 1968a:16).

Phillips Cutright (1973a:400) has estimated the amount of change in the U.S. illegitimacy rates from 1940 to 1960 that may be attributed to improved health conditions. He suggests that 75.7 percent of the nonwhite and 31.5 percent of the white increase in rates is due to improved health and fecundity of the population.

CONTRACEPTION

PROPOSITIONS TO BE EXAMINED

3. When a large proportion of those unmarried women who do engage in sexual intercourse use highly effective contraceptives, low levels of illegitimacy are maintained.

---

[3] For additional evidence on this point, see Kiser (1958).

a. Nonuse of contraceptives, however, does not guarantee high levels of illegitimacy.

b. The greater the (1) knowledge about, (2) availability of, and (3) motivation to use effective contraceptives, the lower the conceptions out of wedlock.

c. Social sanctions promoting or reducing the knowledge, availability and motivation to use contraceptives will affect their use by individuals within societies.

Mary Calderone (1968:42) recently said: "People rarely behave reproductively. They behave sexually with reproduction a by-product of this sexual behavior." Societies or subcultures may facilitate or inhibit the possibility of controlling the reproductive by-product for married and unmarried persons. We know from figure 1 that the countries highest in levels of illegitimacy also have very high crude birth rates. Married and unmarried persons in those countries tend toward high reproduction. An increase in the knowledge about, availability of, and motivation to use contraceptives might help both groups. The relationship between illegitimate and legitimate reproduction is not a linear one, however, since countries with low levels of illegitimacy may also have very high crude birth rates (e.g., all of the Arab countries, India, and some African nations).

KNOWLEDGE ABOUT CONTRACEPTION

One might suppose that the general level of knowledge would influence the knowledge about conception and contraception and thus would help control births out of wedlock. However, if we use the percentage of women aged fifteen and over who are illiterate as a general inverse indicator of the societal level of education, we find no relationship with reported ratios of illegitimacy. Countries with the highest proportions of illiterate women (80 to 90 percent) are at the lowest rank ordering of illegitimacy ratios. The next highest group on illiteracy (50 to 75 percent) are among the highest levels of reported illegitimacy. Those nations in the middle rankings of illegitimacy have a wide variation of female illiteracy (see table 20). I have also examined the proportions of populations enrolled in primary and higher education and per capita newspaper circulation as possible indicators of national educational levels, and these were also unrelated to illegitimacy ratios.

Table 20. Rank Order of Illegitimacy Ratios of Countries, Urban Populations, and Women Illiterate

	Percentage of Births Illegitimate	Percentage of Population Urban[1]	Percentage of Women Illiterate[2]
1964 Jamaica	74.1	25.1	15.2
1967 Panama	70.0	33.1	27.6
1965 Guatemala	67.4	11.2	75.6
1968 El Salvador	67.2	17.7	55.5
1957 Honduras	64.5	26.0	58.5
1968 Dominican Republic	61.8	18.7	37.6
1967 Nicaragua	53.4	23.0	50.4
1967 Venezuela	53.2	47.1	41.6
1969 Peru	48.9	35.2	51.6
1967 Martinique	48.2	30.3	11.8
1968 Paraguay	43.0	46.2	31.3
1967 Guadeloupe	41.6	22.2	17.1
1967 Trinidad and Tobago	41.1	68.9	—
1966 Mozambique	34.3	1.2	—
1963 Angola	32.6	7.0	—
1966 Ecuador	32.2	26.5	37.3
1967 Iceland	30.0	40.0	—
1966 Argentina	26.4	57.7	9.7
1967 Costa Rica	25.8	—	16.0
1967 Colombia	23.4	—	28.9
1965 Puerto Rico	23.2	28.0	21.7
1968 Mexico	22.5	29.6	27.0
1967 Reunion	20.2	65.2	34.7
1963 Uruguay	20.0	62.2	9.2
1967 Chile	17.7	54.7	17.6
1958 Bolivia	17.2	19.7	77.2
1967 Sweden	15.1	44.2	—
1968 New Zealand	13.0	63.2	—
1960 Brazil	12.9	27.0	42.8
1968 Austria	12.0	38.2	—
1967 East Germany	10.7	39.2	—
1966 Denmark	10.2	51.9	—
1968 United States	9.7	47.0	1.8
1968 Bulgaria	9.6	33.9	14.7
1968 England and Wales	8.5	83.4	—
1967 Yugoslavia	8.3	18.8	28.8

Table 20. Rank Order of Illegitimacy Ratios of Countries,
Urban Populations, and Women Illiterate

	Percentage of Births Illegitimate	Percentage of Population Urban[1]	Percentage of Women Illiterate[2]
1967 Canada	8.3	42.7	—
1967 Australia	7.7	68.6	—
1968 Portugal	7.4	17.7	43.4
1968 Scotland	7.4	53.4	—
1956 Congo, Democratic Republic (Zaire)	6.7	9.1	97.2
1967 France	6.1	41.9	—
1968 Norway	5.6	34.8	—
1967 Czechoslovakia	5.4	25.3	—
1967 Finland	5.1	37.8	—
1968 Hungary	5.0	41.8	3.1
1968 Poland	4.9	31.8	6.2
1968 West Germany	4.8	47.6	—
1968 Switzerland	3.8	28.0	—
1968 Northern Ireland	3.8	29.7	—
1968 Ireland (Eire)	2.6	34.5	—
1967 Belgium	2.5	34.8	—
1967 Philippines	2.5	63.2	30.5
1967 Italy	2.0	47.0	11.2
1968 Netherlands	2.0	49.3	—
1968 Taiwan	1.6	80.3	42.0
1968 Spain	1.4	45.4	19.1
1964 Albania	1.4	22.0	36.9
1968 Greece	1.1	37.3	30.0
1967 Japan	0.9	75.7	—
1968 Israel	0.6	62.1	22.3
1965 Tunisia (Moslem)	0.3	23.6	82.4
1968 Mauritius	0.3	44.3	49.4
1965 Algeria (Moslem)	0.2	26.5	96.9
1961 Nigeria (Lagos)	0.1	19.2	88.5 (both sexes)
1967 United Arab Republic (Egypt)	0.0	48.0	87.6
1955 Syria	0.0	—	87.3

SOURCE: *Demographic Yearbook* (1970: tables 9 and 11).
[1]Living in cities of 20,000 or more, latest date.
[2]Women 15 and over unable to read and/or write, latest date.

It is also true, however, that knowledge of conception need not be specific and complete, if in general the possibility of conception as a result of sexual intercourse is recognized. Although young women may have little or no knowledge of "how babies are made," in most societies the necessary condition is very well known. Recognizing the probability of conceiving in any given sexual encounter is something else again. Young people noting the prevalence of two- to three-child families in the advanced countries may assume that conception is unlikely, and sources on which they depend for information may be less than accurate. For example, one of the texts used in college courses on marriage and the family contained the incorrect estimate of 1 chance in 1,825. The correct probability of conception without contraception is one in five (being unequal through the monthly cycle, of course).

Because some recognition of the high probability of conception and the ensuing problems is necessary to motivate persons to an interest in contraception, sex education is often thought to be more directly related than general education to the prevention of conceptions out of wedlock. Yet the National Council on Illegitimacy (1967:11), commenting on both the labeling theory in general and sex education in particular, recently noted: "In Sweden, the fact that the word *illegitimate* has been stricken from the vocabulary in regard to children born out of wedlock seems not to have influenced the rate of such births. Nor, indeed, has compulsory sex education, starting in the first grade, changed the figures."

Sweden is the only country in the world where sex education is compulsory in the public schools (Lee, 1971:83). The first teachers' manuals on sexual education were published by the Swedish National Board of Education in the 1940s, and sex education became compulsory in 1956. The illustrated handbook entitled *Sex Instruction in Swedish Schools* states in its preface: "The purpose of sex instruction in Swedish schools is to present biological information and to impart knowledge in a manner that will help not only in moulding ideals but also in building character. Instruction on these lines is intended to have a pronounced ethical basis" (Linner, 1967:5). Sex education begins with the first school year. Between the ages of 11 and 13, instruction includes the structure and function of the sexual organs, puberty, menstruation, night pollution (wet dreams), masturbation, conception, pregnancy and "traumatic experiences" during pregnancy, development of the fetus, labor, detemination of sex, twins, etc. One of the stated objectives is to counteract less desirable sexual behavior, such as sexual intercourse at too early an age (Ibid., p. 4). If we are to judge by performance, the latter goal has not been met. Although instruction on contraceptives, moral considerations, and illegitimate children are also included in the program, the illegitimacy rate rose from 1950 to 1969 for every age group except the older group who had not been exposed to the special education.

Table 21. Age-Specific Illegitimate Fertility Rates,* Sweden

Age groups	1930	1940	1950	1960	1965	1969
15–19	12.9	12.9	19.5	17.9	27.9	24.5
20–24	31.3	23.6	31.4	28.5	31.9	39.5
25–29	21.5	17.3	23.7	27.4	31.9	32.5
30–34	15.6	12.6	19.0	18.2	21.9	23.5
35–39	10.4	7.9	11.7	10.9	12.8	12.1
40–44	4.5	3.0	4.5	3.9	3.5	3.1

*Rates are the number of illegitimate births per thousand females of specific ages.
SOURCES: Sweden, Statisticka Centralbyran (1970) and computations from raw data from U.N. *Demographic Yearbook* (1960, 1966).

In only five years between 1960 and 1965 the number of births out of wedlock to mothers aged 15 to 19 increased by 60 percent, from 5,083 to 8,166. If we examine table 21 on age-specific rates, it becomes clear that illegitimate fertility rates have increased most rapidly at the early ages. Between 1900 and 1930 the probability of having an illegitimate child decreased in the same proportion as the decline for legitimate childbearing. However, from 1930 through 1969, only the two oldest age groups show little change, the younger age groups show increased illegitimacy rates, and the youngest group shows the greatest change, an increase of almost 100 percent. (For the 15 to 19 year olds in 1965 the Swedish illegitimacy rate was 3.5 times that for whites in the United States.) It is possible, of course, that the increase would have been much greater without sex education, yet it appears that, since a long-term decline in rates had been in effect before 1940, some powerful social forces eliminated the possiblity of sex education reducing illegitimacy rates or that specific education in sex does not have the effect of reducing the level of illegitimacy. Had the Swedish government been inclined to set up experimental and control groups instead of giving the sex instruction to all, we might have a better idea of the effects of such a program.

As it stands, the evidence does not allow us to conclude that sex education, by itself, works to reduce illegitimacy.

Apparently more than mere knowledge about conception and contraception is needed. Even in the slum ghetto studied by Hammond and Ladner (1969:50):

> At least half of the adolescent females in our sample had adequate knowledge of the various types of contraceptives and ways in which they could be obtained. Indeed, one-fourth of the girls could describe in sophisticated language how each of the contraceptives we listed was to be used. Despite this knowledge, the majority of girls do not use them . . . . There seems to be little concern for the consequences of sex. Only a few boys and still fewer girls ever consider protection. . . . The three major reasons given for non-usage are belief in the 'old wives' tale about their ill effects, unavailability of a contraceptive at the time of intercourse, and embarrassment—i.e., reluctance to purchase materials such as EMKO foam on the open market, to secure a prescription for pills, a diaphragm, or an intrauterine device from a doctor, or to ask the partner to use a condom. Moreover, a small number of girls express the desire to have a child to give them a sense of responsibility and a feeling of security. One girl stated: "I would be grown if I had a baby. I'd have something that I could call my own and someone to depend on me." Some express strong moral opposition to controlling fertility, which is another reason for not taking advantage of contraceptives.

A recent large-scale national sample of teenagers found, on the other hand, that of those with sexual experience, blacks were about as likely as whites to report that they had always, sometimes, or never used contraception. The "sometimes" response comprised 63 percent of the total, however. "Use at last intercourse" (an indicator of consistent use) was strongly related to the number of years of formal education the teenagers had had, and again it was similar for blacks and whites. An indication of the difference in effectiveness of use, in spite of similarity of reported use, is found in the report that 10 percent of the white but 40 percent of the black teens with sexual experience had already been pregnant (Kantner and Zelnik, 1973:31).

Perhaps more accurate knowledge would correct the "old wives" tales about the ill effects of various methods of control. Part of the problem, however, is that individuals must first see the information as personally relevant. Contraceptive information often seems more relevant *after* conception occurs (see Kantner and Zelnik, 1973:315). Thus, in Denmark the offer of family planning is compulsory after a childbirth or abortion, and Polish law requires the teaching of contraception to a woman before an abortion is carried out (Lee, 1971:84).

Yet, in general:

> Working-class people tend to have a basic belief that what happens in the world is determined mainly by external forces against which their energies are not likely to be effective. . . . They accept things as given and pour little energy into either self-exploration or exploration of the outer world. They tend to view things negatively, to regard thought and planning as painful activities to be engaged in only under the pressure of great necessity. Even then they are not optimistic since they feel that the best they can do will not be sufficient to overcome adversity (Rainwater, 1966:52).

Knowledge in any area is useful only when individuals see the possibility of its making a real change in their own life situation. As Lorimer indicates:

> The effective control of fertility requires individual initiative and sustained effort. People who do not really believe that it is possible for them to improve conditions of life for themselves or their children will not undertake a radically new venture or put forth the sustained effort required for success in this undertaking. Where hope is weak, contraception will be absent or ineffective (Lorimer, 1963:148-49).

The above holds true for married and unmarried alike. Therefore, knowledge about and availability of contraceptives are necessary but not sufficient conditions for the reduction of births out of wedlock.

AVAILABILITY OF CONTRACEPTIVES

The fact that many societies have changed their laws and the enforcement of their laws on contraceptives makes it clear that the social group really determines the availability of the several means of contraception. Methods of contraception include voluntary sterilization as a means of preventing pregnancy but do not include abortion, which can occur only after the fact of conception. The laws and their enforcement may vary for the different methods, and may be applied differently to persons of different age groups or marital statuses.

Among 23 nations for which data were available, Phillips Cutright (1971a:39) found that declines in the marital fertility rates of women 35 to 39 were associated with declines in illegitimacy rates. The fertility rates of older women are an indirect indicator of the availability of contraceptives in populations where low fertility is preferred. Available contraceptives are presumably used to prevent unwanted births to older women and to unmarried women. One problem with the indicator, however, is that among many groups contraception has been readily available to middle-class married persons, but restricted in knowledge and availability for young unmarried persons.

Pilpel and Wechsler (1971) have reviewed the variety of legal statutes prohibiting the medical treatment of minors for contraception or pregnancy without their parent's consent. For the 50 states of the United States, in years past, unwed minors were generally

> not able to secure medical guidance to avoid unwanted pregnancies at least unless they first paid the penalty of bearing at least one out-of-wedlock child . . . illegitimacy trends in the United States from 1965-1968 seem to confirm this: Illegitimacy rates in older age groups declined during these years coincident with the increase in family planning services available to post partum women. However, illegitimacy rates of girls 15-19 rose by 18 percent in this period, the rise having been particularly marked among white teen-age girls, whose rates increased by 25 percent (p. 37).

Whatever legal restrictions remain, it is significant that since 1965 "there appeared to have been no case in which a doctor or medical facility had been prosecuted criminally or sued for damages for having examined or treated a minor in connection with contraception without parental or guardian consent" (Ibid.). Yet,

> The Ortho Pharmaceutical Corporation recently published the results of a nationwide sample survey of U.S. obstretricians and general practitioners. The survey showed that the young teen-ager will have a difficult time finding contraceptive help (from M.D.s) even if she has her parents' consent, and a most difficult time without it. (Previous studies on physicians' practices had not divided the age groups under 18 or 21 years.) (Goldsmith, 1969:24)

During the 1960s in the United States a few hospitals and a few Planned Parenthood centers set up teen clinics. Of 476 sexually active teen participants in the San Francisco clinic, only 10 had unplanned pregnancies in two years (Ibid, p. 25). Yet these discussion groups and service centers are limited in outreach and follow-up.

Judith Blake (1973) reports that in two recent national surveys of adults in America, respondents were more likely to approve of birth control *information* than of birth control *services* to teenagers. While 71 percent in 1972 said they approved of birth control education in the high schools, only 54 percent approved of making birth control services free to teen-aged girls who requested them. The impracticality of providing information on birth control while limiting availability of contraceptives apparently went unrecognized, since the disjuncture in approval occurred for all age, religious, sex, and educational subdivisions. The disparity in approval was even greater in the 1969 survey.

In 1967 Title IV of the Social Security Act was amended to require local welfare agencies to provide referrals for contraception to recipients without regard to "marital, age or parenthood status." It would be impossible to estimate to what extent the requirement has been carried out. Social workers have leaned toward the psychoanalytic assumptions about illegitimacy; thus they have typically focused on helping the unmarried mother resolve the assumed "unconscious conflicts that motivate these pregnancies" instead of helping women acquire the contraceptive information and tools that would allow the prevention of consciously unwanted births. "It is psychologically naive to presume a (simple causal) relationship between an out-of-wedlock pregnancy and the unconscious motivation to have a child" (Furie, 1966:46). Such notions allow the welfare worker to avoid the subject of birth control. Yet the study by Greenleigh Associates (1960:19-20) of the AFDC program in Cook County, Illinois, indicates that of 619 mothers whose youngest child had been born out of wedlock, 552 did not want to have another baby. Almost half the women either had no information or inadequate information on preventing conception. A study of 2,179 "Families on Welfare in New York City" (Podell, 1968:8) found that over 80 percent of the women under 45 years of age did not want any more children. Unmarried mothers desired fewer children than those presently or formerly married. Furie (1966:48) suggests that "the social work profession has taken too little interest in promulgating birth control programs." Yet, "it would be a mistake to assume that getting social workers to refer patients to a center or even creating free services will be adequate to help this group to practice birth control en masse. Some program of continued information, motivation and education will be necessary" (Bogue, 1963:23).

The various nations of the world all have legal restrictions on the display, advertising, or promotion for sale of contraceptives. Where sales of contraceptives are forbidden by law, their advertisement is also forbidden. "But even where sales are legal, advertisement may remain proscribed as is the case in Belgium, France, the Federal Republic of Germany, and Sweden" (Lee, 1971:83).

Restrictions on the availability of contraceptives may be carried on by strict controls on imports in those nations that do not produce their own supplies. Prohibition of the sale of contraceptives has been absolute in Ireland and Spain (Ibid., p. 84). In contrast Swedish pharmacists are required to stock contraceptives for sale during daylight hours and automatic coin-operated vending machines offer round-the-clock availability of contraceptive devices (Linner, 1967:48).

Because contraceptives are likely to be more available in urban than in rural areas of any nation, the proportions of populations living in cities of 20,000 persons or more are given in table 20. If availability is more widespread in urban areas, it is not evident in consistently lower proportions of births out of wedlock for highly urbanized nations. But we have already seen that the availability of contraceptives is only one factor among many relating to births out of wedlock. Urban areas may positively inflate some of the other factors leading to illegitimacy. For instance, a higher proportion of urban than of rural populations are likely to be unmarried. The greater anonymity of urban life may facilitate nonmarital social and sexual intercourse, and it reduces the social pressures to marry if pregnancy occurs. Because the many aspects of urban life may have contradictory influences on the probability of producing children out of wedlock, there is no direct causal link between urbanization and illegitimacy.

EFFECTIVENESS OF CONTRACEPTIVES

Because of the very great differences in the efficiency of various means of contraception, we must recognize that a society may restrict

or facilitate the use of some means and not others. The most effective
contraceptives are usually those least available to unmarried persons,
especially young, unmarried women.

Sterilization refers to all operations performed on either a male
or a female that physiologically prevent his or her participation in
conception (Presser, 1970:1). The vasectomy for men and tubal
ligation for women are the most effective, complete and lasting means
of preventing conception for those who do not want any future
children. Yet, because of its permanence, it is least likely to be
voluntarily available to or desired by young or unmarried individuals.
The vasectomy is a minor 15- to 30-minute operation that prevents
sperm from being discharged with seminal fluid; sexual potency is
unaffected. The operation is so simple that it is regularly performed
in bus stations in India. A tubal ligation blocks the passage of the
female's egg into the womb. It is common and almost as safe as
vasectomy (or childbirth), but the woman is generally required to
spend a few days in the hospital.

There is some disagreement on the legality of sterilization in the
United States. Lee (1971:87) reports that twenty-eight states have
laws on sterilization. Of these, "26 permit compulsory sterilization
to be performed on mentally infirm persons maintained at State
institutions, while only five states allow voluntary sterilization on
therapeutic or socio-economic grounds." The Planned Parenthood-World Population (1970) brochure on the subject claims that
"sterilization is legal in all 50 states." In the United States by 1970
about 11 percent of couples with wives under 45 years of age reported
a contraceptive sterilization (Presser, and Bumpass, 1973:533).

Scandinavian countries generally have laws allowing voluntary
sterilization on medical, eugenic, or social grounds. East European
countries do not as a rule have laws on sterilization, except for
Czechoslovakia where patient and medical authorities must agree
on the procedure. Japan has the widest possible grounds on which
a sterilization may be performed but requires consent of both patient
and spouse (Lee, 1971:87).

Sterilization has been most frequently *used* as a means of birth
control in India, where over five million vasectomies have been
reported. Governmental encouragement has gone so far as to offer
incentive payments to doctors, solicitors, and patients. We know that
illegitimacy cannot be very high in India, so the availability of

sterilization there cannot be expected to have much influence on levels of births out of wedlock. It is an excellent example, however, of the differential influence of the society on available methods of birth control. In contrast to the situation in India, there was a furor in Colombia when their family planning association, PROFAMILIA, announced that it had performed 160 vasectomies in a 15-month period. Church officials denounced the program and the operation as a criminal and immoral procedure. Yet, not only is Colombian fertility very high, but also about a quarter of all births are out of wedlock. Furthermore, the vasectomies had been offered only to married men over 35 with *more* than six living children (Population Reference Bureau, 1972:4).

Table 22. Women of Childbearing Age Reporting Sterilization
of Selves or Husbands (Selected Areas)

Area	Percent
Puerto Rico (female only, 1965)	30.0 [a]
Thailand, Bangkhen	22.8
Thailand, Bangkok	19.3 [b]
Puerto Rico (female only, 1953)	16.5 [c]
United States	9.8 [d]
Thailand, Photharam (1967)	7.3 [e]
Japan	5.6 [f]
Thailand, Photharam (1964)	3.5 [g]
Thailand, Ban Pong	2.3 [h]

Original Sources:
a. Research Unit, Department of Health of Puerto Rico (1967).
b. Keovichit (n.d.: 17).
c. Hill, Stycos, and Back (1959: 166-67).
d. Whelpton, Campbell, and Patterson (1966: 134).
e. Prachuabmoh and Fawcett (1967).
f. Tietze (1965: 415).
g. Hawley and Prachuabmoh (1965: 541).
h. McDaniel (1967: table 62).
SOURCE: Cowgill et al. (1971: 363-78).

Table 22 summarizes studies in several nations of the proportions of women in the childbearing ages who have reported either themselves or their husbands as having been sterilized. Sterilization is clearly a major method of contraception in Puerto Rico. There is additional evidence of a carry-over for Puerto Ricans living in the United States. In New York City 21 percent of the Puerto Ricans, but only 9 percent of the Negroes and 5 percent of white mothers on welfare reported that they had had an operation that "kept them from getting pregnant" (Podell, 1968:9).

Beyond the effectiveness and permanence of sterilization, Planned Parenthood personnel often suggest that the best method for any particular couple is the most effective method that the couple will use consistently.

Oral contraceptives—pills—are almost 100 percent effective in preventing pregnancies when taken according to the prescribed regimen. Although it is difficult to distinguish between method failure and carelessness on the part of the patient, pregnancy rates range between one per thousand women per year of exposure to one per hundred women per year. "The pregnancy rates among users of diaphragms with contraceptive paste thus appear to be 10 to 30 times higher than those among users of oral contraceptives, those among users of intrauterine devices are 2 to 4 times higher" (Planned Parenthood, 1969:4).

The need for a simple, inexpensive, effective method; independent of coitus; and not requiring sustained motivation, led to a revival of interest in *intrauterine devices* (I.U.D.s). Newly developed "open" devices of inert materials such as plastic and stainless steel are both relatively safe and highly effective, with pregnancy rates (in the United States of from 1.5 to 3 per 100 women during the first year of use. These rates tend to decline during the successive years.

The *diaphragm* with contraceptive jelly or cream offers a high level of protection, but method failures may result from improper placement or displacement during coitus. A rate of two or three pregnancies per hundred women per year is a generous estimate for "perfect users." If motivation is poor, much higher pregnancy rates should be expected (Planned Parenthood, 1969:9).

The *condom* or sheath is ordinarily highly effective but has the danger of slipping or breaking. Sometimes the condom is used in combination with vaginal foams or creams, increasing the security over either used alone. There are a variety of chemical contraceptives for insertion in the vagina. Foams, jellies, creams, foaming tablets, and suppositories are less effective than either the diaphragm used with a chemical or the condom. "Nevertheless, a significant reduction in pregnancy rates may be obtained by the use of these simple methods" (Planned Parenthood, 1969:10).

Coitus interruptus is an ancient technique, available under all circumstances and at no cost. It is the principal method by which historical decline of the birthrate in Western Europe was brought about from the eighteenth century onward. The male must withdraw before ejaculation, and emission of semen must take place completely away from the vagina, or the possibility of pregnancy is as great as if no birth control method had been used.

Rhythm, also called "temporary abstinence" or "periodic continence," is the only method besides total continence presently acceptable to the Roman Catholic Church. Because very few women have absolutely regular menstrual cycles and most women do not remember their irregularities, great care must be taken if the method is to be effective.

> According to the World Health Organization, (rhythm) pregnancy rates range from 0.8-1.4 per 100 women-years for women using basal body temperatures plus calendar, and 14-40 per 100 women-years for women using the calendar method only. According to the World Health Organization, biological variation, failure to understand the method, and unwillingness to abstain from coitus all contribute to failures. The lowest pregnancy rates, of course, are obtainable only by intelligent, highly motivated women (Planned Parenthood, 1969:11).

The probability of births out of wedlock is increased to the extent that social groups restrict the knowledge and availability of the more effective contraceptives for unmarried persons who are sexually active. Subcultural groups may circulate beliefs opposing the more effective means. Less-educated groups may have knowledge about and know where to find contraceptives yet believe superstitions about their disadvantages. Even well-educated persons have a difficult time sorting out the advantages and disadvantages of the pill as reported by the news media. People forget that the possible side effects of the pill must be balanced by the known dangers of pregnancy itself.

The search continues for the "perfect contraceptive." Yet there are sufficient means at hand if individuals are motivated to prevent pregnancy. A once-a-year pill or morning-after pill (actually an abortifact rather than a contraceptive) still must be used in order to be effective; the I.U.D. affords equal protection, if used.

MOTIVATIONS FOR USE OR NONUSE OF CONTRACEPTION

Welfare workers in this country have often followed Leontine Young (1954) in assuming that the unwed mother unconsciously wants a child. But if that were true, the success of preventative programs would be inexplicable. It seems to me more reasonable to assume that human behavior flows from mixed motives and that social groups influence motives and behavior in one direction or another.

Not only can we assume that mixed motives are involved in nonmarital sexual intercourse and the use or nonuse of contraception, but also since male or female or both may use contraceptives, the possible motives of man and women must be examined separately. The following lists are representative, not exhaustive. Not all apply to any individual or within any society; indeed, some are contradictory. The items may be more- or less-recognized or verbalized by participants and may carry great or little weight with specific individuals or within specific societies.

Possible Reasons for Use of Contraception by a Woman

1. She cares about the man and believes pregnancy would jeopardize the relationship.
2. She cares about the potential child (or children in general) and does not want to bring a child into the world without a family unit to care for it.
3. She believes that her future would be jeopardized in some way if she were to become pregnant.
    a. Punishment by the social group may be severe: public flogging or stigmatization, banishment or death; self-recrimination may be a concern: or she may believe that her chances for education, employment, or happy marriage would be lower if pregnancy occurred.
4. She does not care about the particular male partner and does not want to become pregnant by him.
5. She believes that her own loved ones would be disappointed by a pregnancy out of wedlock.

Possible Reasons for Nonuse of Contraception by a Woman

1. She does not want to appear (to herself as well as to her partner) to be ready for sexual intercourse, believing it would imply that she is a "bad girl." (Bowerman, Irish, and Pope (1963) found this reason frequently cited by mothers out of wedlock for not having used contraceptives.)

2. She deliberately avoids birth control because she is afraid it would harm her or because she "just didn't like the idea" (Furstenberg, 1971:196; also Hammond and Ladner, 1969).

3. She does not worry about her or her potential child's future or does not believe that planning can change her prospects for the future. Studies of lower-class persons (Rainwater, 1966; Komarovsky, 1962) find that they are incapable of, or do not see the relevance of, planning for their lives. One line of thinking suggests that "members of the lower-class subculture are too impulsive and present-oriented to anticipate the prospect of pregnancy and too fatalistic and apathetic to care if it does occur" (Furstenberg, 1971:193).

4. She assumes that contraception is the man's responsibility. Reports of attempts at birth control among pregnant teens, interviewed at Baltimore's Sinai Hospital consisted mainly in "getting the boy to use something" (Furstenberg, 1971:195). Yet 54 percent said the boyfriend was either unwilling or unprepared most of the time.

5. She does not believe she will become pregnant. One study found that among 337 unmarried black teenagers pregnancy was the unanticipated consequence of sexual activity. Even in communities where babies out of wedlock are common, "most unmarried girls are upset and incredulous when they first discover that they are pregnant" (Furstenberg, 1971:193).

6. She actually wants the child, whether she is willing to admit it or not.

   a. As something of her own to possess or to care for

   b. As someone to love her

   c. As a means of holding the man or forcing a marriage (some women reported discontinuing contraception only when the man started to lose interest. In Jamaica women are expected to prove a commitment to a man by bearing his child even though there is no commitment by him. In the United States and England the probability of marriage following pregnancy is high for the young and white).

   d. As revenge on her own mother or father (Leontine Young suggests variations on this theme as *the* reason for illegitimacy)

   e. To prove fertility—an historical remnant in northern Europe where the wife's major contribution was to produce children for the working of the farm and continuity of the family (Proof of pregnancy was often enough to guarantee marriage. In most countries or local communities marriage occurred before birth, thus precluding illegitimate status. As strong community and peer pressures became less effective with increased urbanization and mobility in general, illegitimate births were more likely to result.)

f. Because she believes that others will respect her more or give her more attention as an unwed mother (The respondents of Bowerman et al. (1966) were as likely to claim increased as decreased attention. Most felt no loss of respect with the birth out of wedlock. People who had simply ignored her suddenly became sympathetic to the brave little mother. It is important to note that those of the black subculture were more likely than whites to claim increased attention.)

7. Societal support may reduce horrors of bearing a child out of wedlock. Medical care and social services may increase the level of attention received by the mother. Wimperis (1960) found that income supports from welfare in England, though small, averaged the income received for working by these relatively unskilled women. Furthermore, many unwed mothers in England had more attention from agency personnel than poor married mothers received from husbands (Ibid.). In the United States, because so many unwed mothers are very young, they had *no* independent income before childbirth. The $148 monthly payment in California, while not grand, may be more than most college students have to live on. (Payments for books may balance the minimum food requirement of an infant: both groups tend to receive free medical care.)

Possible Reasons for Use of Contraception by a Man

1. He cares about the woman and does not want to place her in an uncomfortable situation. Furstenberg (1971:199) found that contraception was much more likely to be "practiced among couples who had a stable romantic relationship" (contrary to Liebow's (1967) observations; see 3 below).

2. He cares about the potential child and does not want to bring an infant into the world without a unit to care for it.

3. He does not want to be forced to marry the mother. Liebow (1968) observed that men were most likely to use contraception in casual relationships where marriage is not contemplated.

4. He does not want to be forced to support the child. At least in Norway and Germany the very strict enforcement of child support laws (detailed below) seems to encourage prevention of births out of wedlock.

Possible Reasons for Nonuse of Contraception by a Man

1. He does not think conception is very likely.
2. He does not care about the woman.
3. He does not care about the potential child.
4. He thinks contraception is her responsibility.
5. He suggests that spontaneity is a positive value and does not like to organize behavior.
6. He does not expect that any negative sanctions will be applied to him.
7. He does not believe that he has the capacity to plan ahead to affect his own future; he has a sense of powerlessness and drift. Of 350 married Negro men interviewed (Bauman and Udry, 1972) only 10 percent who scored high on powerlessness said they used contraceptives consistently. Eighty-eight percent of those low in powerlessness practiced contraception all the time.
8. He believes that if conception occurs, it would demonstrate his virility. He hopes she will be dependent on him and continue as a dependent partner as long as he wishes. Therefore he has nothing to lose and something to gain. As is the actual case in Jamaica, the man has many potential sexual partners and may require that a woman prove her commitment to him by bearing his child. Having many other possibilities, he need not commit himself to her, to the child, or even to their support.[4]

We have reviewed some of the many reasons why individuals may or may not use those contraceptives that are known, available, and efficient in reducing the probability of conception.

The reasons themselves are often contradictory. Individuals have many motives and are often ambivalent about the importance of any single motive at any given point in time. It is therefore the subtle

---

[4] Although Jamaica has a child-support law, it is not enforced and therefore is ineffective.

interplay of motives in time and space that influence specific behaviors. Small changes in any of the factors may affect the decision to use or not to use contraceptives.

For those who are highly motivated, the use of either of the most effective means of preventing conception would reduce the probability of conceiving out of wedlock to negligible levels. The evidence on effectiveness of contraceptives lends support for proposition 3: When a large proportion of the unmarrieds who engage in sexual intercourse use highly effective contraceptives, low levels of illegitimacy are found.

From our review of the entire concatenated theory, however, we may accept proposition 3a: Nonuse of contraceptives does not guarantee high levels of illegitimacy. We know that there are other preventative measures: early and universal marriage, abstention from extramarital sexual intercourse, and marriage of the persons conceiving out of wedlock or abortion of such conceptions. Some social groups concentrate on one or another of these factors, while sociological analysis requires a recognition of all of these possibilities.

We have seen that neither knowledge about, availability of, nor motivation to use contraceptives is sufficient alone to guarantee use. Rather, as hypothesized in proposition 3b, all three are necessary for widespread prevention of conception out of wedlock. Unfortunately, in some societies it is precisely the unmarried portion of the population that has least access to the knowledge and tools of contraception. Morover, where these are available to unmarrieds, it is sometimes overlooked that the motivation for their use is also a necessary condition.

SOCIAL SANCTIONS

Sanctions are not found in the laws alone, but also in the expectations and actions of the persons in a society. Social groups decide what is to be required in formal law and what may prevail in the informal expectations of the group members. When written laws are not in conformance with informal beliefs and expectations, they are not likely to be enforced either with legal penalties or with the informal pressures of the social group.

Negative sanctions related to the use of contraceptives by unmarried persons have several interesting features. In the first place external punishment for the use or nonuse of contraception by unmarried persons cannot be universally applied, because the behavior is often unknown to others. Yet, because communal standards are typically learned and internalized, an unmarried woman may refuse to be prepared for the use of contraceptives (when these are frowned on by the community) because she does not want to admit to herself that she is ready to break both the group's and her own internalized standards. She is actually in a double bind, because she is punished either by the community or by guilt if she uses contraceptives, and she is often punished by an out-of-wedlock conception if she does not. The response is frequently to take a chance on not becoming pregnant rather than to be burdened by guilt. Studies of

Table 23. Illegitimacy Trends in England and Wales and Norway

	Norway			England and Wales	
Date	Ratio	Index	Date	Ratio	Index
1900	7.2	100.0	1901–5	3.9	100.0
1910	6.6	91.5	1911–5	4.3	110.2
1920	7.6	105.0	1921–5	4.3	110.2
1930	7.0	97.1	1931–5	4.3	110.2
1940				4.3	110.2
1946	5.7	79.5		6.6	169.0
1950	4.1	57.3		5.1	130.0
1955	3.5	47.9		4.7	120.0
1960	3.7	51.0		5.4	138.0
1964	4.2	58.3		7.2	184.6
1968	5.6	77.8	1969	8.4	215.4
	Norway			England and Wales	
	Rate	Index		Rate	Index
1900	17.0	100.0	1901–5	8.4	100.0
1910	13.5	79.4	1911–5	7.9	94.0
1920	14.6	85.9	1921–5	6.7	80.0
1930	8.7	51.2	1931–5	5.5	65.5
1940				5.9	70.2
1946	11.2	65.9		13.8	164.3
1950	8.5	50.0		10.2	121.4
1955	8.5	50.0		10.3	122.6
1960	9.2	54.1		15.1	180.0
1964				20.2	240.5
1969				22.0	261.9

SOURCE: Figures for Norway from Kumar (1969); England from Great Britain, General Registrar Office (1939–1970).

unwed mothers repeatedly find them amazed that they became pregnant; they had assumed it would not happen to them.

One of the most dramatic contrasts in illegitimacy trends and related sanctions (particularly related to paternal responsibility) is that between England and Norway (see table 23). From the turn of the century to the early 1960s illegitimacy rates and ratios were doubling in England and Wales, but were being halved in Norway. One of the major differences was the provision from 1916 to 1956 that all children in Norway have a father's name and support. The state requires the unwed mother to divulge the father's name, with blood tests forming a regular part of the procedure unless the man has already admitted paternity. The father must support the child according to the father's social level. Payments run about 10 percent of the father's income, with an *enforced* normal minimum contribution, but no maximum. Other Scandinavian countries have since adopted most of the provisions of the Norwegian law, but responsibility had been placed in 100 percent of the cases only in Norway. The state, there, steps in to enforce the father's responsibility by attaching his wages if necessary (Nelson, 1953:519). If it was impossible to determine which of several possible sexual partners fathered the child, men could be held jointly responsible for support. (An amendment in 1956 lifted the provision for joint responsibility and universal naming (Krause, 1971); increases in illegitimacy followed.) Other Scandinavian countries have had similar laws but less stringent enforcement. In these countries the mother is not expected to accuse the father in criminal court; agents of the state establish responsibility, and in Norway they enforce support on behalf of the child.

In contrast, in present day England and Wales, as in many other Western nations moving into expanded programs of welfare, sanctions against childbearing out of wedlock are minimal, mild, and rarely enforced. And in those countries levels of illegitimacy have been rising rapidly. In England in 1961, while 48,000 births out of wedlock were reported, only 124 cases of child support were ordered by English courts (U.N. Sub-Commission, 1967). In addition, Wimperis (1960:135-42) found that most men defaulted on such court orders, and that those who actually paid averaged nine shillings, sixpence per week ($1.35 at the then current exchange). The probability of sanction for the male under those circumstances is minimal; he has had little to risk in conception out of wedlock and little motivation for prevention.

These examples exhibit support for proposition 3c: Social sanctions promoting or reducing the knowledge about, availability of, and motivation to use contraceptives will affect their use by individuals within societies.

8. Marriage During Pregnancy

SINCE THERE is a nine-month period following conception before childbirth typically occurs, there is time in which a number of alternatives to birth out of wedlock may be sought. In this chapter we will consider social group and societal variations in the probability of marriage before childbirth.

Births that were premaritally conceived but legitimated by marriage before parturition have a number of interesting features. First, there are two basic types: (1) those in which the marriage occurs because of the pregnancy, and (2) those in which pregnancy occurs when the marriage is already planned, that is, the commitment to the future is made, but the formalization occurs after conception (see Laslett, 1973). We have no means of knowing the relative importance of these two types with the data presently available. Secondly, each marriage during pregnancy reduces the possibility of an outcome in illegitimate birth. Thirdly, the numbers of premaritally conceived but legitimate births in relation to the numbers of illegitimate give us some idea of the probabilities for various national, social, racial, or age categories that premarital conceptions resulting in live births will be legitimated by marriage before birth. Finally, these numbers added to the numbers registered illegitimate give us some idea of the potentialities for reduction of births among these presumably unwanted or unplanned premarital conceptions.

PROPOSITIONS TO BE EXAMINED

4. When a large proportion of those who conceive out of wedlock are married before childbirth, illegitimacy levels will be low.

a. Nonmarriage following conception does not necessarily produce high levels of illegitimacy.

b. The greater the structural and cultural push to marry following conception, the lower the illegitimacy.

c. Social sanctions may push or prevent marriage by the couple conceiving out of wedlock. Those social sanctions may be directed by the families of the partners, by the peer group, by religious organizations or by the state.

VARIATIONS IN NATIONAL PROBABILITIES OF MARRIAGE DURING PREGNANCY

There are two means of examining data on marriage during pregnancy. One relates the number of brides producing a child within 7 or 8 or 8 1/2 months of marriage to the total number of brides in a given time span in a particular area, and the results give us the proportion of brides probably[1] pregnant at marriage. Another use of data is to relate the number of births arriving within 8 to 9 months of marriage to all premarital conceptions issuing in a registered birth. In this case we refer to the proportions of premarital conceptions legitimated before birth or to the probability of marriage during pregnancy, even though strictly speaking the possibility of abortion is eliminated from these calculations so the base figure is only those premarital pregnancies that result in the birth of a child. Some nations list these as proportions of live births, some include stillbirths and thus refer to all maternities. The historical studies to which I have access report only the proportion of brides pregnant at marriage, though I believe that for some local parishes it would be possible to compute the probability of marriage following premarital conception. For more recent dates I have computed both measures for some countries for which raw data are available, and I have reported on other research using one or both measures of the extent of legitimation of premartial conceptions leading to childbirth.

HISTORICAL DATA ON BRIDAL PREGNANCY

England and France

Peter Laslett (1965:139) has nicely summarized the computations of the English and French historical demographers for specific com-

---

[1] For ease of conceptualization we may assume that premature births are balanced by late arrivals, so that aggregate proportions are maintained although we recognize that a few individual cases would thus be incorrectly categorized.

munities with excellent records, intensively analyzed. These are reproduced in table 24. Notice the differences within England, where the parish of Clayworth recorded 10.2 percent of all first baptisms as occurring within eight months of marriage, while 46.2 percent were so reported in Colyton. In France the proportions of births occurring in the first eight or nine months of marriage were also significantly different in the two areas reported, being almost twice as common in the three villages of the Ile de France as in Crulai in an earlier time period.[2] The variation in prenuptial pregnancies among local communities within countries reminds us that the customs, culture, and structural patterns of most people were limited to very small geographical areas in *The World We Have Lost.*

Table 24. Prenuptial Pregnancy (England and France)

	Percentage of First Baptisms Recorded (in months from date of marriage)					
	8	8½	9	10	11	12
England						
Cartmel (Lancs.)						
1660-75 (173 cases)	13.2	17.8	24.7	35.6	47.7	57.5
Wyley (Wilts.)						
1654-1783 (76 cases)	28.9	34.2	40.0	48.5	63.0	66.4
Clayworth (Notts.)						
1650-1750 (127 cases)	10.2	13.4	15.7	22.0	44.9	49.8
Colyton (Devon)						
1538-1799 (976 cases)	46.2		61.3		83.4	
France						
Crulai (France)						
1674-1742 (323 cases)	9.5		20.3	33.0	42.2	45.4
Three villages in the Ile de France late 18th century						
(206 cases)	19.90		35.9	47.1	54.4	63.6

SOURCE: Laslett (1965: 139).

---

[2] In a recent recalculation of a sample of northwestern France for 1670 to 1769, Louis Henry (1973) estimated that in about 13 percent of his 1,963 cases an infant was born within eight or fewer months of the marriage.

Since 100, 200, and more years were represented in these summary proportions, one might well wonder about variation over the time span covered. Hair (1966) has sampled 4- to 10-year periods between 1550 and 1820 for 77 rural or semirural parishes in 25 counties in England. The 1,855 marriage records thereby sampled were matched with baptismal registrations of the same parish. Hair found that before 1700, 13 to 27 percent of all baptisms were recorded as falling within 8 1/2 months of the date of marriage. The average for the entire period before 1700 was about 20 percent. After 1700, 29 to 36 percent of baptisms were reported within 8 1/2 months of marriage. The baptismal date gives "a great deal of grace to the married couples [since] there was an interval of something like a fortnight [two weeks] on average at most times in most parishes between the date of birth and date of baptism" (Laslett, 1965:139). Hair estimates that after 1700, 36 to 42 percent of actual first births were within 8 1/2 months of marriage and that an additional 4 to 10 percent of brides may have been pregnant at marriage but either aborted spontaneously or produced a stillbirth. He concludes, therefore, that up to 50 percent of brides in the eighteenth century (specifically 1700-1820) were pregnant at marriage and that bridal pregnancy has fallen in the last 80 years because of efficient contraception.

I would like to point out that bridal pregnancy could also decline because of a decline in the probability of legitimating a conception out of wedlock. These probabilities must have been very high throughout the entire period investigated by Hair, because the registered illegitimacy ratios in fifteen rural parishes reported by Laslett (1967:17) were very low, ranging from 1 to 5 percent of all births. Hair's data imply that there is a very significant decline in brides pregnant at marriage—18 and 20 percent for 1938 and 1963 respectively—but at least for these recent years in England there has been a decline in the probability of a premaritally conceived maternity being legitimated by marriage before birth and a rise in the illegitimacy ratio (see table 24). Not efficient contraception alone, therefore, but that together with the variation in probability of pregnancy leading to marriage, abortion, or a birth out of wedlock must be considered in the analysis of a decline or rise in premarital pregnancies.

In England historically, the probability of legitimation of premarital conceptions and the relatively high probability that brides were already pregnant at marriage implies something about the customs prevailing:

> It is plain that no ceremony in church, no ecclesiastical marriage, is in question here, but a contract to marry—an espousal, a troth plight, a *handfasting* as it was called in some localities—what we would term an engagement. . . .
>
> In spite of local variations in the words used and the actions taken, it is possible to make the following tentative generalization about espousals or contracts in England in relation to marriage. A contract publicly entered into before witnesses and marked by two overt actions, the kissing of the woman by the man and the presentation of gifts—often a gold ring, or, oddly enough, half a gold ring—constituted a binding marriage, provided only that the couple then proceeded to sexual intercourse. In the Roman Church after 1564 such an action between an affianced couple was a grave sin. In the English church it was a much less serious matter (Laslett, 1965:142-43).

Northern and Western Europe

There are bits of evidence that somewhat similar customs prevailed over much of northern and western Europe. Until the eighteenth century the region covered by southern Sweden and Denmark officially regarded engagements as a legal institution. The beginning of intercourse during this phase was expected. Vance Packard (1968:319) claims that "in 1880 two-thirds of all brides already had children at the time of marriage or were pregnant." He suggests that the custom was a test of the woman's fecundity, since for peasant populations the woman's ability to bear children may have been one of her primary contributions to the family unit. In fact, throughout less-developed societies historically, death rates were so high that all societies had to have high fertility goals for mere survival (Hartley, 1972). Although the idea that premarital sexual intercourse may have historically been a test of the woman's fecundity is not universally accepted, it is known that many of the countries reporting this socially recognized practice have had very low illegitimacy rates but high bridal pregnancy rates.

Tomasson (1971) stresses that what he has called the "Nordic ethic" has its roots in *rural* society rather than in the liberality of urban society. Alva Myrdal suggests that in the old agrarian society of northern Europe:

There was a structuralized system of mores controlling the meeting and mating of the young within which sexual experimentation could occur.... Youth could be given great relative freedom in playful mating experimentation in the stable society of yore. Such experimentation could be tolerated because it was always "safe," meaning that, if sex relations were involved and if a pregnancy occurred, the male partner was practically always known and marriage followed (Myrdal, 1945:42).

One of the fascinating aspects of these patterned relationships is that the "controlling authority rested with the youth group rather than with parents" (Ibid.). Yet, a good deal of self-control was also required. In the custom called "bundling" an unmarried couple who were courting would occupy the same bed without undressing. A more elaborate pattern of "night courting" (frieri) involved organized groups of young men who would together go "calling" on a girl who was in bed in the separate "girl house" traditional for maturing girls. The group would spend some time sitting around her joking and singing and then leave one young man as her bedfellow for the night. The pattern was institutionalized in that it was a regularized form of flirtation, of chaste entertainment, with shared norms and patterned behavior expected of the participants.

Shame and in some places even fines and other forms of punishment were provided by group regulations for the young man who broke one of the many rules: who went courting alone without the company of the youth guild, who came from another village, who removed other than prescribed items of clothing (never the skin apron), who lay otherwise than on top of the bedclothes the first time, who was too young or who broke the rule of sexual integrity of the girl he visited in this way. For the girl the risks were even greater, as a girl who was known to have "slept herself away" had practically forfeited her right to a suitable marriage (Myrdal, 1945:43).

As two young people would indicate their preference for one another over time, there were specific indications to the youth guild that they were serious. With an exchange of presents the couple were left alone more often and even allowed to court in the middle of the week. An official proposal and marriage typically followed. It is not certain how often, during the later stages of this gradual commitment, sexual relations preceded marriage. "There is no doubt that the initial period with changing young men was one of restraint. Such training in self-control was highly valued in Scandinavian culture" (Myrdal, 1945:43). Croog (1951) notes the crucial importance of the "ring engagement," which had almost the status of a formal marriage, including rights to sexual intercourse. Most important for our consideration is that in almost all cases where pregnancy occurred, marriage followed. Illegitimacy could remain at very low levels over hundreds of years under such a system.

RECENT PROBABILITIES OF LEGITIMATION

With the advent of industrialization and increased geographic mobility it became easier for either partner to avoid a marriage he or she did not fully desire. The declining cohesion of the local community made it easy for people to avoid commitments. If marriage is increasingly avoided following pregnancy (as it becomes easier to do so in urban-industrial societies), and there is no sharp drop in premarital conceptions, or increase in abortions, or both, there would be a corresponding rise in births out of wedlock.

England and Wales

The above situation does describe a part of "The Amazing Rise in Illegitimacy in Great Britain" from 1938 onward (Hartley, 1966). In some areas of England the custom of "bundling" was said still to be common. As long as the pattern was surrounded by community controls to back up self-controls, pregnancies out of wedlock were overwhelmingly followed by marriage rather than births out of wedlock. As recently as 1938, over 70 percent of all premarital conceptions carried to term were legitimated by marriage before birth. From 1964 to 1970, about 54 percent were similarly legitimated[3] (see tables 25 and 26).

---

[3] At the same time that the probability of marriage following conception was declining, the number of extramaritally conceived maternities per thousand unmarried women was rising dramatically, and the proportion of women unmarried was declining (Hartley, 1969a). The first two factors tend to inflate levels of illegitimacy, the latter to depress these levels. Altogether they indicate the complexity of the events involved in the analysis of the phenomenon.

Table 25. Illegitimate and Premaritally Conceived Legitimate Maternities (1938–60) and Live Births (1961–70), England and Wales

(1)	(2)	(3)	(4)	(5)	(6)
			Total maternities/live births conceived extramaritally		Percentage of extramaritally conceived maternities/ live births legitimated by marriage of parents before birth of child
Year	Illegitimate maternities/ live births	Premaritally conceived legitimate maternities/ live births (within 8 mos.)	Numbers	Percentage of all maternities/ Live Births	

			Maternities		
1938	27,440	64,530	91,970	14.4	70.2
1939	26,569	60,346	86,915	13.8	69.4
1940	26,574	56,644	83,218	13.7	68.1
1941	32,179	43,362	75,541	12.7	57.4
1942	36,597	40,705	78,302	11.8	52.0
1943	44,881	37,271	82,152	11.8	45.4
1944	56,477	37,746	94,223	12.3	40.1
1945	64,743	38,176	102,919	14.9	37.1
1946	55,138	43,488	98,626	11.8	44.1
1947	47,491	59,633	107,124	12.0	55.7
1948	42,402	62,304	104,706	13.4	59.5
1949	37,554	59,185	96,739	13.1	61.2
1950	35,816	54,188	90,004	12.8	60.2
1951	33,444	50,477	83,921	12.3	60.1
1952*	33,088	50,740*	83,828	12.3	60.5
1953	33,083	50,266	83,349	12.1	60.3
1954	32,128	50,901	83,029	12.2	61.3
1955	31,649	50,638	82,287	12.2	61.5
1956	34,113	54,895	89,008	12.6	61.7
1957	35,098	56,203	91,301	12.5	61.6
1958	36,787	56,581	93,368	12.5	60.6
1959	38,792	57,638	96,430	12.8	59.8
1960	43,281	60,972	104,253	13.2	58.5
			Live Births		
1961**	48,490	66,596	115,086	14.2	57.9
1962	56,023	70,202	126,225	15.1	55.5
1963	59,655	71,456	131,111	15.4	54.5
1964	63,925	75,328	139,253	15.8	54.1
1965	66,249	77,775	144,024	16.7	54.0

(1)	(2)	(3)	(4)	(5)	
1966	67,056	79,254	146,310	17.2	
1967	69,928	81,004	150,932	18.1	
1968	69,806	81,309	151,115	18.4	ɔɔ.8
1969	67,041	78,559	145,600	18.3	54.0
1970	64,744	76,696	141,440	18.0	54.2

SOURCES: Great Britain, General Register Office (1960: pt. III, table 26, p. 43; 1961–68: pt. II, tables AA and II) and computations therefrom.

*From 1952 onward the figures relate to women married once only.

**From 1961 onward column (3) records live births within the first 8 months of marriage.

One of the most interesting aspects of table 25 is the clear complementarity between the probability of legitimation and births out of wedlock during the war years. Illegitimacy levels (numbers, ratios, and rates) peak in 1945 for England and Wales. While many observers have assumed these data indicated an increase in "immorality" during the war, the more complete information contained in table 25 indicates a very different set of facts. In the early years of the war, maternities conceived out of wedlock actually declined in numbers, rising during the later war years but at a lower pace than illegitimacy levels alone would imply. The figures indicate that it was not an increase in premarital conceptions, but a very sharp decline in the legitimation of those conceptions, that was the main cause of the 1945 peak in illegitimacy. In that year the probability of legitimation of a premarital conception carried to term was only about half what it had been only seven years earlier. For the English people the war brought destruction not only to homes, industry, and public buildings, but also to human relationships. Those who might have married following conception were often physically separated and unable to do so. Nevertheless, the illegitimate fertility rates, or births per thousand unmarried women, were lower for every age group in 1945 than through the 1960s when there was no wartime dislocation (Hartley, 1969a:49).

Although the probability of marriage for nonmaritally conceived maternities has never returned to the pre-World War II level, it is not now nearly as low as at the 1945 depths. Overall, the decrease in the proportion of premarital conceptions legitimated by the parents before the birth of the child has pushed illegitimacy levels higher. If 70.2 percent of the mothers conceiving premaritally had married before the birth of the child in 1964, as they had in 1938, illegitimate births would have been 35 percent fewer than were actually registered in England and Wales in that year.

Table 26. Percentage of Premaritally Conceived Births Legitimated by Marriage, England and Wales.

Age at Maternity	1950	1960	1970
Under 20	73.8	71.6	63.5
20–24	72.1	67.2	60.2
25–29	48.2	42.2	31.2
30–34	34.2	26.1	16.7
35–39	25.6	22.0	11.2
40–44	21.1	20.1	7.7
15–44	60.5	58.5	54.2

SOURCES: Great Britain, General Register Office (1950: pt. III; 1960: pt. III; 1970: pt. II, tables AA and IIb).

Another interesting aspect of the probability of legitimation is the variation by age of mother at maternity. Table 26 allows a comparison of the probability of marriage before birth for premaritally conceived maternities by age of mother in England and Wales for the years 1950, 1960, and 1970. More than 60 percent of those in the two youngest groups married before childbirth. That percentage declines drastically with increasing age, but because the total group of women involved in these calculations is heavily weighted by the younger groups, the overall probability is closer to the probability at younger than at older ages. Although probabilities of marriage have declined over time for each age group, the reductions are far greater in the older groups, whose probabilities of legitimation were already lowest. As I have shown elsewhere, a significant portion of those in the later age groups were not free to marry (Hartley, 1969b; see also Wimperis, 1960).

Northern Europe

Sidney Goldstein (1967:999) analyzing premarital pregnancies in Denmark, computed "Births Out of Wedlock as a Percent of all Premarital Conceptions." The reciprocal of those percentages, of course, gives us the probability of legitimation of a premarital conception that does result in birth. For 1950, 1955, 1960, and 1964, the overall probabilities of legitimation were 60.4, 65.7, 63.4, and 60.5 percent. These are more stable over time than in England and Wales for a similar time span. It is probably possible to obtain these figures over a longer period, at least for Sweden, Norway, and Denmark, and to compute age-specific probabilities as well. Nevertheless, the number of nations publishing the data necessary for these calculations is very limited for the world as a whole. My goal is not to do these for every possible country but to offer a scheme of analysis so that national specialists will have a full range of variables to consider in their own analysis.

The United States

For the United States, even published data are not uniformly reported for all states, and births within the early months of marriage by age of mother are unavailable. There are, however, estimates from sample surveys that allow computation of the probability of legitimation of premarital conceptions issuing in live births for whites and nonwhites. A special publication of the Bureau of the Census (1969) on "Marriage, Fertility and Childspacing: June 1965" gives an estimated rate of first births occurring before or within the eighth month of marriage. Subtracting the rate for first births entirely outside of marriage we obtain a rate within the first eight months of marriage for first births. Applying that rate to marriages occurring in the same time period, we are able to estimate the numbers of legitimate births within eight months of marriage. Relating these figures to estimates of illegitimate births allows computation of the probability of legitimation (see table 27).

For the white category over the years 1940 to 1964, over 60 percent of premaritally conceived births were legitimated by marriage before childbirth. Therefore, the overall proportion for whites in the United States is somewhat higher than the current probability of such a resolution in England and Wales. For the nonwhite category only there was a decline from 25.8 to 17.7 percent of nonmarital conceptions carried to term that were legitimated before first birth. A very different structural and cultural pattern among nonwhites is implied in the far less frequent use of marriage as an alternative to births out of wedlock. Although the nonwhite category is itself made up of a multiplicity of subcultures, blacks make up about 90 percent

Table 27. Probability of Legitimating a Premarital Conception,
United States, Specified Time Periods

White Women	1940–44	1945–49	1950–54	1955–59	1960–64
Number of births within 8 months of first marriage	352,625	522,240	537,495	739,198	854,633
Number of illegitimate births	216,600	286,600	279,500	356,700	487,200
Total premaritally conceived	569,225	808,840	816,995	1,095,898	1,341,833
Probability of legitimation	61.9%	64.6%	65.8%	67.5%	63.7%

Nonwhite Women	1940–49		1950–59		1960–64
Number of births within 8 months of first marriage	215,306		264,509		163,240
Number of illegitimate births	619,300		1,147,600		756,700
Total premaritally conceived	834,606		1,412,109		919,940
Probability of legitimation	25.8%		18.7%		17.7%

Total	1940–49		1950–59		1960–64
Number of births within 8 months of first marriage.	1,090,171		1,541,202		1,017,873
Number of illegitimate births	1,122,500		1,783,800		1,243,900
Total premaritally conceived	2,212,671		3,325,002		2,261,773
Probability of legitimation	49.3%		46.4%		45.0%

SOURCE: Computations from U.S. Bureau of the Census (1969: 39, 41) and U.S., H.E.W. (1968a: 8).

of the nonwhites nationwide. The decline in probability of legitimation among the nonwhites over time is reflected in the decline for the nation as a whole.

A study of the Detroit area in 1960 by William Pratt (1965:31) estimates slightly higher probabilities of legitimation there. For white women 69.6 percent, and for nonwhites 23.8 percent of conceptions carried to term appeared to have been resolved by marriage before childbirth. In Massachusetts in 1966-1968, the percentage of nonmaritally conceived first births legitimated by marriage before birth was estimated to be 71.7 for whites and 33.3 for nonwhites (Whelan, 1972a:22).

From a one in 1,000 sampling of all births in the United States for the years 1964 to 1966 conducted by the National Center for Health Statistics, Mary Grace Kovar (1970:12) has computed the proportion of first births assumed to have been conceived outside marriage and legitimated by marriage before birth. For white respondents 64.7 percent and for "all others" 33.3 percent of premarital conceptions issuing in a live birth were born in wedlock.

Differences in these computed probabilities may be due to differences in the population sampled, the time period, and the adequacy of the estimates. As more data become available we may reduce our insecurity in reporting estimates.

One intersting feature of both the Kovar and the Pratt proportions is their computed differences by age for white and nonwhite categories. For the whites the highest probability of legitimation is in the 15- to 19-year-old age group with a gradual decline in the probability of marriage as age increases. For the nonwhite category, however, the 15 to 19 year olds appeared less likely than 20 to 21 or 20 to 24 year olds to have premarital conceptions legitimated by marriage.. Although tempting, speculation on the reasons for such differences cannot be based on a very firm foundation at this time. It is clear from these data, however, that age and racial groups with lower proportions marrying after pregnancy have higher levels of illegitimacy, while those with higher proportions marrying have lower illegitimacy.

Noting that the higher the rate of conceptions out of wedlock the lower the probability of legitimation for 11 populations in seven countries, Cutright (1973a:405) concludes that "it is the out of wedlock conceived birth rate, rather than the probability of legitimation, that will best explain differences in illegitimacy rates among the two [white and nonwhite] populations" of the United States. From the information available for this country it is not clear whether the probabilities of legitimation have changed greatly over a much longer period of time. We do know from a number of surveys that the proportions of brides pregnant at the wedding date has risen at the same time that births out of wedlock have been on the increase. Therefore, the two possibilities are not offsetting one another in the United States, but we must conclude that the numbers and rates of premarital conceptions carried to term have generally been on the increase both within and outside marriage.[4]

PROPORTIONS OF BRIDES PREMARITALLY PREGNANT

Table 28, reproduced from two publications of the Bureau of the Census, contains estimates of the percentage of women married in specified years whose first child was born before the eighth month of marriage, by color. It includes not only those born within eight months of marriage, but also those born before marriage, the births out of wedlock to those women who did later marry in the time period indicated.

Note that these data exclude altogether the very small proportions of women never marrying. The illegitimate births before marriage are included with those within eight months of marriage for women ever married in the given years. The data are interesting in adding a bit of information on the changes that have occurred over a long time period.

Given the information already at hand, it is not surprising that the proportion of married white women conceiving out of wedlock and carrying to term has more than doubled, even since 1940-44 (with relative stability from 1900 to 1944). It is more difficult to understand why nonwhite women have had so great a proportional increase. There is reason to suspect that part of that increase may be due to improved reporting of births among a population that was largely rural, southern, and poor at the turn of the century. Another part of the apparent rise in the proportion of ever-married nonwhite women who gave birth before or within eight months of marriage may be an increase in fecundity due to some improvements in health and nutrition and a decline in sterility.

---

[4] Remember, however, the recent decline in the *rate* of illegitimacy among non-whites in the United States.

In contrast to the indicators within the United States, very recent data for Sweden (a 35 percent drop in the number of marriages between 1966 and 1971 together with a sharp rise in illegitimacy) may indicate a trade off in premarital conceptions born outside of rather than within wedlock.

Earlier sample surveys of United States women report similar results. In 1939 Raymond Pearl reported that 9.3 percent of his sample of 25,316 white mothers and 36.6 percent of his sample of 5,635 Negro mothers had had premarital conceptions born either in or out of wedlock (Pearl, 1939:181). Gebhard (1958:35) reported that 16.8 percent of Kinsey's white female respondents had had premarital conceptions. Monahan (1970), reporting on domestic relations cases in Philadelphia in 1954, found that 20 percent of white and 45 percent of Negro first marriages had been preceded by pregnancy carried to term. Finally, a sample of all first births occurring from 1964 through 1966 (Kovar, 1970) indicated that about 22 percent of all first births within first marriages arrived less than eight months after marriage and were apparently premaritally conceived. This had been the case for about 20 percent of whites and for about 42 percent of nonwhites (U.S., H.E.W., 1970:2).

Table 28. Percentage of Women Married Whose First Child Was Born before or within Eight Months of Marriage, United States

Marriage Date	Percent premaritally pregnant
White women	
1960–64	20.5
1955–59	18.3
1950–54	13.0
1945–49	10.8
1940–44	8.7
1935–39	8.6
1930–34	9.0
1925–29	8.1
1920–24	8.3
1910–19	8.9
1900–1909	7.4
Nonwhite women	
1960–64	49.6
1950–59	47.9
1940–49	35.1
1930–39	25.5
1920–29	21.8
1910–19	20.7
1900–1909	11.8

SOURCE: Data for first marriages occurring 1900–39 from U.S. Bureau of the Census (1961: tables 16 and 17). Data for first marriages contracted 1940–64 from U.S. Bureau of the Census (1969: tables 17 and 18).

In his cross-cultural comparison of the timing of pregnancy, Christensen (1953:55; 1963:121) found that over 30 percent of the Danish marriages examined were apparently preceded by pregnancy. His Indiana and Utah marriage samples, when matched with births, showed that 24.5 and 15.7 percent, respectively, produced first births within 266 days (the normal period of uterogestation) following marriage.

The Kinsey group has the only set of data I have found that includes abortion as a possible outcome of premarital conceptions. Since these do not result in births, the above data generally refer to actual births within or outside marriage. In the next chapter we will examine the outcome ratios reported by Gebhard (see table 31). Of all premarital conceptions (including those aborted) reported by the white Kinsey respondents, a greater proportion resulted in marriage before childbirth than in live births out of wedlock. Many more resulted in spontaneous or induced abortion.[5] For those respondents, illegitimate births were the least likely of the possible outcomes following nonmarital conception. The probabilities of legitimation referred to above relate only to those conceptions that ended in childbirth.

Proposition 4

It appears from the wealth of data above that there is sufficient, if not complete, information to confirm proposition 4: When a large proportion of those who conceive out of wedlock are married before childbirth, illegitimacy levels will be low. Historically, in England and many of the northern and western European countries, very large proportions of brides were pregnant on the wedding day, yet levels of illegitimacy were very low. A pattern of premarital conceptions followed almost uniformly by marriage appears to have been socially sanctioned. Declines in the probability of legitimation since 1940, at least in England, have paralleled recent increases in levels of illegitimacy, although very great increases in premaritally conceived maternities have also occurred.

---

[5] Because nonwhite respondents (except those with some college education) were less likely to report abortion, they were more likely than whites to report premarital conceptions resulting in marriage *or* in births out of wedlock (varying by age and education).

Although nonmarriage following conception may lead to increased illegitimacy, is it necessarily the case? In Jamaica I have noted that premarital conceptions do not seem to be regarded as a reason for marriage (Hartley, 1971:182). Births by months of marriage are not reported for Jamaica, yet 94.9 percent of all births to women in the youngest age group in that country are out of wedlock. If all the remainder had been premaritally conceived but legitimated by marriage, the probability of legitimation would be only 5 percent. In contrast, however, the situation in Japan indicates that the alternative of abortion means that nonmarital conceptions need not be followed by birth out of wedlock even if marriage is avoided (for details, see Hartley, 1970b). The acceptance and legalization of safe abortion in Japan appears to be a factor in the decline in illegitimacy there. The technical indicators imply that births within the early months of marriage are rare in Japan,[6] that nonmarriage following conception does not lead to increased illegitimacy; and that birth is avoided by abortion. We may therefore accept proposition 4a: Nonmarriage following conception does not necessarily produce high levels of illegitimacy.

Proposition 4b suggests that the greater the structural and cultural push to marry following conception the lower the illegitimacy. Perhaps the most interesting evidence favoring this proposition is provided by Christensen's data from Denmark, Indiana, and Utah (1963:121). If the rush to marry following pregnancy can be taken as an indicator of the degree of cultural push to marry following conception, the following statistics are pertinent. In Utah 79 percent of all births within the first nine months of marriage were within the last three of those months. Marriages were apparently hurried when pregnancy was discovered. In Indiana 62 percent, but in Denmark only 21 percent, of such maternities were followed by a

---

[6] Although, information on months of marriage at time of childbirth is not available, we do have some indirect information indicating that premarital conceptions legitimated before birth cannot be used as an alternative to illegitimacy in Japan as often as in England and Wales: (1) the age-specific legitimate birth rates for Japan are similar to the rates for England *after* removal of births conceived before marriage (Hartley, 1969a:214); (2) the vital statistics for 1964 show that only about 4 percent of all births were recorded to parents married in the same year. Yet, because five months is the *modal* month after marriage for the birth of a premaritally conceived offspring (in England, Denmark, and the United States), if bridal pregnancy were common in Japan, far more than 4 percent of all births would be recorded in the same year as marriage (even allowing losses at year ends).

similarly hurried marriage. It is important that Utah has one of the lowest ratios of illegitimacy in the United States. Indiana is about average for the United States (see U.S., H.E.W., 1968a; table 18), and Denmark is much higher than either for proportions of white births out of wedlock.

In a recent study of the timing of births in Massachusetts, it was found that whites were more likely than nonwhites to rush the marriage after pregnancy was discovered. "Nonwhite premaritally conceived babies were born sooner after the wedding of their parents than were white babies, with the mean number of days between marriage and the birth of the premaritally conceived child being 147 (about 5 lunar months) for whites and 101 (about 3 1/2 lunar months) for nonwhites" (Whelan, 1972b).

In all of these comparisons the groups evidencing the greatest push or rush to marry following conception are also those with lower levels of illegitimacy. In addition, the historical data discussed above lend weight to confirmation of Proposition 4b. I know of no negative evidence.

SOCIAL SANCTIONS

A discussion of the structural and cultural "push" to marry implies that some kinds of sanctions exist. Proposition 4c suggests that social sanctions may encourage or prevent marriage by the couple conceiving out of wedlock. Those social sanctions may be directed by the families of the partners, the peer group, religious organizations, the state, or combinations of these.

Research indicates that the most effective sanctions are the informal approval or disapproval of members of one's primary groups: friends or family. These become less effective if geographical mobility and secondary relationships predominate. We have seen that in Europe historically the peer group forced marriage if there was hesitation following conception out of wedlock. In the United States, parents have been expected to encourage marriage when conception occurred out of wedlock.[7] Now, however, some parents or friends, recognizing the recent evidence on the high probability of divorce

---

[7] Parenthetically, it is not beyond the recognition of the young that parents who forbid marriage may become only too eager to consent if the couple conceive first.

in cases of marriage following pregnancy, discourage marriage for couples in that situation.

Differences in sanctions of the English Anglican and French Catholic churches with regard to the previously accepted pattern of sexual intercourse during the formal, legal engagement period are credited by Laslett (1965:142) as one of the basic factors in the much lower probability of French than English brides being pregnant at the wedding day. Following the decree of the Council of Trent in 1564, the Catholic hierarchy declared the ancient practice not merely inadvisable but one of the "grave sins." It is clear that religious beliefs form powerful sanctions among the faithful. Even contemporary studies consistently indicate that the religiously devout are less likely than others questioned to engage in premarital sexual intercourse, to conceive out of wedlock, and to be pregnant at the time of marriage.

Knodel reports (1967) an interesting example of the fluctuations that may occur with changes in state-imposed sanctions. Early in the nineteenth century a number of German states, hoping to reduce fertility among the poor, imposed minimum age and property restrictions on marriage. A rise in births out of wedlock followed as partners in conception were unable to follow the traditional path to the altar. Between 1860 and 1890 the states involved repealed the restrictions, and a decrease in illegitimacy resulted. Meanwhile, among those nearby German states that had not imposed the initial restrictions, illegitimacy rates remained stable.

We have already seen that state or government regulations or national emergencies that have nothing to do with the focus of these studies may influence the results. During World War II conscription and the movement of troops, temporary stationing of troops, and so on, affected the ability of persons to legitimate premartial conceptions, with the result that a great part of the 1945 peak in illegitimacy was due to the very sharp decline in the probability of legitimation of nonmarital conceptions. Further national studies will uncover more examples than are reported here. Disconfirming evidence would include instances of a push to marriage being followed by lowered probability of legitimation or social rejection of marriage following conception being accompanied by an increased probability of that result. While these are unlikely results, there is, nevertheless, a fertile field for future studies. In the meantime, evidence already at hand favors tentative acceptance of proposition 4c. Not simply random individual decisions, then, but also the weighting of those decisions by social group sanctions leads to varying probabilities of marriage following conception, and we have seen that these probabilities are inversely related to levels of illegitimacy.

9. *Abortion as an Alternative*

ALTHOUGH we may talk and write about abortion as an alternative to a live birth—legitimate or illegitimate—for many persons it is not a substitute at all. For some the societal prohibition of abortion is complete in both physical and mental terms. Constraints include legal restrictions, the unwillingness of the medical profession to perform abortions, problems of access to an abortionist (the knowledge network) and the woman's access to money for payment. Abortion may also be restricted psychologically. That is, if individuals and groups define abortion (even when physically available) as out of the question for them, it is not a considered choice.

Abortion is the last of the alternatives to an illegitimate birth to be considered, because for many persons it is the last possibility when all else fails. Many women apparently hope to resolve a premarital conception in marriage before childbirth. And, we have seen that social groups vary in the degree to which they encourage a hurried marriage. Thus Christensen found that in two different communities in the United States, marriage (if it was to occur at all) followed very quickly after recognition of pregnancy. In Denmark the modal month of marriage was four months after conception. Wherever so long a delay is common and some people back out at the last minute, it is usually too late for an abortion. Not only is it more difficult to obtain legal or illegal abortions after the third month, but also complications are more likely after that time.[1]

---

[1] However, research indicates that for the last 30 to 40 years "risk to life from abortion carried out in a hospital by an experienced physician upon a healthy woman in her first trimester of pregnancy is far smaller than the ordinary risks of pregnancy and birth" (Tietze and Lehfeldt, 1961: 1154).

DEFINITIONS AND PROPOSITIONS

Abortion may be defined as the termination of pregnancy before independent viability of the fetus has been attained, that is, before there is capacity for life outside the womb. The loss of embryonal and fetal organisms may occur at any stage of pregnancy.

"It has traditionally been assumed that viability is attained at 28 weeks of gestation, corresponding to a fetal weight of approximately 1000 g. This definition is based on the observation that infants below this weight have little chance of survival, while the mortality of infants above 1000 g. [2 pounds, 3 1/3 ounces] declines rapidly" (World Health Organization (WHO), 1970:6). The expulson of a dead fetus later in pregnancy is called a stillbirth or late fetal death. Birth of a living infant before term is called premature birth. Miscarriage is a popular term for spontaneous abortion.

Unfortunately the 28-week distinction between abortion and still birth is not treated uniformly by all registrars and governments, but United Nations agencies have been making some attempt to encourage uniform reporting.[2]

SPONTANEOUS ABORTION

When allowance is made for very early, unrecognized losses there are probably about 15 to 20 percent of all conceptions terminated spontaneously (WHO, 1970:20).[3] There are a variety of physical, hormonal, or infectious abnormalities in the fetus itself or in the relationship of the pregnant woman to fetus that may result in fetal death. The probabilities of such an outcome would vary not only among societies, but also among subcultures and social strata within societies. The Kinsey sample (Gebhard et al., 1958) of nonprison Negroes indicated that their spontaneous abortions were inversely

---

[2] In recent years, some authorities have placed the upper limit of abortion at 20 weeks or at 500 or even 400 grams because some infants of this weight have in fact survived, and the term "immature" has been used to describe fetuses weighing between 500 (or 400) and 1,000 grams. The choice of upper gestational limit is relatively unimportant in terms of the incidence of abortion, since fetal deaths at 20 to 27 weeks are far outnumbered by those occurring before 20 weeks (WHO, 1970:6-7).

[3] Other researchers have placed the estimate for spontaneous fetal loss at four weeks or more of pregnancy at between 20 and 40 percent of conceptions (James, 1970; Shapiro et al., 1971).

related to education and to induced abortions. Although results of this small, nonrepresentative sample cannot be generalized to the larger population, it alerts us to the possibilities of categorical differences. Of those with zero to eight years of education, 27 percent of pregnancies were said to have been spontaneously aborted, while only 3.8 percent of such pregnancies were said to have been aborted by Negro respondents with thirteen years or more of formal education. Although the differences would be assumed to be related to the general level of health of the women (or their unwillingness to report induced abortion), the inverse relationship between education (and presumably health) and spontaneous abortion did not appear for the white respondents, who had much lower overall tendency to report spontaneous abortion and a very much higher reporting of induced abortion (see table 31).

THERAPEUTIC OR "INDUCED" ABORTION

In most countries medical ethics and the law allow the deliberate termination of pregnancy for one reason or another, as, by local definition, when the woman's health, life, or sanity are seriously jeopardized by the pregnancy or when grossly deformed offspring are highly probable. Great variation occurs, however, in the liberality of definition of the legal and medical terms involved.

An indication of that variation comes from the data on legal abortions in comparison to live births. A survey of 26 hospitals in San Francisco and Los Angeles for 1952 through 1956 found only one therapeutic abortion for each 418 live births (Foote et al., 1966:611). By way of contrast, in the first quarter of 1971 California reported 257 abortions per 1,000 live births and New York State reported 781 abortions (including those to out of state residents) for every 1,000 live births (see table 33). Some countries of eastern Europe have reported more abortions than live births. In Hungary from 1961 through 1971 there were 140 to 165 registered abortions per 100 live births. It has been estimated that in 1965 Romania had 400 legal abortions per 100 live births. (Severe restrictions on abortion were instituted in the following year.) Although no official statistics are available it is estimated that the USSR also has more legal abortions than live births (Heer, 1965). The historically separate cultures that make up the subdivisions of present day Yugoslavia report widely different abortion rates and ratios (David et al., 1973). It has been claimed that some Yugoslav women have experienced as many as 40 abortions, with costs there at about five to ten dollars each. Women in some nations are clearly using abortion as a major means of birth control, even though governments and medical personnel claim they are offering contraceptive training as an alternative. Freedman (1964:10) feels that "abortion has been the principal means used in all countries with major fertility declines since World War II."

PROPOSITIONS CONNECTING ABORTION AND ILLEGITIMACY

5. When a large proportion of those who conceive out of wedlock abort the fetus, illegitimacy levels will be low.

a. Freely available, safe abortion does not guarantee elimination of illegitimacy.

b. Restriction of the availability of abortion does not necessarily lead to high levels of illegitimacy.

c. Societies that facilitate (in structural opportunity and cultural beliefs) abortion as an alternative to childbearing outside of wedlock, will tend to have low levels of illegitimacy.

d. The greater the economic and emotional burden of illegitimate children on the mother and father, and the fewer the potential rewards of such childbirth, the greater the motivation to avoid, and the lower the levels of illegitimacy.

SOCIETAL NORMS RELATING TO ABORTION

CULTURAL BELIEFS ABOUT ABORTION IN PREINDUSTRIAL SOCIETIES

The best example of the wide variety of cultural pre- and proscriptions about abortion comes from the report by Devereux (1960) on abortion in 400 preindustrial societies. Culturally acceptable reasons for inducing abortion include:

1. Medical and biological considerations encompassing factors such as: fear of birth, belief that the fetus is guilty of causing illness in the mother, "youth" or "advanced" age of the mother (though the definition of what ages are too young and too old vary greatly), and eugenic reasons for limitations on the number of births.

2. Political causes for abortion may operate to safeguard or limit dynastic lines, may relate to conquest or miscegenation, or may depend on the whims of absolute rulers.

3. Social structural reasons including cultural definitions of "improper paternity" are closely tied to the cultural definition of illegitimacy. Those reasons accepted by specific tribes:

    a. The father is unknown.

    b. The father raped the mother.

    c. The father had access to the woman through "error."

    d. The father is not married to the girl (widespread motivation).

    e. There are "several fathers."

    f. The father is a close relative of the girl (incest taboo).

    g. The father is an alien.

    h. The father is neither a native nor an acceptable colonial.

    i. The father is a prisoner of war or a slave.

    j. The father's marriage to the mother is unlawful.

    k. The father is a prince, and the mother is his slave concubine.

    l. The father is the owner of the slave-girl.

    m. The father, though the lawful husband, is dead.

    n. The father is not the married woman's husband.

    o. The father is neither the woman's husband nor a person who has lawful sexual access to her.

    p. The father is believed to be a demon.

4. Economic factors. Nomadic groups are seldom able to support unlimited numbers of births, and poor soils in many parts of the world lead to a cultural acceptance of abortion as a means of limiting numbers of those within tribal support limits.

Although abortion is extensively and rather openly practiced in many primitive societies, few groups give it unqualified approval. The most widespread approval is in the case of premarital pregnancies, indicating a preference for abortion over illegitimacy.

LAWS ON ABORTION IN CONTEMPORARY SOCIETIES

Although there is an obvious disparity between the law and actual practice within the nations of the world, the laws themselves are at least an indicator of the acceptance or rejection of abortion by the society.

Legal statutes do not often grant abortion on the basis of a request of the mother alone. Yet, in practice, an already liberal law may be interpreted in such a way that requests are not denied. The grounds for abortion may be subsumed under two broad categories (see also table 29).

Medical Grounds

The most widely accepted grounds for abortion fall into the medical category. The strictest laws are those that authorize abortion only to save the life of the woman or permit such a ground to be raised as the reason. This has been a feature until 1973 of some of the state laws of the United States, of a number of Latin American laws, and of French Law (Lee, 1971:85).

Some countries allow abortion to preserve the health of the prospective mother. The laws of Czechoslovakia provide long lists of specifically approved "pathological conditions in which continued pregnancy constitutes a hazard to the health of the woman" (Grzybowski, 1971:242, 254-61).

Liberality of interpretation of the law may depend on the precise wording used in the statute. The wording in Peru, "to avoid *serious* and *permanent* damage to her [woman's] health" (emphasis added), allows less room for judgment than the wording of the Thai law permitting abortion performed by a medical practitioner "if it is necessary for the sake of the woman's health" (Lee, 1971:85).

> It is significant that even in those East European countries where the indications for abortion cover a wide range of medical, eugenic, social, and economic reasons, the legal controls nevertheless prohibit abortion in a number of cases, for example, when there are medical contraindications of a specified nature, where pregnancy has exceeded three months, or where an induced abortion has been performed within the immediately preceding six months (Ibid.).

Eugenic grounds for abortion may include the probable transmission of an hereditary disease, deformity (or probable deformity as a result of interuterine damage), or retardation, the wish being to keep the live population in good condition.

Table 29. Current Status of Worldwide Abortion Legislation

Country	Illegal (No Exceptions)	Medical			Eugenic (Fetal)	Social		Elective (Within time limit)	Law and Practice
		Absolute (Life)	Relative (Health)	Physical/Mental		Juridical (Rape, incest)	Socioeconomic		
Algeria		x							Ordinance No. 66–156 of 8 June 1966.
Argentina		x	x			x			Law No. 17567 Penal Code of 6 December 1967.
Australia		x		x					
South Australia		x		x	x		x		Criminal Law Consolidation Act, Amendment Act 1969.
Austria		x	x						Criminal Code Section 144–148.
Bangladesh		x							
Belgium	x								Penal Code Section 348–353.
Bolivia	x								
Brazil		x				x			Decree-Law No. 2848 of 7 December 1940. (Nonmedical abortion widespread.)
Bulgaria		x		x	x	x	x		Decree No. 220 of 16 March 1968.
Cambodia, Federal Republic of		x							Crown Ordinance No. 103 of 23 July 1934.
Cameroon		x	x			x			Law 67-LF-1 of 12 June 1967, Section 339.
Canada		x							Criminal Law Amendment Act 1968–1969.
Chile		x							December 1967. (Nonmedical abortion widespread.)

Table 29. Current Status of Worldwide Abortion Legislation

Country	Illegal (No Exceptions)	Legal Grounds						Elective (Within time limit)	Law and Practice
		Medical				Social			
		Absolute (Life)	Relative (Health)	Physical/Mental	Eugenic (Fetal)	Juridical (Rape, incest)	Socioeconomic		
China, People's Republic of								x	Regulation of 15 May 1957. (Elective if within first three months and if no other abortion during prior 12 months.)
Colombia	x		x						Decree No. 2831 of 23 September 1954. (Non-medical abortion widespread.)
Costa Rica		x	x						Penal Code of 21 Aug. 1941, Sec. 199
Cuba		x	x			x	x		Social Defence Code of 10 October 1938, Sec. 443. (About 95% of all requests are granted, regardless of reason.)
Czechoslovakia		x		x	x	x	x		Decree No. 54 of 6 July 1966.
Denmark		x		x	x	x	x		Law No. 120 of 24 March 1970.
Dominican Republic	x								Law No. 1690 of 19 April 1948. (Non-medical abortion widespread.)
Ecuador		x	x			x			Penal Code of 22 March 1938 Section 423.
Ethiopia		x	x						Penal Code of 23 July 1957, Sections 534–546.
Finland		x		x	x	x	x		Law No. 239 of 24 March 1970.

Table 29. Current Status of Worldwide Abortion Legislation

| Country | Illegal (No Exceptions) | Medical | | | | Social | | Elective (Within time limit) | Law and Practice |
		Absolute (Life)	Relative (Health)	Physical/Mental	Eugenic (Fetal)	Juridical (Rape, incest)	Socioeconomic		
France		x							Decree of 11 May 1965. (Nonmedical abortion widespread.)
German Demo-cratic Repub.								x	Law of 9 March 1972. (Elective within 1st 12 weeks if no other abortion during prior 6 months.)
German Federal Repub.		x	x						Law of 1935, Section 14.
Ghana		x	x						British Law prior to 1967. (Not difficult to obtain in urban areas.)
Greece		x	x			x			(Easily available from physician on quasi-legal grounds.)
Guatemala	x								Penal Code Article 304.
Honduras		x	x						Decree No. 94 of 25 June 1964.
Hong Kong	x								(Socially unacceptable but available from physicians.)
Hungary								x	Ordinance No. 2/1956 of 24 June 1956. (Elective under 12 weeks.)
Iceland		x		x	x	x			Law No. 16 of 13 January 1938.
India		x		x	x	x	x		Medical Termination of Pregnancy Act 1971. (Contraceptive failure is an additional indication.)

ABORTION AS AN ALTERNATIVE

Table 29. Current Status of Worldwide Abortion Legislation

Country	Illegal (No Exceptions)	Medical		Social			Elective (Within time limit)	Law and Practice
		Absolute (Life)	Relative (Health)	Physical/Mental	Eugenic (Fetal)	Juridical (Rape, incest)	Socioeconomic	
Indonesia	x								Penal Code
Iran		x							Public Code of 1962, Sections 180–183. (Abortion easily available from physicians.)
Ireland	x								
Italy		x	x						Penal Code Article 54. (Nonmedical abortion widespread.)
Ivory Coast		x							Law No. 62-248 of 31 July 1962, Section 36.
Jamaica	x								(Abortion easily available from physicians.)
Japan		x		x	x	x	x		Eugenic Protection Law of 21 April 1960. (Abortion easily available from physicians.)
Jordan						x			(Nonmedical abortion widespread.)
Kenya		x	x						
Korea, Republic of		x	x						Criminal Code of 3 October 1953. Articles 269–270 and certain court decisions. (Abortion easily available from physicians.)
Liberia		x							Based on French law of 1810.
Luxembourg		x							
Malaysia		x							(Nonmedical abortion widespread.)
Mauritius		x	x						(Nonmedical abortion widespread.)

Table 29. Current Status of Worldwide Abortion Legislation

Country	Illegal (No Exceptions)	Medical			Eugenic (Fetal)	Social		Elective (Within time limit)	Law and Practice
		Absolute (Life)	Relative (Health)	Physical/Mental		Juridical (Rape, incest)	Socioeconomic		
Mexico		x				x			Penal Code of 13 August 1931, Sections 333–334.
Morocco		x	x						Crown Decree No. 181–66 of 1 July 1967.
Netherlands		x							(Abortion easily available from physicians.)
New Zealand		x							Crimes Act of 1961, Sections 182–187.
Nigeria		x							Nigerian Penal Code, Section 232.
Norway		x		x	x	x	x		Law No. 2 of 11 Nov. 1960; implementation of law by decree of 20 December 1963.
Pakistan		x							Penal Code, Chapter 16, Sections 312–316.
Panama	x								Penal Code Articles 329–330.
Paraguay		x							Penal Code of 18 June 1914, Section 352.
Peru		x							Sanitary Code, Sections 19–23, promulgated by Decree-Law No. 17505 of 18 March 1969.
Philippines	x								Revised Penal Code of the Philippines, Book 2, Articles 256–259. (5th ed., 1963)
Poland		x		x		x	x		Law No. 61 of 27 April 1956.

Table 29. Current Status of Worldwide Abortion Legislation

Country	Illegal (No Exceptions)	Absolute (Life)	Relative (Health)	Physical/Mental	Eugenic (Fetal)	Juridical (Rape, incest)	Socioeconomic	Elective (Within time limit)	Law and Practice
		Medical	Medical	Medical	Medical	Social	Social		
		Legal Grounds							
Portugal		x							Decree-Law No. 40651 of 21 June 1956.
Romania		x		x	x	x	x		Decree No. 770 of 29 Sept. 1966.
Senegal		x							Decree No. 67–147 of 10 Feb. 1967. Section 35.
Sierra Leone		x		x					British law prior to 1967.
Singapore		x		x	x	x	x		Abortion Act of 1969.
South Africa		x							
Spain		x							Decree of 23 December 1944.
Sweden		x		x	x	x	x		Law No. 172 of 20 March 1964.
Switzerland		x	x						
Syria		x							Legislative Decree No. 96 of 26 September 1952, Section 8.
Taiwan	x								Criminal Code 1935. (Abortion easily available from physicians.)
Thailand		x	x			x			Act of 13 November 1956.
Tunisia		x	x				x		Law No. 65–24 of 1 July 1965.
Turkey		x	x		x				Decision No. 6/8305 of 12 June 1967.
Uganda		x		x					British Law prior to 1967.
USSR								x	Decree of the Supreme Soviet of the USSR, 23 Nov. 1955. (Elective within 1st 3 months if no other abortion during prior 6 months.)

Table 29. Current Status of Worldwide Abortion Legislation

| | | Legal Grounds | | | | | | |
| | | Medical | | | | Social | | |
Country	Illegal (No Exceptions)	Absolute (Life)	Relative (Health)	Physical/Mental	Eugenic (Fetal)	Juridical (Rape, incest)	Socioeconomic	Elective (Within time limit)	Law and Practice
UAR-Egypt		x							
United Kingdom		x		x	x		x		Abortion Act 1967.
Uruguay		x	x			x	x		Penal Code of 24 Jan. 1938, Sec. 328.
Venezuela		x							Decree of 22 June 1964, Section 435 (Non-medical abortion wide-spread.)
Vietnam (Dem. Rep.)								x	
Yugoslavia		x		x	x	x	x		Decree of 26 April 1969.

SOURCE: David, Alam, and Kalis (1972).

Abortion statutes have been classified into three major groupings: (1) *Illegal* with no exceptions permitted; (2) *Conditional/legal* if any one or a combination of six specified medical and/or social conditions prevail; and (3) *Elective/legal* with abortion on request, provided the pregnant woman requests termination within a legally specified time period. The six conditional situations for legal abortion are:

Condition	*Definition*
Medical	
Absolute	Life threatening for the pregnant woman
Relative	Threatening the woman's health (without definition)
Physical/mental health	Danger to the woman's physical/mental health (with mental health specified in the statute)
Eugenic	Danger of fetal abnormality
Social	
Juridical	Usually encompassing pregnancy resulting from rape or incest
Socioeconomic	Threatening the well-being of the woman and/or her family in terms of health or the total life situation

Social and Economic Grounds

Size of the family or problems in child support are sometimes permitted as reasons for legal termination of pregnancy. Bulgaria and Tunisia permit abortion on request to women with three or five children, respectively. Czechoslovakia does not generally permit abortion on request although permission is granted to mothers of three children. Czechoslovakia also allows as a ground for abortion "risk to the standard of living in cases where predominant economic responsibility for the maintenance of the family or the child devolves upon the woman" (Roemer, 1967:1911).

In Japan economic and health factors together may provide legal grounds for abortion. A strict interpretation of the law would not permit termination of pregnancy on economic grounds alone, yet the difficulty of proving adverse effect in the future has led to a liberal interpretation of the law, so that in practice "every wealthy *and* healthy women can obtain abortion" (Lee and Larson, 1971:16).

Some laws allow abortion on one or more of the following humanitarian grounds: where conception is the result of criminal acts, such as rape or incest, of sexual intercourse with a mentally defective person or a girl below the minimum age.

Grounds for Abortion in the United States

The abortion laws of the United States have been particularly confusing, since these have been state laws and have had many different versions. In addition, the laws have been changing very rapidly in recent years. While there has been an overall tendency to liberalization, the campaign for more restrictive legislation has also heightened. For instance, after only two years of a liberalized law in New York, the state legislature, under heavy pressure, voted for repeal (even though, or because, the governor promised his veto).

Table 30 lists eight major categories of American abortion laws as of April 1, 1971. The liberalization of state laws via legislative enactment began in earnest only in 1969 and 1970. Even then most states allowed abortion only when necessary to save the life of the woman. By 1973, however, judicial review made abortion within the first three months of pregnancy legal in all states of the union.

Table 30. Major Categories of United States Abortion Laws, April 1, 1971

Major Categories of State Abortion Laws	States Having Similar Abortion Laws
I. Abortion allowed only when necessary to preserve the life of the pregnant woman.	Arizona, Connecicut, Florida, Idaho, Illinois[1], Indiana, Iowa[2], Kentucky, Louisiana[3], Maine, Michigan, Minnesota, Missouri, Montana, Nebraska, Nevada, New Hampshire, North Dakota, Ohio, Oklahoma, Rhode Island, South Dakota, Tennessee, Utah, Vermont, West Virginia, Wyoming
II. Indications for legal abortion include threats to the pregnant woman's life and forcible rape	Mississippi
III. "Unlawful" or "unjustifiable" abortions are prohibited	Massachusetts, New Jersey, Pennsylvania
IV. Abortions allowed when continuation of the pregnancy threatens the woman's life or health	Alabama
V. American Law Institute Model Abortion Law; "A licensed physician is justified in terminating a pregnancy if he believes that there is substantial risk that continuance of the pregnancy would gravely impair the physical or mental health of the mother or that the child would be born with grave physical or mental defect, or that the pregnancy resulted from rape, incest, or other felonious intercourse"	Arkansas, California (does not include fetal deformity), Colorado, Delaware, Kansas, Maryland (does not include incest), New Mexico, North Carolina, South Carolina, Virginia
VI. Abortion law based on the May 1968 recommendations of the American College of Obstetricians and Gynecologists. Allows abortion when the pregnancy resulted from felonious intercourse, and when there is risk that continuance of the pregnancy would impair the physical or mental health of the mother: "In determining whether or not there is substantial risk (to the woman's physical or mental health), account may be taken of the mother's total environment, actual or reasonably foreseeable"	Oregon

Table 30. Major Categories of United States Abortion Laws, April 1, 1971

Major Categories of State Abortion Laws	States Having Similar Abortion Laws
VII. No legal restriction on reason for which an abortion may be obtrained prior to viability of the fetus	Alaska, Hawaii, New York, Washington
VIII. Legal restrictions on reasons for which an abortion may be obtained were invalidated by court decision	District of Columbia, Georgia, Texas, Wisconsin[4]

[1]A Federal District Court Decision, *Doe vs. Scott* 321 F. Supp. 1385 (N.D. Ill., Jan. 29, 1971), holding the Illinois abortion statute unconstitutional has been stayed pending appeal in the United States Supreme Court.

[2]In *State vs. Dunklebarger,* the Iowa statute which is couched in terms of saving the life of the woman, has been interpreted to suggest that preservation of health is sufficient. 221 N.W. 592 (Iowa, 1928).

[3]Although the Louisiana abortion statute does not contain an express exception to the "crime of abortion" the Louisiana Medical Practice Act authorizes the Medical Board to suspend or institute court proceedings to revoke a doctor's certificate to practice medicine in the state when the doctor has procured or aided or abetted in the procuring of an abortion "unless done for the relief of a woman whose life appears imperiled after due consultation with another licensed physician." La. Rev. Stat. Ann. 37:1261.

[4]The abortion laws of several other states have been ruled unconstitutional by lower state trial courts; however, these decisions are binding only in the jurisdiction in which the decision was rendered.

SOURCE: U.S., H.E.W. (1972:9).

The Supreme Court rendered a landmark decision (No. 70-18) on the constitutionality of state abortion legislation on January 22, 1973. The opinion of the court, delivered by Justice Blackmun, said in part:

> We do not agree that, by adopting one theory of life, Texas may override the rights of the pregnant woman that are at stake. We repeat, however, that the State does have an important and legitimate interest in preserving and protecting the health of the pregnant woman, whether she be a resident of the State or a nonresident who seeks medical consultation and treatment there, and that it has still *another* important and legitimate interest in protecting the potentiality of human life. These interests are separate and distinct. Each grows in substantiality as the woman approaches term and, at a point during pregnancy, each becomes "compelling."
>
> With respect to the State's important and legitimate interest in the health of the mother, the "compelling" point, in the light of present medical knowledge, is at approximately the end of the first trimester. This is so because of the now established medical fact, . . . that until

the end of the first trimester mortality in abortion is less than mortality in normal childbirth. It follows that, from and after this point, a State may regulate the abortion procedure to the extent that the regulation reasonably relates to the preservation and protection of maternal health. Examples of permissible state regulation in this area are requirements as to the qualifications of the person who is to perform the abortion; as to the licensure of that person; as to the facility in which the procedure is to be performed, that is, whether it must be a hospital or may be a clinic or some other place of less-than-hospital status; as to the licensing of the facility; and the like.

This means, on the other hand, that for the period of pregnancy prior to this "compelling" point, the attending physician, in consultation with his patient, is free to determine, without regulation by the State that in his medical judgment the patient's pregnancy should be terminated. If that decision is reached, the judgment may be effectuated by an abortion free of interference by the State.

With respect to the State's important and legitimate interest in potential life, the "compelling" point is at viability. This is so because the fetus then presumably has the capability of meaningful life outside the mother's womb. State regulation protective of fetal life after viability thus has both logical and biological justifications. If the State is interested in protecting fetal life after viability, it may go so far as to proscribe abortion during that period except when it is necessary to preserve the life or health of the mother."

The decision of the Supreme Court has already had widely different impacts in various parts of the country. As this book goes to press Congress is considering several constitutional amendments to negate the court decision. Thus, while the trend over time is unmistakable, the issue is not permanently settled. We cannot know the effect of this recent decision, or of current changes in law, on illegitimacy levels until some time has passed. There are some relevant data over time, however, on different state and national laws, and on reports of both legal and illegal abortions. How have these influenced births out of wedlock?

DATA ON REPORTED ABORTIONS

Two important sources of hard data on abortions became available recently. The United Nations *Demographic Yearbook, 1971* (1972:656) includes for the first time, numbers of legally induced abortions by age of woman and number of previous live births. The number of countries reporting is very small in comparison to the total members of the United Nations. These early reports must be taken as indicating a social, rather than physiological, event, since differences among countries in definition and in record keeping preclude truly comparative analysis.

The report of the International Reference Center for Abortion Research (David et al., 1973) offers more detailed data over time for almost the same nations listed in the *Yearbook*. All countries with data on abortion and illegitimacy for the same years are included in tables 34 through 36. The countries offering information are mainly those that have four or five legal grounds for abortion, or where it is purely elective (see table 29). The nations group themselves into (1) the east Europeans, (2) the Scandinavians and (3) the United States, England, Canada, Australia, and New Zealand, all of whose data are so recent that we cannot very well compare them with illegitimacy over time. In addition, Japan, as a unique case, offers many details on both illegitimacy and abortion.

Changes in the United States abortion laws are so recent that it will be some time before it will be possible to make national comparisons of the effects on births out of wedlock. In the meantime, there are several types of information that offer clues as to the possibilities.

THE UNITED STATES

There are three distinctly different types of data on abortion in the United States. First we will examine information from interviews of women who had at some time in their lives a premarital pregnancy, and who have reported the resolution in live birth—legitimate or illegitimate—or in abortion—either spontaneous or induced. A recent survey of medical hospitals furnishes a second source of information on age, marital status and race of women receiving legal abortions. Finally, we will review very recent data from all states reporting on abortion to the Department of Health, Education and Welfare.

Interviews of United States Females

Although they were able to interview only volunteers for their female sample, the Kinsey group does provide the only data I have found on proportional outcomes among all alternatives following premarital conception.

Table 31. Outcome Ratios For Premarital Conceptions

	Premarital Conceptions				
	Type of premarital outcome			Outcome in marriage	Total conceptions
Categories	Live birth	Spont. Abortion	Induced abortion		
White Nonprison Sample	Percent			Percent	Number
Marital status at interview					
Never married	8.3	5.0	86.7		121
Married once, still married	2.9	5.7	70.8	20.6	175
Div., Wid., or Sep.	4.1	2.4	70.7	22.8	123
Age period					
−20	6.2	3.4	69.2	21.2	146
21–25	4.6	5.3	74.3	15.8	152
26+	3.4	5.0	85.7	5.9	119
Total	4.8	4.5	75.8	14.9	417
Educational level					
9–12	10.1	3.7	63.3	22.9	109
13–16	2.4	4.3	81.7	11.6	164
17+	1.6	6.2	82.9	9.3	129
Decade of birth					
1900–1909	1.6	4.8	81.7	11.9	126
1910–1919	6.2	3.1	76.5	14.2	162
1920–1929	6.5	7.5	67.7	18.3	93
Religious devoutness					
Protestant devout	8.1	8.1	64.9	18.9	37
Protestant moderate	5.6	3.3	68.9	22.2	90
Protestant inactive	5.1	5.1	79.1	10.7	178
Jewish inactive	0	3.5	84.2	12.3	57
Negro Nonprison Sample					
Educational level					
0–8	25.9	27.6	18.9	27.6	58
9–12	40.8	8.6	24.7	25.9	81
13+	7.5	3.8	81.2	7.5	53
Prison Samples					
White females					
Prison A	38.7	14.1	9.9	37.3	142
Prison B	42.2	17.8	23.3	16.7	90
Negro females	51.7	20.0	5.5	22.3	145

SOURCE: Gebhard et al. (1958:78,161,178).

In examining the data for *white females* (table 31) note first (under "Total" age category) that less than 5 percent of all premarital conceptions reported ended in a birth out of wedlock. Another small (4.5) percentage was reputed to have aborted spontaneously while over three-fourths reported induced abortions (at a time when these were illegal in *all* states). About 15 percent of premarital conceptions were reportedly legitimated by marriage before birth. Because Kinsey did not have a probability sample, we cannot extrapolate these to the entire population. Nevertheless, we can make some comparisons according to other demographic characteristics. It appears that abortion was chosen more often by the never-married respondents, and more often by those pregnant at older than younger ages. Over 80 percent of those with more than a high school education reported that premarital pregnancies were resolved by induced abortions; for these more educated women, 86 to 89 percent of premarital conceptions were aborted, either spontaneously or by induction. The less educated were more likely to have the pregnancy end in live birth—either legitimate or illegitimate—than those with a higher level of formal education.

When the responses are compared according to the decade in which the premaritally pregnant respondent was born, it is interesting that the earlier in the century the woman was born the less likely that a premarital conception would end as a birth out of wedlock. In fact there appears a fourfold increase over time in the probability that such a conception would end as an illegitimate birth. The probability of marriage had also increased for these respondents over time.

The religiously devout in the Kinsey sample were least likely to have been involved in premarital coitus, and thus they reported only 37 conceptions, a small number on which to base the percentage breakdowns in table 31. The births out of wedlock, indicated as 8.1 percent, are made up of only three such outcomes for the Protestant devout category. Devouts and moderates are rather similar in outcomes, reporting a lower tendency to induced abortion and a higher tendency to legitimate the conception before birth than the inactive Protestant or Jewish respondents.

The Negro nonprison sample looks like not one but two distinct groupings when subdivided by education. Those with thirteen or more years of formal education reported outcomes that look proportionately like the white females of similar education. They are vastly different from the less well educated black females. For Negro females in the highest educational category, 85 percent of premarital conceptions were ended by spontaneous or induced abortion, with an even division of the remainder as illegitimate and legitimate live births. Although Negro women with twelve years or less of formal education were much less likely than those of any other category (except prison respondents) to report induced abortion, those with eight or fewer years of schooling had the highest proportional reporting of spontaneous abortion of any group interviewed. An outcome of marriage or birth out of wedlock was more likely than for the more-educated Negro conceiving premaritally or for any of the categories of white nonprison respondents.

The *prison women* who had conceived premaritally are interesting in a number of ways. Whether white or black they are much more likely than their nonprison counterparts to report premarital conceptions as resulting in a birth out of wedlock. The outcome ratios for black and white prison respondents are more like each other than like their nonprison racial category. They are least likely as a group to choose induced abortion to resolve a conception out of wedlock. They are more likely than any but the least-educated Negro respondent to report spontaneous abortion. This may indicate their lower level of knowledge about care during pregnancy, lower levels of health and nutrition, and reduced access to adequate medical facilities; or it may be that this group was less willing to say that the abortion was induced.

With regard to the very low reports of induced abortion by less-educated Negro and prison respondents, in comparison to others, Gebhard of the Kinsey research team suggests that among those of the lowest socioeconomic level:

> Since there is relatively little social disapproval of illegitimacy, the women do not have such strong reason to seek an abortion. Also for these people the cost of an abortion is often prohibitive, and many of them have a general distrust and fear of physicians. A pregnant woman may attempt self-abortion and, when repeated efforts fail, she may overcome her misgivings and scrape together enough money for an operative abortion, only to find that her pregnancy is too far advanced for the professional abortionist. . . .
>
> As a rule induced abortion is strongly connected with status-striving.

Abortion is practiced to preserve reputation, to provide much for a few children rather than little for many children, to maintain or raise a level of living, and the like. These motives are weak or even absent in the people of the lowest social stratum, and one often has the impression that they are passive, resigned, and prone to follow the path of least effort (Gebhard, 1958:181).

The most important aspect of the Kinsey-Gebhard data is the way in which marriage, abortion, and illegitimate births counterbalance one another as possibilities whenever premarital conception occurs. Evidently those categories of respondents most likely to report the outcome as a birth out of wedlock had the lowest proportion reporting abortion or marriage during pregnancy.

Survey of Medical Hospitals

In June 1972 the first report of a new "Joint Program for the Study of Abortion" was made available by the Population Council (Tietze and Lewit, 1972). Sixty-six hospitals participating in the program reported a total of 72,988 abortions performed from July 1, 1970, to June 30, 1971. These were about one-seventh of all legal abortions in the United States during that time period. Table 32 and figure 16 exhibit the proportional breakdown of abortion patients according to such demographic characteristics as age, marital status, prior pregnancies, and so on. More than half the pregnant women were in their twenties, and 24 percent were 19 or under.

Of particular interest to this study is the indication that only 30 percent of the women were married. If the fifty-one thousand abortions to women not presently married represents one-seventh of all legal abortions, something like 357,000 births out of wedlock or illegal abortions were averted in the one-year period under study. We have no way of knowing how many of these might have been terminated by an illegal abortion if the legal route had been closed. Nor do we know how many women might have hurried marriage or even terminated their own lives without the alternative of legal abortion.

Reporting States: 1970, 1971

It is difficult to interpret the meaning of reported abortions in the early 1970s in the United States. Since estimates of *illegal* abortions

Table 32. Patients with Induced Abortions by Selected Characteristics

Characteristic	Number	Percent
Age (years)		
14 and under	760	1.0
15–17	6,412	8.8
18–19	10,524	14.4
20–24	26,818	36.8
25–29	14,033	19.2
30–34	8,049	11.0
35–39	4,569	6.3
40 and over	1,823	2.5
Prior pregnancies		
None	34,354	47.1
1 abortion only	2,455	3.4
2 + abortions only	374	0.5
1 birth	11,328	15.5
2 births	10,606	14.5
3 births	6,808	9.3
4–5 births	5,383	7.4
6 + births	1,680	2.3
Marital status		
Single	40,814	55.9
Married	21,843	29.9
Wid./div./sep.	10,331	14.2
Ethnic group		
White	50,590	69.3
Black	18,930	25.9
Other	3,468	4.8
Type of service		
Private	42,787	58.6
Nonprivate	30,201	41.4
Residence		
Local	45,129	61.8
Out-of-area	27,859	38.2
All patients	72,988	100.0

SOURCE: Tietze and Lewit (1972:100).

have hovered around the one million per year figure, we do not know whether reported *legal* abortions are merely replacing the more dangerous illegal abortions or whether the total may itself have increased. For New York City alone, Christopher Tietze (1973) estimated that "approximately 70 percent of the legal abortions of resident women performed under the 1970 law replaced illegal abortions—about 50,000 illegal procedures each year." No doubt some illegal abortions still occur.

Figure 16. Percent Distribution of Patients with Induced Abortions,
by Age, Prior Pregnancies, Marital Status, Ethnic Group,
Type of Service, and Residence

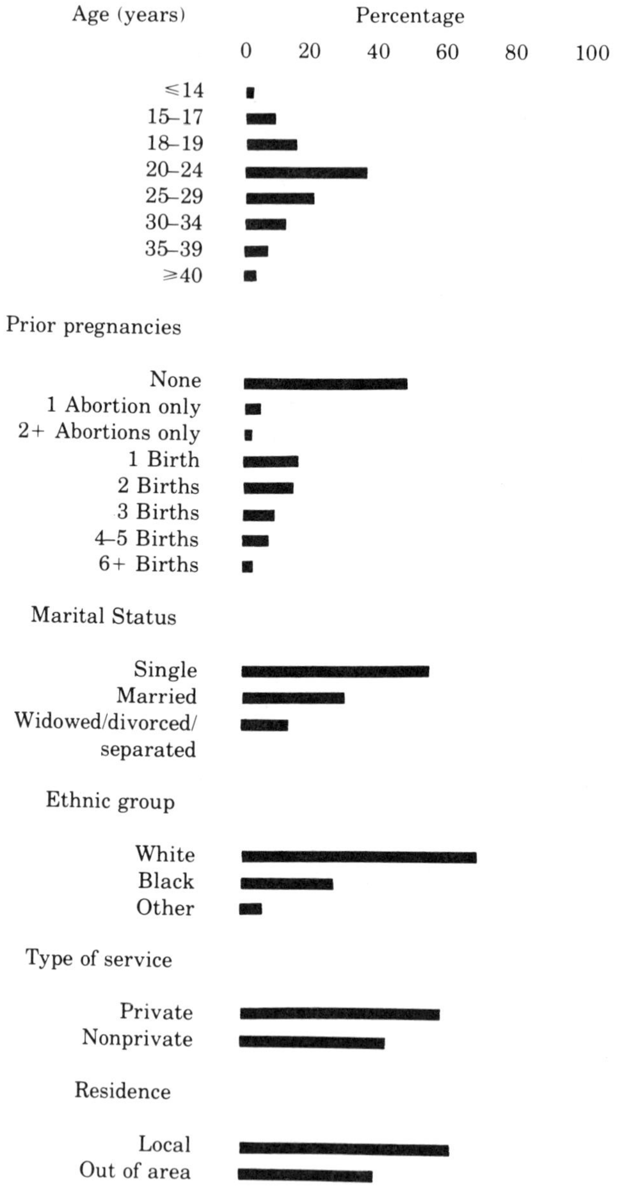

SOURCE: Tietze and Lewit (1972:100).

Table 33. Reported Legal Abortion Ratios by State of Occurrence,*
January—March 1971

State	Abortions	Live Births[1]	Abortions/1,000 Live Births
Alaska	237	1,926	123
Arkansas	130	9,212	14
California	23,880	92,911	257
Colorado	678	10,223	66
Delaware	252[2]	2,658	95
Georgia	320	25,307	13
Hawaii	938	3,978	236
Kansas	2,772	8,881	312
Maryland	1,880	14,716	128
New York	57,737	73,888	781
(Upstate)	(12,004)	(39,062)	(307)
(City)	(45,733[3])	(34,826)	(1,313)
North Carolina	561	24,305	23
Oregon	1,809	8,723	207
South Carolina	192	13,814	14
Virginia	875	20,597	42
Washington	2,158	12,132	178
TOTAL	94,419	323,271	292

[1]Live birth data for all states except Hawaii taken from *Monthly Vital Statistics Reports Provisional Statistics* 20, no. 3 (May 26, 1971) published by the National Center for Health Statistics. Hawaii live birth data from Hawaii State Department of Health.

[2]Abortions performed in three hospitals that reported more than 95 percent of state's abortions in 1970.

[3]Estimate from City of New York Department of Health.

*All states with data available.

SOURCE: U.S., H.E.W. (1972:2).

The number of abortions for all fifteen states reporting between January 1 and March 31, 1971, are given in table 33. Legal abortion ratios for those states range from 13 per thousand live births in Georgia to 781 per thousand in New York State. "Every state that reported abortions for both 1970 and first quarter of 1971 had a higher abortion ratio in 1971. . . . Although the largest number of abortions were performed on women in the 20 to 24 age group, the proportion of abortions obtained by women less than 20 years old has increased to 31 percent, up from 24 percent in 1970" (U.S., H.E.W., 1972:1). More than one-fourth of the reported abortions were to women who normally resided outside the state in which the abortion was performed. In New York State over 40 percent of the legal abortions

were to women from out of state, so that the total ratio of 781
abortions per thousand live births reduces to 464.4 for residents of
the state (see figure 17).

Figure 17. Ratios of Reported Legal Abortions to Live Births, by State of Residence,
January — March 1971

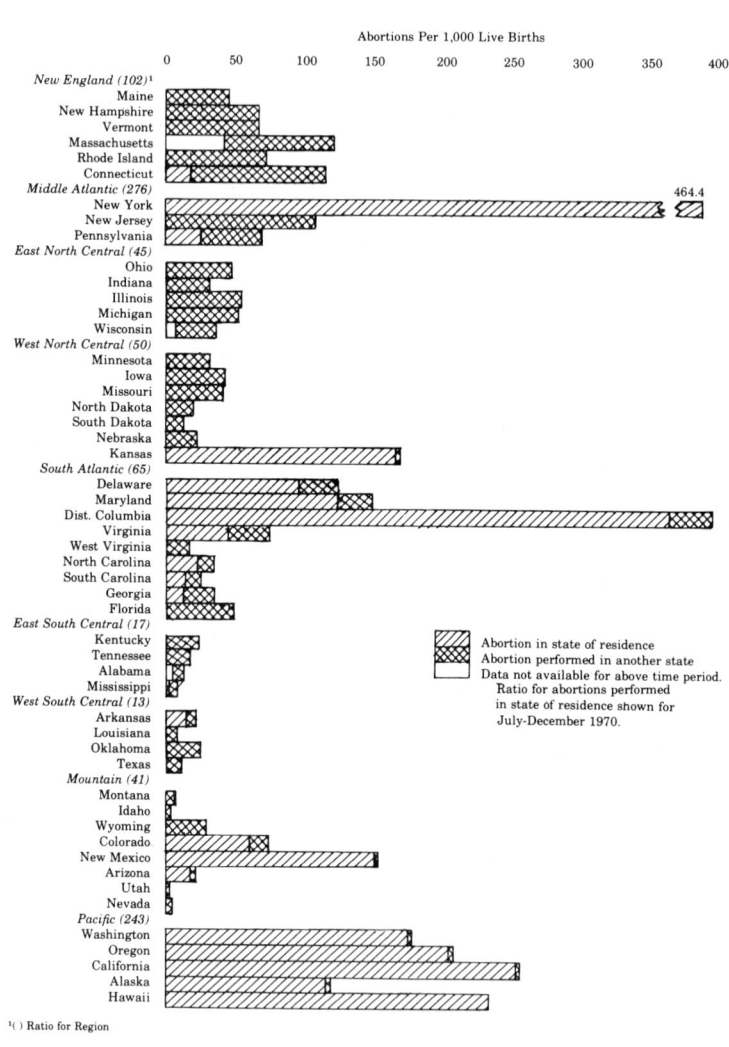

¹( ) Ratio for Region

SOURCE: U.S. H.E.W. (1972:8).

Reporting on the first two years' experience with the liberal abortion law, Christopher Tietze (1973) estimates that in New York City:

> legal abortion has been a major factor accounting for the unprecedented decline in the numbers of illegitimate births in 1971 (a drop from 31,900 to 28,100 or nearly 12 percent—the first year-to-year *decline* reported since 1954 when such records first were kept . . . Fragmentary data suggest that the (abortion) ratio may have been on the order of 1,000 abortions per 1,000 first births conceived out of wedlock, and about 125 abortions per 1,000 first births conceived after marriage. The discrepancy becomes even greater if the ratios are computed in terms of the woman's marital status at the time of abortion or birth—approximately 1,500 per 1,000 births for unmarried women compared with 100 for married women (p. 39).

Thus even the partial information we have indicates that legalizing abortion has reversed the upward trend in illegitimacy, at least in part of the United States.

EASTERN EUROPE

Table 29 indicates that the countries of eastern Europe report few legal restrictions on abortion. Following the U.S.S.R. lead in permitting abortion on demand in 1955,[4] Bulgaria, Hungary, and Poland legalized abortion in 1956, and Romania did so in 1957. Czechoslovakia's easy abortion law was amended in 1962 to require that abortion must take place in the early months of pregnancy and that none should have been performed in the previous six months. Yugoslavia—included here with the east Europeans for convenience—adopted a modified legal abortion law in 1960 (David, 1970).

Although these countries have no more restrictions on unmarried than married women, there has been no consistent pattern in the relationship between legal availability of abortion, the numbers and ratio, and the reported measures of illegitimacy (see table 34). In Bulgaria, following legalized abortion, the ratio of illegitimate births continued to increase from 4.8 to 9.6 percent of all births. In

---

[4] The Russian revolution was an initial impetus for the legalization of abortion, in November 1920. The government did a complete reversal, however, banning abortion in 1936. The laws of 1955, then, are another reversal of policy (Heer, 1965; David, 1970).

Table 34. Comparison of Abortion Ratios[1] and Illegitimacy Ratios,[2] Eastern Europe, 1949–71

Year	Bulgaria Abortion Ratio	Bulgaria Illeg. Ratio	Czechoslovakia Abortion Ratio	Czechoslovakia Illeg. Ratio	Germany D. Rep. Abortion Ratio	Germany D. Rep. Illeg. Ratio	Hungary Abortion Ratio	Hungary Illeg. Ratio	Poland Abortion Ratio	Poland Illeg. Ratio	Yugoslavia Abortion Ratio	Yugoslavia Illeg. Ratio
1949					270.1	11.9						
1950					269.8	12.8	184.1	8.5				
1951					**205.9	13.2	198.3	8.4				
					(rescinded)							
1952					202.6	12.8	235.2	8.1				
1953	113.6	3.7	112.6	5.1	214.1	12.9	*206.4	8.2				
1954	124.1	4.8	125.2	5.3	214.5	13.1	261.0	7.8				
1955	126.5	6.4	132.4	5.3	171.5	12.8	373.0	7.0	128.0	4.7		
1956	*270.4	7.2	130.2	5.4	166.7	13.1	*641.1	6.6	*133.7	5.6		
1957	327.7	7.4	148.4	5.4	161.7	13.1	974.3	6.4	155.7	5.3		
1958	401.3	7.6	*379.2	5.1	162.9	12.1	1155.1	5.7	167.3	5.2		
1959	466.0	7.7	486.2	4.9	151.7	11.8	1241.5	5.7	223.4	5.0	263.5	8.7
1960	528.9	8.0	527.4	4.8	133.1	11.4	1338.2	5.5	334.3	4.5	*308.1	8.7
1961	643.2	8.0	550.8	4.5	134.6	10.9	1451.2	5.5	345.1	4.3	473.7	8.4
1962	729.3	8.1	**532.9	4.5	136.2	9.9	1519.4	5.4	351.5	4.2	484.2	8.2
1963	785.8	8.4	423.3	4.7	–	9.1	1571.0	5.3	442.5	4.1	527.7	8.5
1964	857.3	8.8	411.1	4.9	151.1	9.4	1655.1	5.2	438.5	4.1	567.4	8.4
1965	922.1	9.4	456.6	5.1	*		1608.9	5.2	429.4	4.5	601.2	8.3
1966	971.5	9.6	*520.2	5.3			1591.5	5.1	426.2	4.6	663.3	8.3
1967	966.3	9.7	560.7	5.4			1493.8	5.0	423.7	4.9	708.9	8.3
1968	**770.5	9.6	580.5				1520.5	5.0	419.1	4.9		
1969	–		570.9				1548.9		400.8			
1970	1026.2		546.2				1464.1		391.9			
1971							1431.5					
1972					*							

SOURCES: David, et al. (1973); U.N. Demographic Yearbook (1954, 1959, 1965, 1969).
[1]Abortion ratios = number of recorded abortions per thousand live births, including legal plus "women admitted to a hospital for treatment of incomplete abortions or other complications following illegal or spontaneous abortions."
[2]Illegitimacy ratios = number of births out of wedlock per hundred births.
*Laws liberalized
**Restrictions in law

Czechoslovakia and Hungary there were only slight declines in the ratio of births out of wedlock in spite of the report that unmarried women in Czechoslovakia in 1966 had 141.6 abortions for every 100 live births (David, 1970:168). In Yugoslavia and Poland there were insignificant fluctuations in ratios. In the German Democratic Republic there was actually a decline in illegitimacy ratios as abortions became more difficult to obtain.

Examining rates of illegitimacy, Cutright (1973a:424) found that there were declines of 31, 46, and 41 percent for Czechoslovakia, Hungary, and Poland, respectively, between 1956 and 1965. There must be a larger proportion of women who are unmarried, if the rates have declined while the ratios have remained fairly stable in these countries.

In spite of the fact that two of these countries have reported more abortions yearly than live births, they still maintain illegitimacy ratios ranging from 5 to 9.5 percent of all births out of wedlock. Providing the alternative of legal abortion, therefore, does not elimi- nate births out of wedlock, unless persons are motivated to use the alternative available.

SCANDINAVIAN COUNTRIES

Although the stated legal grounds for abortion in the Scandinavian countries appear to be very similar to those of eastern Europe, the interpretation of those grounds has been more restrictive. This is indicated by the lower overall abortion ratios, by the increase in abortions in Denmark and Finland with the 1970 liberalization, and in the estimates for Sweden, (from 1953 to 1964) of two to four times as many "other abortions" as legal abortions. These "others" referred to estimates based on "women admitted to a hospital for treatment of incomplete abortions or other complications following illegal or spontaneous abortions" (David et al., 1973).

In spite of recourse to legal abortion for a variety of reasons, the Scandinavian countries, like those of eastern Europe have maintained historical levels of illegitimacy, and in some cases, e.g., Denmark and Sweden, report increasing percentages of births out of wedlock (see table 35). Since abortion is increasingly available, why is it not *used* as a means of preventing illegitimate births? We have already sug- gested that the social structuring of sanctions that motivate people to prevent births out of wedlock varies among societies. In studying premarital pregnancy in Denmark, Croog (1951) suggested that the historical emphasis on the rights to sexual intercourse with the "ring engagement" spread to include going steady. Not only was the pattern accepted by a liberal clergy, but also, he says, welfare laws made "unmarried motherhood relatively easy." If Croog's assumptions are correct, there is less need to prevent births out of wedlock in Scandinavia by either the belief system or structural patterns. In reviewing differences within the Nordic countries Tomasson (1971) found the lowest levels of illegitimacy in the communities influenced by Pietism. Further research would be needed to determine whether individuals in those areas were less likely to be unmarried or to engage in nonmarital sexual intercourse. Or are there differences in the likelihood of using effective contraception, promoting marriage if conception occurs, or using abortion as a final alternative?

Table 35.Comparison of Abortion Ratios and Illegitimacy Ratios, Scandinavian Countries, 1949–71

Year	Denmark Abortion[1] Ratio	Illeg. Ratio	Finland Abortion[1] Ratio	Illeg. Ratio	Iceland Abortion[1] Ratio	Illeg. Ratio	Norway Abortion[1] Ratio	Illeg. Ratio	Sweden Abortion[2] Ratio	Illeg. Ratio
1949	42.6	7.4								
1950	49.0	7.4	³11.8	5.2	13.9	27.9				
1951	61.4	7.0	30.7	4.9	12.8	27.5				
1952	65.0	6.7	33.1	4.7	16.2	25.2				
1953	61.3	6.8	41.7	4.5	15.3	25.4			151.5	9.8
1954	66.8	6.7	41.1	4.4	14.9	27.6			152.2	9.8
1955	70.3	6.6	40.8	4.2	10.7	26.5			150.4	9.9
1956	³58.8	6.8	45.7	4.2	9.1	25.2			141.9	10.2
1957	53.1	6.9	52.3	4.3	12.1	24.9			133.4	10.1
1958	52.1	7.2	65.0	4.0	9.9	25.5			129.9	10.2
1959	48.5	7.3	69.3	4.1	8.1	25.4			134.1	10.4
1960	51.5	7.8	75.3	4.0	11.2	25.3			132.8	11.3
1961	54.0	8.0	71.5	4.1	14.2	25.3			131.9	11.7
1962	51.4	8.3	73.8	4.0	11.0	24.5			133.9	12.4
1963	48.2	8.9	68.3	4.2	19.1	25.1			130.6	12.6
1964	54.3	9.3	61.2	4.4	22.8	26.7	44.0	4.2	³134.7	13.1
1965	60.5	9.5	61.4		14.4	26.9	–	4.6	137.4	13.8
1966	64.8	10.2	67.2		15.3	28.4	66.3	4.9	58.8	14.6
1967	77.7		72.7		17.3	30.0	75.1	5.1	80.0	15.1
1968	80.3		85.4		17.5		76.5	5.6	¹ 96.2	15.8
1969	102.4		118.7		24.3		92.6		127.6	16.3
1970	³127.1		³230.0		22.3				146.2	
1971									168.6	

SOURCES: David, et al. (1973); U.N. *Demographic Yearbook* (1954, 1959, 1965, 1969).
[1]Legal abortions
[2]All abortions
[3]Liberalized law

ENGLAND

The formal and informal sanctions that historically operated to minimize illegitimacy in England have been declining recently in overall effectiveness. At the same time, sanctions against abortions before 1968 worked to increase illegitimacy as an outcome.

The old laws, dating from 1803, 1829 and 1861, declared that abortion was a crime under all circumstances. In practice, however the court might permit an abortion when the woman's physical or mental health was in danger. The medical doctor could be challenged to prove the danger in a particular case, however, and thus abortion was not a generally available alternative to illegitimate birth.

Estimates of "backstreet" illegal abortions have ranged from 20,000 to 200,000 per year in England and Wales. Roy Jenkins, the Home

Secretary, placed his educated guess at 100,000 per year. Arguments favoring a liberalization of legal abortion largely revolved around the goal of eliminating the "backstreet abortion mills." Arguments against liberalization suggested that medical doctors might be tempted to set up their own abortion "mills."

Nevertheless, on July 14, 1967, after thirteen hours of debate, the House of Commons voted 167 to 83 to approve the reform measure, "The Medical Termination of Pregnancy Bill." Not only did the new act legalize abortions beginning in April 1968, but also it permitted an abortion to be performed free of charge under the National Health Service, if two physicians find that "continuance of pregnancy would involve risk to the life or of injury to the physical or mental health of the pregnant woman or the future well-being of herself and/or the child or her other children." Furthermore, "in determining whether or not there is such a risk of injury to health or well-being, account may be taken of the patient's total environment, actual or reasonably foreseeable" (*New York Times* 1967).

As presently worded the bill seems to offer no greater bar to an unmarried than to a married woman, except that the less educated and the young may be less aware of their rights under the new law. The original wording of the law, as submitted by David Steel, specified that any woman who became pregnant under the age of sixteen or as a result of rape would be entitled to an abortion (*London Times*, July 2, 1967). The final wording is less specific, but it certainly leaves room for an interpretation favoring legal abortion in such cases.

The number of registered abortions since legalization has climbed yearly from 35,000 for the eight months in 1968, to 55,000 in 1969 and 86,600 in 1970. In 1971 a total of 126,800 legal abortions were reported, but if we exclude nonresidents, the number is reduced to 95,300 (David et al., 1973). Madeleine Simms (1972:7) supposes that if the number of illegal abortions formerly estimated at 100,000, were added to previously legal numbers, at 30,000 in 1967, the new medically safe legal abortions are just beginning to approach the old legal and illegal combined.

Furthermore, the 1971 peak finds only 12.2 abortions per hundred live births for residents of England and Wales combined. Availability appears to be uneven among hospital regions, and Simms (1972:10) reports a consultant psychiatrist in the London area who was unable to obtain National Health Service abortions "even for patients with a record of battering their babies, who recognized that further babies might meet a similar fate." Liberalization, then, has not necessarily meant easy availability.

Published details of abortions by age and marital status are available for 1969 in a Supplement on Abortion. Of the 55,000 legal abortions, less than half (24,403) were to married women. Some 30,000 illegal abortions or illegitimate births were thus avoided (Great Britain, General Register Office, 1969:2). By 1971 there were 9.7 legal abortions for residents for every thousand women in the 15- to 44-year-old group. Partial returns for 1972 show continued increases (David, et al., 1973).

The latest available data on illegitimacy indicates that in 1969, for the first time in twenty years, there was a significant decline in the number of live births out of wedlock. While the number decreased by only 2,500 or about 3.5 percent out of almost 70,000 illegitimate registrations, the fact of decline instead of continued increase is significant. The decline may be interpreted as demonstrating the power of legal abortion to aid in reducing illegitimacy, or it may be viewed as slight in comparison to both the number of abortions registered and the numbers of births out of wedlock. Although the numerical decline and the reversal in direction are significant in themselves, the decline in illegitimacy ratios amounted to only 0.1 percent in 1969 and 1970. Only the future will tell whether English women are increasingly motivated to use induced, legal, and free abortion to terminate conceptions out of wedlock.

JAPAN

The liberalization of abortion laws in Japan beginning in 1948 and 1949 apparently facilitated an already present motivation to prevent births out of wedlock. The data presented in table 36 indicate declines in illegitimate births beginning about the turn of the century and accelerating after legalization of abortion. It is important to note that during the years of declining measures of illegitimacy, Japan was becoming rapidly urbanized and industrialized, implying that increasing illegitimacy is not a necessary accompaniment to the process of modernization.

Table 36. Illegitimate Birth Rates and Ratios, and Numbers
and Ratios of Reported Abortions[1], Japan

Illegitimacy			Abortions		
Date	Rate	Ratio	Date	Number	Ratio per 100 Live Births
1900		8.8			
1920		8.2			
1940	13.5	4.1			
1947		3.8			
1948		3.2			
1949		2.7	1949	246,104	
1950	6.9	2.5	1950	489,111	
1951		2.2	1951	638,350	
1952		2.0	1952	798,193	40
1953		1.9	1953	1,068,066	57
1954		1.7	1954	1,143,059	65
1955	3.1	1.7	1955	1,170,143	68
1956		1.6	1956	1,159,288	70
1957		1.5	1957	1,122,316	72
1958		1.4	1958	1,128,231	68
1959		1.3	1959	1,098,853	68
1960	2.0	1.2	1960	1,063,256	66
1961		1.2	1961	1,035,329	65
1962		1.1	1962	985,351	58
1963		1.1	1963	955,092	58
1964	1.6	1.0	1964	878,748	51
1965		1.0	1965	843,200	46
1966		1.1	1966	808,400	59
1967		0.9	1967	747,500	39
1968		1.0	1968	757,400	41
1969		0.9	1969	744,500	40
1970		0.9	1970	732,000	38

SOURCES: 1900: Wimperis (1960); 1920–54: Taeuber (1958); 1955–70: Japan Ministry of Health and Welfare. Rates computed from data in U.N., *Demographic Yearbook* (1954, 1959, 1965) and Japanese census documents; David (1973).

[1]Substantial numbers of abortions still go unreported. At the 1955 peak the registration of abortions was estimated to have been only 50 to 75 percent complete. See Muramatsu (1960: 152–66).

When the means of eliminating births out of wedlock are freely available, and the motivation to use them is built into the social system, the reduction in illegitimate births can be spectacular. In Japan, with changes in the legal codes in 1949 and an increase in the availability of family planning and safe abortion, the legitimate birth rates decreased in 1964 to little more than one-half the 1940 rate, and the general illegitimate fertility rate decreased by 1964 to only 12 percent of the 1940 rate. One of the most rapid declines in illegitimacy anywhere in the world is that recorded by Japan. Not only has the illegitimacy ratio dropped from about 9 percent at the beginning of the century to 1 percent in 1964, but the general illegitimacy rate has also declined sharply, until in 1964 there were only 1.6 births reported as illegitimate for each thousand unmarried women. No nation with detailed statistics reports such a low illegitimacy rate (see figure 13).

All available data on abortions and on illegitimacy rates and ratios for specified years are exhibited in table 36. The ratio, or percentage of all births that were recorded as illegitimate, was only half as great in 1940 as it had been in 1920. The postwar decline merely continues a trend already well in evidence. Moreover, the decline in the ratio early in the century was accompanied by a very rapid rise in the age of marriage. With a 50 percent drop in the ratio and an increase in the number and proportion of unmarried women we can be sure that the general rate of illegitimacy was also declining from 1920 to 1940, the first year for which I have been able to compute the rate. In 1940 there were 13.52 births recorded as illegitimate for each thousand unmarried women aged 15 to 44. The decline in rate, which we know was already underway, continued at a rapid pace with the help of legal abortion. The illegitimate fertility rate actually declined by 88 percent from 1940 to 1964. There is no other case I know of that has registered this phenomenal drop.

From table 36 we see that the number of yearly reported abortions rose dramatically from 1949 to a peak in 1955. The decline in number and ratio of abortions from the mid-1950s onward does not seem to make sense in view of the continued decline in both rate and ratio of illegitimacy. However, as is obvious by now, there are in our scheme of analysis a number of escape routes from the path towards births out of wedlock. The decline in total fertility in Japan is clearly related to an early rise in abortions followed by an increased use of contraceptives. It was in 1952, several years after the legalization of abortion, that the government began an aggressive family-planning campaign. Results of national surveys on family planning led government experts to estimate an increase from 20 percent (in 1949 and 1950) to 50 percent (in 1965) of all couples who were "current users" of contraceptives (Japan, Ministry of Health and Welfare, 1966:20). Muramatsu (1970) has calculated that there were about 2 1/2 times as many births prevented by contraception in 1965 as in 1955. The decline in reported abortions over the same period of time is believed to have been accompanied by a rise in unreported abortions. The total number of abortions was estimated to have been about the same in 1965 as it was a decade earlier (Ibid.).

Although we do not know what proportion of abortions occurs to unmarried women, table 20 of the Japanese *Vital Statistics,* 1964 reports "late foetal deaths," at seven completed months or more, according to legitimacy status. From 1955 to 1964, from 7 to 9 percent of the reported late foetal deaths were classified as illegitimate. If so large a proportion of all reported induced abortions were to unmarried mothers, 1955 could have seen well over 100,000 such abortions. Without these, illegitimacy rates would have risen sharply instead of exhibiting a sharp decline.[5]

Why should the Japanese be more willing than northern or eastern Europeans to use abortion as a means of avoiding births out of wedlock? A number of cultural and structural factors unique to Japan will be reviewed below. The study of the decline in illegitimacy in Japan is all the more interesting when we remember that concubinage had been a legal contractual relationship in Japan historically. Apparently concubinage was largely responsible for the relatively high percentage of births out of wedlock in 1900, the first year for which we have such data. The leaders of the Meiji Restoration (1868) regarded concubinage as an antiquated and unacceptable relationship and made no mention of it in the civil codes of the Restoration period. However, the omission of it in the codes, which made the relationship

---

[5] Note, however, that one woman could have several abortions during the normal nine-month gestation period. Thus each abortion does not necessarily equal one birth prevented.

nonexistent in law, did not result in its elimination (Taeuber, 1958: chapter 6).

Before 1948 the Japanese reported whether a birth was a "recognized" illegitimate birth (by the father from his concubine) or a "strictly" illegitimate birth.[6] The new civil code effective in 1948 did not mention the separation of illegitimate births by type according to recognition. Thereafter births were divided into the categories of legitimate or illegitimate.

After World War II the decline in both legitimate and illegitimate fertility was so sharp that it would be easy to conclude that the decrease was due to the reorganization of Japanese society by the occupation forces. Yet the statistics indicate quite clearly that whatever postwar factors contributed to the reduction of births out of wedlock, similar forces were underway long before the war. Furthermore, it is claimed that occupation leaders ignored or worked against the spread of contraceptive information and the availability of abortion (Kitaoka, 1957).

The use of abortion was desired by the Japanese people; voted into law by their representatives in the Diet, or parliament; and used to reduce both legitimate and illegitimate fertility. Japan is the only nation to have gone through the demographic transition in this century and the only non-Western nation ever to do so. The declines in measures of illegitimacy are without parallel anywhere, at any time known to man.

REVIEW OF PROPOSITIONS

Proposition 5: When a large proportion of those who conceive out of wedlock abort the fetus, illegitimacy levels will be low.

The best evidence on this point is that supplied by Gebhard of the Kinsey group. White respondents indicated that premarital pregnancies overwhelmingly (up to 90 percent, by categories) were

---

[6] In 1920 the recognized illegitimates made up 3.4 percent and the strictly illegitimates 4.8 percent of all births; together 8.2 percent were out of wedlock. The strictly illegitimate births declined at a much more rapid pace than the recognized category, in spite of the government attempt to downgrade concubinage. The last year for which there are separate statistics, 1947, finds the strictly illegitimate at 1.6 percent and the recognized at 2.2 percent, for a total of 3.8 percent of births out of wedlock (Taeuber, 1958).

resolved by abortion; and over that period of time illegitimacy ratios for whites were very low, at 2 percent and less of all births. Well-educated black women reported outcome ratios for premartial pregnancies that closely resembled those for whites. Yet the much larger category that was less well educated was far less likely to report an induced abortion following premarital pregnancy: only 18.9 and 24.7 percent of such conceptions were so resolved (table 30). For that time period, births out of wedlock represented 16 to 17 percent of all nonwhite births, and an unmarried black woman was ten times more likely than an unmarried white woman to produce a birth out of wedlock (U.S., H.E.W., 1968a:4).

It is too early to know whether the recent liberalization of abortion in the United States will mean that unmarried women will take that option in preference to giving birth out of wedlock. There is evidence of a small decline in numbers of illegitimate births to public assistance mothers in New York City, but the decline was small and not as great as for married mothers. This seems to present a contradiction to proposition 5, for when illegitimacy "levels" are measured by number of births, they appear to have declined, yet these unmarried females seem less inclined than married women to birth prevention. It may also be the case that there is a greater proportion of unmarried women, and thus at a stable rate they could contribute both larger numbers and a higher proportion of all births out of wedlock. However, the lower numbers of such births in New York City could even imply a lower *rate* (illegitimate births per thousand unmarrieds) combined with a higher proportion of women unmarried. Such a situation seems to have prevailed between 1960 and 1970 in Washington, D. C. (Gendell and Van der Tak, 1973), where illegitimacy rates went down for nonwhites and up slightly for whites, but nonwhites with much higher illegitimacy rates to begin with increased to 75 percent of the female population aged 15 to 44, and both groups increased dramatically in the proportion unmarried in the childbearing ages. It will be interesting to watch the trends as they may be affected by the recent liberalization of abortion. For the District of Columbia in the first quarter of 1971 there were about 360 abortions reported for every 1,000 live births (see figure 17); these included many abortions for women in neighboring states.

In California, Sklar and Berkov (1973:282) note that the increased availability of abortion led to a decline of 16.3 percent in the rate of illegitimacy in 1971 but only a 2.7 percent drop was recorded for 1972. (The decreases were greater for legitimate than illegitimate fertility rates.) Black illegitimacy rates fell more consistently than the rates for white women. One might suppose that whites with greater past acceptance of illegal abortion (Gebhard, 1958) would be disposed to take advantage of legal abortion as it becomes more easily obtainable. The early data on trends in the United States are not consistent on this point, however.

For Japan, we have not had data on the extent of premarital conceptions or the proportions aborted. We do have indicators that marriage during pregnancy is not very common, and we know that contraceptive use was not very widespread until after the large number of abortions led to encouragement of contraception. Although we do not know what proportion of all abortions are to unmarried women, we may assume that the available and inexpensive abortion of Japan has meant that large proportions of premaritally pregnant women actually use that alternative to achieve low rates and ratios of births out of wedlock.

Proposition 5a: Freely available, safe abortion does not guarantee elimination of illegitimacy.

Although the people of Japan have used abortion as an aid in the very rapid reduction of illegitimacy, not all peoples are so motivated to reduce or virtually eliminate births out of wedlock. In the United States, we have noted that the reductions in births out of wedlock following liberalized abortion have been surprisingly slight and incon-sistent. Unmarried women do not seem to be increasingly motivated to use the more liberal abortion laws of recent years to prevent births out of wedlock. Unless they define birth prevention as advantageous to themselves and their future, and unless they define abortion as an acceptable alternative, the legalization of abortion will play little part in eliminating illegitimacy.

In England abortion was not only legalized under a variety of indications but made available free of charge through the National Health Service and it still has not played a significant part in the reduction of illegitimacy there, the decline in numbers of births out of wedlock being only 3.5 percent per year. Still abortions are not always granted under legal and medical restrictions. Perhaps the change will be more rapid in future years, or perhaps the motivation to prevent births out of wedlock is simply too mixed to be effective. In an earlier chapter a long and still incomplete list of possible motives favoring and opposing conceptions and births out of wedlock pointed up the multiplicity of considerations and probable ambivalence of individuals with regard to births out of wedlock.

The data for the countries of northern and eastern Europe also imply that easy availability of abortion does not guarantee reduction or elimination of illegitimacy. Even those countries that report more abortions than live births yearly maintain considerable proportions of all births that occur out of wedlock.

Proposition 5b: Restriction of the availability of abortion does not necessarily lead to high levels of illegitimacy.

I take this proposition to be self-evident from the total scheme of analysis presented in chapter 4. Since national cultures may concentrate on any one of the other alternatives to the path toward illegitimacy, they may restrict the availability of induced abortion and still maintain low levels of illegitimacy. Moslem and Hindu societies that impose early and near universal marriage reduce or virtually eliminate the possibility of premarital conceptions. Societies may guard the unmarried female before marriage by seclusion and exclusion from interaction with males, or they may provide chaperones for such encounters as are allowed, so that opportunity for nonmarital sexual relations are minimized. To minimize the likelihood of conception out of wedlock, other societies or social groups may accept and promote the use of contraceptives in case of pre- or nonmarital coitus but strongly encourage or even "force" marriage on those partners who conceive outside of marriage.

Proposition 5c: Societies that facilitate, in structural opportunity and cultural beliefs, abortion as an alternative to childbearing outside of wedlock, will tend to have low levels of illegitimacy.

Proposition 5c suggests that, since easy access to abortion does not seem to guarantee the elimination of illegitimacy, both structural opportunity and cultural acceptance or motivation to use abortion are necessary to its use as an alternative to births out of wedlock.

Japan is the only example I have of a society that clearly has maximized both the structural opportunity of easily available, medi- cally safe, and inexpensive abortion and a cultural system favorable to abortion as an acceptable alternative to childbirth with family unity, loyalty, and lineage placed above individualistic considerations. What are the combination of factors relevant to the unique situation of Japan in this regard?

In the first place, we have already noted some evidence that the only other alternative to illegitimate childbirth once premarital conception occurs—a quick marriage—does not seem to be an important aspect of the Japanese scene. Unless we are willing to assume a rapid decline in nonmarital sexual intercourse with increasing industrialization and urbanization in Japan (an assumption noticeably lacking in any discussion of the subject), the increase in availability of contraceptives and abortion seems to be the best explanation for the very sharp decrease in illegitimacy rates and ratios specified earlier. It is interesting in this regard that an aggressive contraceptive campaign began several years *after* the legalization of abortion.

The rapid rise in the number of legal abortions to over a million a year is surely related to the cultural acceptance of abortion as a means of birth control. In ancient Japan, and up to the Meiji Restoration in 1868, there was no sharp differentiation among contraception, abortion, and infanticide either as biological procedures or as ethical concepts. Contraception occupied the least important place as a technique for limitation, followed by abortion (Taeuber, 1958:29). The Confucian and Buddhist influences in Japan taught that "men should take life as given and that if death should come, whether to the living or to the fetus, it would be but a natural phenomenon. Furthermore, Confucianism teaches children to revere their parents as life givers. Abortion and infanticide were regarded as parents' self-inflicted punishment—rather than a sin against God or a crime against humanity" (Lee and Larson, 1971:33). After the Meiji Restoration, both abortion and infanticide were outlawed, but clearly the background of the culture left a receptivity to abortion that is not present in most "Westernized," especially Catholic, nations.

Abortion is a legal means of terminating pregnancy in many countries. Why are the Japanese especially motivated to use the available means to prevent births out of wedlock? We have previously noted that in England and Wales and in northern and eastern Europe the knowledge and availability of means of prevention, including abortion, does not necessarily mean that these are used.

Authors who have written on Japan are in agreement that the individual has been historically deemphasized in that nation. In the transition from a traditional, agrarian economy to an industrial, urban one, Matsumoto (1960:7) claims that "the sense of familial-collectivity *still* prevails over the sense of individual rights in political as well as social life." Another social scientist says, "The Japanese family is conceived of as existing continuously from the past into the future, unceasingly and independent of the birth and death of its members. Ancestors and offspring are linked together by the idea of geneology, not based merely on blood relationship but rather by the bond of relationships, inherent in the maintenance and continuance of the family as an institution" (Ariga, 1954:362).

Under the post-World War II occupation the old civil code was revised in line with democratic principles. The legal status of women was greatly improved. There was provision of free choice of marriage partners, equal property rights, equal rights to divorce, and equal obligations to chastity (Matsumoto, 1960). But legal codes, especially when they embody new radical changes, tell us not what is, but what some people think ought to be. We can get a better idea of what a population thinks about a subject by questioning a large, representative sample; and there are behavioral measures that tell us even more.

Attitude surveys since the war indicate that the greatest changes have occurred in the direction of individual choice of a marriage partner. However, the individual's reliance on family old age support over state support is indicated by the response of over seven thousand married persons in 1950 who overwhelmingly lacked plans to be independent of their children in old age (Matsumoto, 1960:18). Stoetzel (1955:166-190) found that Japanese respondents in every age group indicated family preoccupations. The adults, heads of families, think primarily of their children, while the young think primarily of the home in which they were raised. Japanese young adults said that they expected their greatest future satisfactions to come from family relationships and 97 percent expected to get married. Only 17 percent of male and 3 percent of female students at the University of Kyoto agreed that the idea of trial marriage should be expanded, to allow greater sexual freedom among young people. These attitudes alone do not prove anything about the family system in Japan. It is only when they link consistently to behavioral indices that we can say something concrete about the position of the individual and the family in Japan.

Although the age at marriage has risen, almost everyone in Japan does eventually marry. In 1965, for instance, only 2.1 percent of women aged 45 to 64 and 5.8 percent of women 35 to 44 had never been married. The proportions single were 1.3 and 3.4, respectively, for males (U.N., *Demographic Yearbook,* 1970:543). Yet, in spite of the high proportion of the population married and the new legal freedoms given to women, we do not find an increase in the divorce rate as in other industrialized nations.

Divorce may now be obtained by either of two methods: (1) by mutual consent without any other legal process, or (2) by suit of either husband or wife (Koyama, 1961). By allowing the woman an equal right to divorce, the new laws immediately doubled the number of persons capable of suing. Yet the divorce rates per thousand married couples have fallen from 5.3 in 1949-1951 to 4.4 in 1954-1956 and then to 3.6 in 1960 (U.N., *Demographic Yearbook,* 1958:473; and calculation from raw data for 1960 in Japan, Bureau of Statistics, 1960).

The Japanese government provides little in the way of welfare provisions that would free the individual from the family unit. The individual is still forced to rely on the family collectivity, which links the individual to the extended family, the "ward" or neighborhood organization (Dore, 1962:1-20), the occupational community,[7] and the nation (Vogel, 1963:chapter 5; Hulse, 1963:298).

These closely interrelated systems exert extralegal control over individualism. Self-orientations connote selfish, nonsocial or antisocial attitudes (Matsumoto, 1960:60). Collectivity-orientations are

---

[7] The family and family relationships play a large part in the procurement of a job for the young person. Even the highly educated person, then, remains obligated to the family unit, while his own achievement is secondary in both job placement and advancement. The occupational world is organized on paternalistic lines, with all sorts of subsidiary payments made on the basis of family and seniority rather than production (Abegglen, 1958:; Vogel, 1963; Yamane and Nonoyama, 1969). Taeuber (1958:chapter 7) points out that the employment of women does not mean their independence as in the West. In Japan, following the the required nine years of schooling, a girl typically works under a contract arranged by her father who receives most of her wage. The girls often live in dorms provided by industry until they are of marriage age. Free hours may be spent in educational or artistic improvement.

stressed throughout life. Occupational, educational, and political groups are modeled on family loyalty (Dore, 1958). The entire social system, then, is such that it is very difficult for the individual to escape his responsibilities to others. Group sanctions carry more weight in a society in which the individual has a difficult time existing on his own. The Japanese social system makes it difficult for the individual to escape the sanctions of the group, but alternatives to births out of wedlock, especially the ease of obtaining an abortion, facilitate the avoidance of childbirth out of wedlock.

It would be difficult, if not impossible, for governments alone to impose the strong family model of Japan. Yet there are other means of motivating individuals and couples to prevent births out of wedlock. That points leads us directly into a consideration of the next proposition.

Proposition 5d: The greater the burden of illegitimate children on the mother and father, and the fewer the potential rewards of such childbirth, the greater the motivation to avoid and the lower the levels of illegitimacy.

Norway is the only country I know of that has attempted to place responsibility for child support on the father in 100 percent of the cases. Presumably, if the male partner knows that he will be responsible for approximately eighteen years, he is likely to want to prevent conception or childbirth with the woman he does not want to marry. The woman who is expected to work to support herself and share the childrearing expenses is likely to feel the same. When responsibility is immediately and consistently placed, persons recognizing the probable outcome may use a variety of means of prevention. When only a few fathers are occasionally held responsible, each may suppose he will not be one of these. Thus in Norway, while responsibility *and* father's name were assigned consistently (1916-1956), illegitimacy levels were halved. In England they doubled over approximately the same time span. In the latter case, paternal responsibility was rarely established by the courts. In one case the state provides a strong motivation for preventing, in the other there is little need to bother.

Similarly, in some cases the mother is given a lot of help through life, and in other societies she is expected to support and care for the child in addition to herself. In England and the United States where welfare payments to unwed mothers are not large in total, they may be as much as the mother earned on the average before she had the child (Wimperis, 1960) and (as many of my students have been eager to point out) more than most college students survive on while working and going to school. The Scandinavian countries and the eastern European nations expect mothers of children out of wedlock to work, but they typically supply excellent maternity benefits and child allowances of small amounts. The working woman, who must still perform childrearing duties in spare time, may find it disadvantageous to produce very many children without a husband's support.

10. Societal Levels of Illegitimacy as a Result of Restriction or Promotion of Alternatives to Births Out of Wedlock

I HAVE attempted to study illegitimacy as a societal phenomenon or "social fact" rather than using the more typical psychological or social welfare approach to the subject. Although a great deal more research is needed on all aspects of illegitimacy, we have seen that there is a wide variety of evidence on the questionable or negative consequences of illegitimacy for the child, the mother, the father, the social group and larger society.

While cross-cultural studies indicate that all societies prefer that childbearing occur within socially recognized family units responsible for the care and support of the child, we have seen that cross-national measures of the actual behavior of parents in this regard vary widely. Although illegitimacy measures differ among the many societies of the world, within societies and social groups they are patterned in both time and space, and thus can be termed a "social fact." Each country and social group tends to maintain its levels of births out of wedlock, and where changes have occurred, they tend toward unidirectionality, that is, they are not random. Not only are the data patterned for individual nations and subcultures, but also there are similarities in patterning for some large geographical and cultural areas. We have seen that there are parallels among the Caribbean group of nations that contrast greatly with those of the Far East. In the case of similar cultural heritage, we find that countries as widely separated geographically as England, the United States, and Australia, report similar levels and trends in births out of wedlock. The various measures of illegitimacy, then, may be viewed as the product of social forces that can be examined as potential causes of behavioral processes leading to the production of births out of wedlock.

A great many "causes" of illegitimacy have been suggested previously. These were reviewed under the general headings of physical features and psychological, structural, and cultural explanations. While some of these may contribute to our understanding or interest in the subject, none by itself was found capable of truly "explaining" illegitimacy. Some are a part of the complex of factors that underlie social phenomena and thus may be incorporated into a multidimensional analysis.

The concatenated scheme of analysis is an attempt to draw together the multiple factors underlying societal summary measures of illegitimacy. The scheme may or may not be intuitively satisfying (or helpful in an attempt to understand the wide variations in societal levels of illegitimacy) for individual readers, but it is only when the scheme is translated into a series of specific hypotheses that any researcher is able to prove or disprove the propositions making up a theory of illegitimacy.

We have set out a list—by no means exhaustive—of hypotheses related to the general proposition that whenever a society or social group, in the patterning of social relationships (social structure) and its cultural adjuncts (culture), promotes one or several of the alternatives to childbearing out of wedlock, the levels of illegitimacy will be low. The specific propositions derived from the more general one were related to the ways in which societies might promote or deny alternatives to the path toward births out of wedlock. Thus there were a series of hypotheses about the social organization of marriage, nonmarital coitus, contraception, marriage following pregnancy, and abortion. A society need not promote all these alternatives. If there is a heavy emphasis on even one (such as early and universal marriage), illegitimacy will be low. On the other hand, it is probably more usual, especially in the more complex, advanced, industrial societies, that there is a mix of the factors leading away from the path toward illegitimacy. Each of the possible alternatives, the cluster of specific hypotheses, and the available evidence relating to them were presented in the final chapters of this book.

It is clear that if all women in a society are rigidly controlled and marriage is arranged at puberty, there will be little or no apparent illegitimacy. Social groups influence marriage in many ways. Marriage patterns alone, however, do not explain levels of illegitimacy, since societies with large proportions of women unmarried do not necessarily have high rates or ratios of illegitimacy. The sexual behavior of unmarried persons is itself a variable.

Of course, if a large proportion of the unmarried avoid sexual intercourse, there will be low levels of illegitimacy. Coitus is still a necessary if not sufficient cause of conception. Nations also differ according to whether they prohibit, promote, or are ambivalent about nonmarital sexual intercourse. Actual behavior is influenced by the beliefs, values, and expectations of the group; the structural opportunities; and the positive and negative sanctions relating to the phenomenon. Because sexual behavior typically occurs in private, we have only scattered bits of information from volunteer respondents on nonmarital sexual behavior. There is some evidence that variations in behavior among people in the advanced nations and some variations across time are related to different levels of illegitimacy.

Knowledge about, availability of, and motivations to use contraceptives among those who engage in nonmarital coitus is another variable that has been considered in our analysis of factors related to illegitimacy. Again social groups and whole societies may promote or restrict accurate knowledge, availability, and motivation to use all or some of the means of avoiding conception. Because the effectiveness of contraceptives varies so greatly, it makes an enormous difference which ones are promoted or banned. It is not that any social group is able to obtain 100 percent conformity, but that the availability and use may be made easy or difficult.

When conception out of wedlock occurs, one resolution that has found favor in some societies historically, and to a varying degree today, is the parent's marriage before the birth of the child. In some areas when childbearing was an important contribution to the farm family premarital pregnancy may have insured the fecundity of the bride. When marriage almost always followed, the extent of premarital conceptions might be great while illegitimacy ratios and rates were low. As individuals in such societies become more mobile, it is increasingly difficult for the social group, peers, church, or family to guarantee that a wedding will follow pregnancy, and births out of wedlock could rise. Some historical data on bridal pregnancy was presented, and some new computations on the probabilities of legitimating a nonmarital conception resulting in birth were given for the United States and England. A variety of positive and negative group sanctions influences the extent to which this alternative to illegitimacy is used.

When all else fails, the final alternative to a birth out of wedlock is abortion. Even when societies are highly restrictive of legal, medically supervised abortion, some unknown numbers occur. Because the extent of legal and illegal abortions combined remains questionable, it is difficult to assess the effect of induced abortion on societal levels of illegitimacy. The data that are available were sifted for clues pertinent to the specific propositions examined. Societies that allow legal, medically safe, and inexpensive abortions certainly facilitate the decline of illegitimacy or its maintenance at low levels. A number of nations and states of the United States that had experienced long-term increases in births out of wedlock, evidenced a turnaround in past trends within recent years with the lifting of restrictions on induced abortions. The Japanese case remains unique, however, in the extent to which legal abortion was used to reduce the levels of illegitimacy. The reasons for this may be found in Japanese cultural beliefs and values and patterning of social relationships. Rapidly changing abortion laws in other parts of the world should encourage continued study of the relationships suggested. Having reviewed the alternatives and the evidence pertaining to social group influence on the extent to which the alternatives are actually used in various societies, we are brought to the end of the line in the registration and reporting of societal levels of births out of wedlock. The numbers of such births registered, together with other required statistical data, allow the calculations of general illegitimate fertility rates, age-specific illegitimate fertility rates and ratios, or percentages of births out of wedlock. The final data are imperfect, but they are indicative of actual differences among the societies of the world. Those who specialize in the study of single nations will best be able to evaluate particular data. The demographers of the United Nation's Population Division have indicated in their publications the specific nations whose data are thought to be of questionable reliability. In a study as broad as this one, it is necessary to rely on their expert judgment. The perfection of the data at this time was considered to be second in importance to the presentation of a scheme of analysis thought to be useful to other researchers in the field.

USE OF THE CONCATENATED SCHEME

INDIVIDUAL CASES OF BIRTHS OUT OF WEDLOCK

If one is interested in analyzing why a particular person or several individuals have been involved in a birth out of wedlock, the concatenated series of variables may be applied on the individual level. What factors contributed to the fact that the person was not married at a given age? Under those circumstances what conditions led to nonmarital sexual activity? Why was conception not avoided by using one of the many types of contraceptives, or why were less rather than more efficient means of avoiding pregnancy used? Once pregnancy was confirmed, why were the partners in conception not married in order to provide a home for the child? Finally, what forces negated the alternative of abortion as a resolution to the conception out of wedlock? Most of these factors have been discussed at various times by those interested in the subject of illegitimacy. All must be reviewed in order to understand the phenomenon at the individual as well as at the group level.

SUBCULTURAL VARIATIONS

No contemporary nation could be considered "homogenous" in characteristics of the internal population. All exhibit social class differences and many also have racial and religious differences. These may or may not lead to variations in the forces at work at each of the stages in the concatenated scheme used in the analysis of illegitimacy.

Social class differences may or may not lead to differences in the probability of universal or early marriage. Because Rodman's explanation of lower-class family organization and illegitimacy admittedly applies only to certain societies (Rodman, 1971:185) it is a particularistic rather than universal or general explanation. Are the crucial differences educational, economic, or occupational? How can we blame lower-class membership for low marriage rates in Trinidad or Jamaica when lower classes in the Middle and Far East are overwhelmingly committed to marriage and childbirth within wedlock? Among those who are not married, why should one class be more likely to engage in sexual intercourse than another? What social factors lead some to use highly effective contraception in such a situation and not others? Is the probability of marriage following pregnancy different among the different social classes? How does the likelihood of abortion as a resolution differ by social class? Are the differences related to education, income, occupation, residential area, or other dimensions of the social class construct?

Racial differences in measures of illegitimacy cannot be due to physiological differences (see chapter 3), so an explanation of variation must be sought in the social realm. How much of the measured differences are due to social class, especially educational, differences? We have reviewed available data on racial differences within the United States. It is possible to analyze the extent to which these differences are due to different proportions married; differences in nonmarital coitus, especially at an early age; differences in likelihood of consistent use of effective contraception; and great differences in the probability of marriage among those conceiving out of wedlock. Evidence points to a much lower probability of abortion following nonmarital conception among blacks than among whites. For well-educated blacks, however, the probability of different outcomes resembles the white category more than looking like less-educated blacks. Separating out the racial and educational differences, therefore, becomes very complex, particularly in view of the imperfect bits of information contributing to the analysis. The study will become more difficult if those who wish to do away with racial or illegitimate "labels" are successful. Had they had their way, we would not now know that rates of births out of wedlock have actually declined for blacks in recent years, even though proportions married have declined, allowing continued increase in illegitimacy ratios.

Religious differences are a part of overall cultural variation. It is difficult to extract those differences due to religion alone without better data than is presently available. Within any nation one could research the questions relevant to religious differences in proportions of persons married at given ages, the proportions of unmarried persons participating in nonmarital coitus and the frequency of such, the consistency and efficiency of contraceptive use, the proportion of those marrying if conception occurs, and the probability of abortion as an outcome. Not only must the researcher be concerned with religious or denominational differences, but consideration must also be given to strength of religious commitment, measured by beliefs or practices. Could differences among religious groups be explained by their differences in education, income, or occupation? To what extent may different religions share the same ethical principles and thus produce similarities rather than differences in measured behaviors?

Social movements appealing to subgroups within a nation may also produce differential behavior among members of the movement. To what extent does the rhetoric of the Black Power movement, the Women's Liberation movement, or the *Playboy* devotees contribute to differences in the actual behavior of individuals?

Each of the subgroups of a society may be studied in the same way that we have studied the differences among whole nations. In all cases we must be careful to distinguish what people say from what they do.

SOCIETAL DIFFERENCES

We have seen that all societies seem to support the "principle of legitimacy" as an ideal. Yet behavioral measures of births out of wedlock vary so greatly that the phenomenon of illegitimacy becomes one of the more interesting social facts open to sociological investigation.

This scheme of analysis, or theory, may become the basis for prediction by simultaneous consideration of all the variables discussed. One looks to the future of a social group or society with respect to present levels and past trends in illegitimacy. In general, any social group that would restrict or reduce the potential escape mechanisms (early and universal marriage, sexual abstinence or the use of contraceptives in nonmarital coitus, marriage before birth, and abortion) would be expected to experience increased levels of illegitimacy. Our examination of the details of the social encouragement or restrictions on these mechanisms, however, has indicated that groups may prohibit some and facilitate others. Other things being equal, restrictions on marriage would be expected to produce increased proportions of births out of wedlock; increased motivations to use contraceptives would be expected to lower illegitimacy, etc. A social group that presses for any of the escape mechanisms or alternatives to illegitimacy would be expected to record low levels of births out of wedlock.

As is true in most sociological analysis, however, we are rarely able to look at the effects of change in one variable while the "other things remain equal." Thus in examining the details for any given society, we are more commonly dealing with a variety of simultaneous changes—a decline in proportions of women married and an increased availability of contraception and abortion, for instance. The challenge of analysis of the details of these countervailing forces may maintain or stimulate an interest in the ongoing study begun here. As data continue to improve for the many nations and subcultures of the world, the utility of the scheme of analysis presented may be tested by national and international specialists. It is hoped that the theory presented here may form a base on which elaboration and corrections can be made.

Bibliography

Abegglen, James C. 1958. *The Japanese Factory: Social Organization.* Glencoe, Illinois: Free Press.

———. 1970. "The Economic Growth of Japan." *Scientific American* 222 (March):31-37.

Allport, Gordon W. 1950. "Prejudice: A Problem in Psychological and Social Causation." *Journal of Social Issues.* Supplement Series, 4 (November):4-21.

Anderson, O. W. 1965. *Syphilis and Society: Problems of Control in the United States,* 1912-1964. Research Series 22. Chicago: Center for Health Administration Studies.

Ariga, K. 1954. "The Family in Japan." *Marriage and Family Living* 16 (November):362.

Arriaga, Eduardo E. 1968. "Some Aspects of Family Composition in Venezuela." *Eugenics Quarterly* 15, no. 3 (September):177-90.

Back, Kurt W., and J. Mayone Stycos. 1959. *The Survey Under Unusual Conditions: The Jamaica Human Fertility Investigation.* New York: Society for Applied Anthropology, Cornell University.

Barclay, Allan G. and D. R. Cusumano. 1973. "Testing Masculinity in Boys Without Fathers." In *Social Psychology* edited by E. Aronson and R. Helmreich, pp. 26-28. New York: D. Van Nostrand Company.

Barclay, George W. 1958. *Techniques of Population Analysis.* New York: Wiley.

Batten, Thelma F. 1971. *Reasoning and Research.* Boston: Little, Brown.

Bauman, Karl E., and J. Richard Udry. 1972. "Powerlessness and Regularity of Contraception in an Urban Negro Male Sample: A Research Note." *Journal of Marriage and the Family* 34, no. 1 (February):112-14.

Behrens, Carl. 1972. "Abortion: The Continuing Controversy." *Population Bulletin* 28, no. 4 (August).

Bell, Robert R. 1966. "Parent-Child Conflict in Sexual Values." *The Journal of Social Issues* 22, no. 1 (January):34-44.

Bell, Robert R., and Leonard Blumberg. 1959. "Courtship Intimacy and Religious Background." *Marriage and Family Living,* 21 (November).

Bell, Robert R., and Jay B. Chaskes. 1970. "Premarital Sexual Experience Among Coeds, 1958 and 1968." *Journal of Marriage and the Family* 32 (February):81-84.

Benson, Leonard. 1968. *Fatherhood: A Sociological Perspective*. New York: Random House.

Berger, Morroe. 1962. *The Arab World Today*. New York: Doubleday.

Berkov, Beth. 1968. "Illegitimate Births in California." *Milbank Memorial Fund Quarterly* 46, no. 4 (October).

———. 1971. "Illegitimate Fertility in California's Population." In *California's Twenty Million* edited by K. Davis and F. Styles. Berkeley: University of California, Institute of International Studies.

Bernstein, Blanch, and Mignon Sauber. 1961. *Deterrents to Early Prenatal Care and Social Services Among Women Pregnant Out-of-Wedlock*. Albany: New York State Department of Social Welfare (April).

Billingsley, Andrew, and Amy Tate Billingsley. 1966. "Illegitimacy and Patterns of Negro Family Life." In *The Unwed Mother*, edited by Robert W. Roberts, pp. 131-57, New York: Harper & Row.

Blake, Judith. 1961. *Family Structure in Jamaica*. Glencoe, Illinois: Free Press.

———. 1965. "Demographic Science and the Redirection of Population Policy." In *Public Health and Population Policy*, edited by M. C. Sheps and J. C. Ridley, pp. 41-70. Pittsburg, Pennsylvania: University of Pittsburgh Press.

———. 1973. "The Teenage Birth Control Dilemma and Public Opinion." *Science* 180, no. 4087 (May 18):708-12.

Blake, Judith, and Kingsley Davis. 1964. "Norms, Values and Sanctions." In *Handbook of Modern Sociology*, edited by E. Faris, pp. 456-84. Chicago, Illinois: Rand McNally.

Bock, Philip K. 1964. "Patterns of Illegitimacy on a Canadian Indian Reserve: 1860-1960." *Journal of Marriage and the Family* 26, no. 2 (May):142-48.

Bogue, Donald J. 1963. "How Low-Income Families Feel About Family Planning." In *Birth Control Services in Tax-Supported Hospitals, Health Departments and Welfare Agencies*, pp. 23-24. New York: Planned Parenthood Federation of America.

Bowerman, Charles E.; Donald P. Irish; and Hallowell Pope. 1966. *Unwed Motherhood: Personal and Social Consequences*. Report on Project No. 006, Soc. Sec. Admin. U. S. Dept. H.E.W. Mimeographed. Chapel Hill: University of North Carolina, Institute for Research in Social Science.

Bowlby, John. 1951. *Maternal Care and Mental Health*. Geneva, Switzerland: World Health Organization.

Briffault, R. 1927. *The Mothers*. New York: Grosset & Dunlap.

Brinton, Crane. 1936. *French Revolutionary Legislation on Illegitimacy, 1789-1904*. Cambridge, Massachusetts: Harvard University Press.

Bromley, Dorothy D., and Florence H. Britten. 1938. *Youth and Sex: A Study of 1300 College Students*. New York: Harper & Row.

Bronfenbrenner, Urie 1964. "The Changing American Child—A Speculative Analysis." In *Personality and Social Systems*, edited by N. Smelser and W. Smelser, pp. 347-56. New York: Wiley.

Bumpass, Larry, and Charles F. Westoff. 1970a. "The 'Perfect Contraceptive' Population." *Science* 169 (September):1177-82.

———. 1970b. "Unwanted Births and U.S. Population Growth." *Family Planning Perspectives* 2, no. 4 (October):9-12.

Burgess, Ernest, and Paul Wallin. 1953. *Courtship, Engagement and Marriage*. Philadelphia: J. B. Lippincott.

Calderone, Mary. 1968. "The Sex Information and Education Council of the United States." *Medical Aspects of Human Sexuality* 2, no. 8.

Callahan, Daniel. 1970. *Abortion: Law, Choice and Morality*. New York: Macmillan.

Campbell, Arthur A. 1968. "The Role of Family Planning in the Reduction of Poverty." *Journal of Marriage and the Family* 30, no. 2 (May):236-45.

Campbell, Arthur A., and James D. Cowhig. 1967. "The Incidence of Illegitimacy in the United States." *Welfare in Review* (May):1-6.

Cannon, Kenneth L., and Richard Long. 1971. "Premarital Sexual Behavior in the Sixties." *Journal of Marriage and the Family* 33, no. 1 (February):36-49.

Cattell, James P., M.D. 1966. "Psychodynamic and Clinical Observations in a Group of Unmarried Mothers." In *The Unwed Mother*, edited by Robert W. Roberts, pp. 95-104. New York: Harper & Row.

Chaskel, Ruth. 1967. "The Unmarried Mother: Is She Different?" *Child Welfare* (February):65-75.

Chesser, Eustace. 1956. *The Sexual, Marital and Family Relationships of the English Woman*. England: Hutchinson's Medical Publications.

Christensen, Harold T. 1953. "Studies in Child Spacing: I—Premarital Pregnancy as Measured by the Spacing of the First Birth From Marriage." *American Sociological Review* 18 (February):53-59.

———. 1958. "The Method of Record Linkage Applied to Family Data." *Marriage and Family Living* 20 (February):38-43.

———. 1960. "Cultural Relativism & Premarital Sex Norms." *American Sociological Review* 25 (February):35-39.

———. 1963. "Timing of First Pregnancy as a Factor in Divorce: A Cross-Cultural Analysis." *Eugenics Quarterly*, 10 (September):119-30.

Christensen, Harold T., and G. R. Carpenter. 1962. "Timing Patterns in

Development of Sexual Intimacy." *Marriage and Family Living* 24:30-35.

Christensen, Harold T., and Christina F. Gregg. 1970. "Changing Sex Norms in America and Scandinavia." *Journal of Marriage and the Family* (November):616-27.

Christensen, Harold T., and H. Meisner. 1953. "Studies in Child-Spacing III: Premarital Pregnancy as a Factor in Divorce." *American Sociological Review* 18, no. 6 (December):641-44.

Christensen, Harold T., and Bette Rubinstein. 1956. "Premarital Pregnancy and Divorce: A Follow-Up Study by the Interview Method." *Marriage and Family Living* 114 ff.

Clarke, Edith. 1966. *My Mother Who Fathered Me*. London: George Allen & Unwin.

Clausen, John A. 1961. "Drug Addiction." In *Contemporary Social Problems,* edited by R. K. Merton and R. A. Nisbet. New York: Harcourt, Brace & World.

———. 1968. "Perspectives on Childhood Socialization." In *Socialization and Society*, edited by J. Clausen, pp. 130-81. Boston: Little, Brown.

Collver, O. Andrew. 1965. *Birth Rates in Latin America: New Estimates of Historical Trends and Fluctuations*. Berkeley: Institute of International Studies, University of California (Research Series No. 7).

Coombs, Lolagene; Ronald Freedman; Judith Friedman; and William F. Pratt. 1970. "Premarital Pregnancy and Status Before and After Marriage." *American Journal of Sociology* 75, no. 5 (March):800-20.

Coopersmith, Stanley. 1967. *The Antecedents of Self-Esteem*. San Francisco: W. H. Freeman.

Coser, Lewis, A. 1964. "The Case of the Soviet Family." In *The Family*, edited by Rose Coser, pp. 526-45. New York: St. Martin's Press.

Coser, Rose Laub, and Lewis A. Coser. 1970. "The Principle of Legitimacy and its Patterned Infringement in Social Revolutions." Paper read at the meetings of the International Sociological Association, Varna, Bulgaria, September 14-19.

Cowgill, Donald O.; Srisomang Keovichit; Robert G. Burnright; J. Richard Udry; and Charas Yamarat. 1971. "Sterilization, A Case of Extensive Practice in a Developing Nation." *Milbank Memorial Fund Quarterly* 49, no. 3, pt. 1 (July):363-78.

Croog, Sydney H. 1951. "Aspects of the Cultural Background of Premarital Pregnancy in Denmark." *Social Forces* 30 (December):215-19.

Cutright, Phillips. 1967. "Inequality: A Cross-National Analysis." *American Sociological Review* 32, no. 4 (August):562-77.

———. 1970. "AFDC, Family Allowance and Illegitimacy." *Family Planning Perspectives* 2, no. 4 (October):4-9.

————. 1971a. "Illegitimacy: Myths, Causes and Cures." *Family Planning Perspectives* 3, no. 1 (January):26-38.

————. 1971b. "Economic Events and Illegitimacy in Developed Countries." *Journal of Comparative Family Studies* 2 (Spring):33-53.

————. 1973a. "Illegitimacy in the United States, 1920-1968." In *Demographic and Social Aspects of Population Growth*, edited by C. F. Westoff and R. Parke, Jr. Washington, D. C.: U. S. Government Printing Office.

————. 1973b. "Illegitimacy and Income Supplements." Joint Economic Committee, Subcommittee on Fiscal Policy, U. S. Congress. Washington, D.C.: Government Printing Office.

David, Henry P. 1970. *Family Planning and Abortion in the Socialist Countries of Central and Eastern Europe*. New York: Population Council.

David, Henry P.; Zahur Alam; and Mary G. Kalis. 1972. *Abortion Legislation: A Summary International Classification*. Silver Spring, Maryland: IRCAR Transnational Family Research Institute (July).

David, Henry P.; Mary G. Kalis; and Christopher Tietze. 1973. *Selected Abortion Statistics, an International Summary*. Silver Spring, Maryland: IRCAR Transnational Family Research Institute, (January).

Davis, Kingsley. 1939a. "Illegitimacy and the Social Structure." *American Journal of Sociology* 45, no. 2 (September):215-33.

————. 1939b. "The Forms of Illegitimacy." *Social Forces* 18, no. 1 (October)76f.

————. 1948. *Human Society*. New York: Macmillan.

————. 1955. "Institutional Patterns Favoring High Fertility in Underdeveloped Areas." *Eugenics Quarterly* II (March):33-39.

————. n.d. "Problems and Solutions in International Comparison for Social Science Purposes." Berkeley: International Population and Urban Research Center, University of California.

————. 1963. "The Theory of Change and Response in Modern Demographic History." *Population Index* 29, no. 4 (October):345-66.

————. 1965. "Demographic Aspects of Poverty." In *Poverty in America*, edited by Margaret S. Gordon. San Francisco: Chandler.

Davis, Kingsley, and Judith Blake. 1956. "Social Structure and Fertility: An Analytic Framework." *Economic Development and Cultural Change* 4 (April):211-35.

Devereux, George. 1960. *A Study of Abortion in Primitive Societies*. London: Thomas Yoseloff.

Dixon, Ruth B. 1970. "The Social and Demographic Determinants of Marital Postponement and Celibacy: a Comparative Study." Ph. D. dissertation, University of California, Berkeley.

————. 1971. "Explaining Cross-Cultural Variations in Age at Marriage and

Proportions Never Marrying." *Population Studies* 25 (July):215-54.

Dodd, Peter C. 1970. "Women's Honor (il-'ird) in Contemporary Arab Society." Mimeographed paper presented at the Seventh World Congress, International Sociological Association, Varna, Bulgaria, September 14-19.

Dodd, Peter C. 1973. "Family Honor and the Forces of Change in Contemporary Arab Society." *International Journal of Middle East Studies* 4:40-54.

Dore, Ronald P. 1958. *City Life in Japan.* Berkeley: University of California Press.

———. 1962. "The Ward." In *Japanese Character and Culture,* edited by Bernard S. Silberman, pp. 1-20, Tuscon: University of Arizona Press.

Durkheim, Emile. 1949. *The Division of Labor in Society.* Translated by G. Simpson. New York: Free Press.

———. 1961. *The Elementary Forms of Religious Life.* New York: Collier Books.

———. 1962. *The Rules of Sociological Method.* Glencoe, Illinois: Free Press.

Ehrmann, Winston W. 1964. "Marital and Nonmarital Sexual Behavior." In *Handbook of Marriage and the Family,* edited by Harold T. Christensen, pp. 585-622. Chicago: Rand McNally.

Encyclopaedia Brittannica. 1969. Chicago: William Benton.

England, L. 1949-50. "Little Kinsey: An Outline of Sex Attitudes in Britain." *Public Opinion Quarterly* 13:567-600.

Erikson, E. H. 1963. *Childhood and Society.* New York: Norton.

Family Planning Federation of Japan. 1967. *Japan's Experience in Family Planning—Past and Present.* Edited by Minoru Muramatsu. Tokyo, Japan.

Fogarty International Center. 1969. *The Family In Transition.* Bethesda, Maryland: National Institutes of Health.

Foote, Caleb; Robert Levy; and Frank Sander. 1966. *Cases and Materials on Family Law.* Boston: Little, Brown.

Foote, Nelson N. 1954. "Sex as Play." *Social Problems* 1, no. 4 (April):159-63.

Ford, C. S., and F. A. Beach. 1951. *Patterns of Sexual Behavior.* New York: Harper.

Forssman, Hans, and Inga Thuwe. 1971. "120 Children Born after their Mothers' Application for Therapeutic Abortion had been Refused." In *Readings in Population,* edited by W. Petersen, pp. 401-410. New York: Macmillan.

Francis, O. C. 1963. *The People of Modern Jamaica.* Jamaica: Department of Statistics.

Freedman, Mervin B. *The College Experience.* San Francisco: Jossey-Bass.

Freedman, Ronald. 1964. *Population: The Vital Revolution.* Garden City, New York: Doubleday, Anchor Books.

French Institute of Public Opinion. 1961. *Patterns of Sex and Love: A Study of the French Woman and Her Morals.* New York: Crown.

Frisch, Rose E. and Roger Revelle. 1969. "The height and weight of adolescent boys and girls at the time of peak velocity of growth in height and weight: longitudinal data." *Human Biology* 41:536-59.

————. 1970. "Height and weight at menarche and a hypothesis of critical body weights and adolescent events." *Science* 169 (July 24):297-99.

Furie, Sidney. 1966. "Birth Control and the Lower-Class Unmarried Mother." *Social Work* 11, no. 1 (January):42-49.

Furstenberg, Frank F., Jr. 1971. "Birth Control Experience Among Pregnant Adolescents: The Process of Unplanned Parenthood." *Social Problems* 19, no. 2 (Fall):192-203.

Garcia, Celso-Ramon. 1963. "Clinical Studies on Human Fertility Control." In *Human Fertility and Population Problems*, edited by Roy O. Greep. Cambridge, Massachusetts: Schenkman.

Gebhard, P. B.; W. Pomeroy; C. Martin; and C. V. Christensen. 1958. *Pregnancy, Birth and Abortion.* New York: Harper & Brothers.

Gendell, Murray, and Jean van der Tak. 1973. "Illegitimacy Ratios in Large Cities: Determinants and Implications." *American Journal of Public Health* (December).

Glass, D. V., and E. Grebenik. 1954. *The Trend and Pattern of Fertility in Great Britain.* Papers of the Royal Commission on Population London: pp. 138-44.

Goldsmith, Sadja. 1969. "San Francisco's Teen Clinic." *Family Planning Perspectives* 1, no. 2 (October):23-26.

Goldstein, Sidney. 1967. "Premarital Pregnancies in Denmark, 1950-1965." In *The Contributed Papers of the International Union for the Scientific Study of Population*, pp. 993-1001. Sydney, Australia: IUSSP, August.

Goldstein, Sidney, and Kurt B. Mayer. 1965. "Illegitimacy, Residence, and Status." *Social Problems* 12, no. 4 (Spring):428-36.

Goode, William, J. 1960a. "A Deviant Case: Illegitimacy in the Caribbean." *American Sociological Review* 25 (February):21-30.

————. 1960b. *Die Struktur der Familie*, Koln und Opladen: Vestdeutscher Verlag.

————. 1961. "Illegitimacy, Anomie & Cultural Penetration." *American Sociological Review* 26 (December):910-25.

————. 1963. *World Revolution and Family Patterns.* Glencoe, Illinois: Free Press.

————. 1964. *The Family.* New Jersey: Prentice-Hall.

Gough, E. Kathleen. 1959. "Is the Family Universal?–The Nayar Case." *Journal of the Royal Anthropological Institute* 89, pt. 1.

Gough, Harrison. 1961. "Theory and Measurement of Socialization." In *Studies in Behavior Pathology*, edited by T. R. Sarbin, pp. 141-48, New York: Holt, Rinehart & Winston.

Great Britain, General Register Office. 1939-1972. *The Statistical Review of England and Wales* 1938 *through* 1971. Yearly series. London: General Register Office, pts. 1 and 3.

Greenleigh Associates. 1960. *Facts, Fallacies and Future–A Study of the ADC Program of Cook County, Illinois*. New York: Greenleigh Associates, pp. 19-20.

Grzybowski, Kazimierz. 1971. "Czechoslovakia." In *Population and Law*, edited by L. Lee and A. Larson, pp. 235-66, Durham, North Carolina: Rule of Law Press.

Hair, P. E. H. 1966. "Bridal Pregnancy in Rural England in Earlier Centuries." *Population Studies* 20, no. 2 (November):233-43.

Hamady, Sania. 1960. *Temperament and Character of the Arabs*. New York: Twayne.

Hammond, Boone E., and Joyce A. Ladner. 1969. "Socialization into Sexual Behavior in a Negro Slum Ghetto." In *The Individual, Sex, and Society*, edited by C. Broderick and J. Bernard, pp. 41-51. Baltimore: Johns Hopkins Press.

Hardin, Garrett. 1968. "Abortion–or Compulsory Pregnancy?" *Journal of Marriage and the Family* 30, no. 2 (May):246-51.

Harlow, Harry F., and Margaret K. Harlow. 1962. "Social Deprivation in Monkeys." *Scientific American* 207 (November):138-44.

Hartley, Shirley Foster. 1966. "The Amazing Rise of Illegitimacy in Great Britain." *Social Forces* 44, no. 4 (June):533-45.

———. 1969a. "Comparative Differences and Changes in Levels of Illegitimacy." Ph. D. dissertation, University of California, Berkeley, and University Microfilm, Ann Arbor, Michigan.

———. 1969b. "Illegitimacy Among 'Married' Women in England and Wales." *Journal of Marriage and the Family* 31, no. 4 (November):793-98.

———. 1970a. "Standardization Procedures in the Analysis of Cross-National Variations in Illegitimacy Measures." *Journal of Biosocial Science* 2 (April):95-109.

———. 1970b. "The Decline of Illegitimacy in Japan." *Social Problems* 18, no. 1 (Summer):78-91.

———. 1971. "The Contributions of Illegitimate and Pre-Maritally Conceived Legitimate Births to Total Fertility." *Social Biology* 18, no. 2 (June):178-86.

————. 1972. *Population: Quantity vs. Quality.* Englewood Cliffs, New Jersey: Prentice-Hall.

Hawley, A. H. and V. Prachuabmoh. 1965. "Family Growth and Family Planning in a Rural District of Thailand." In *Family Planning and Population Programs*, edited by B. Berelson. Chicago: University of Chicago Press.

Heer, David M. 1965. "Abortion, Contraception, and Population Policy in the Soviet Union." *Demography* 2:531-39.

Heer, David M., and Judith G. Bryden. 1966. "Family Allowances and Population Policy in the USSR." *Journal of Marriage and the Family* 28, no. 4 (November):514-19.

Helfer, Ray E., and C. Henry Kempe. 1968. *The Battered Child.* Chicago and London: University of Chicago Press.

Heltsley, Mary, and Carlfred Broderick. 1969. "Religiosity and Premarital Sexual Permissiveness: Reexamination of Reiss's Traditionalism Proposition." *Journal of Marriage and the Family* 31, no. 3 (August):441-43.

Henriques, F. M. 1952. *Family and Color in Jamaica.* London: Eyre and Spottiswoode.

Henry, Louis. 1961. "Some Data on Natural Fertility." *Eugenics Quarterly* 8:81-91.

————. 1973. "Intervalle Entre le Mariage et la Premiere Naissance. Erreurs et Corrections." *Population* 28, no. 2 (March, April):261-83.

Herzog, Elizabeth. 1962. "Unmarried Mothers: Some Questions to be Answered and Some Answers to be Questioned." *Child Welfare* (October).

Herzog, Elizabeth, and Cecelia E. Sudia. 1968. "Fatherless Homes; a Review of Research." *Children* 15:177-82.

Hill, Adelaide Cromwell, and Frederick S. Jaffe. 1965. "Negro Fertility and Family Size Preferences." In *The Negro American*, edited by Talcott Parsons and Kenneth Clark, pp. 205-224. New York: Daedalus Library.

Hill, R.; J. M. Stycos, and K. Back. 1959. *The Family and Population Control: A Puerto Rican Experiment in Social Change.* Chapel Hill: University of North Carolina Press.

Hill, Reuben, and Rene Konig, eds. 1970. *Families in East and West.* International Sociological Association, The Hague: Mouton.

Himes, Norman E. 1936. *Medical History of Contraception.* Baltimore, Maryland: Williams & Wilkins.

Hobhouse, L. T.; G. C. Wheeler; and M. Ginsberg. 1915. *The Material Culture and Social Institutions of the Simpler Peoples.* London: Chapman and Hall.

Hopkin, W. A. B., and J. Hajnal. 1947. "Analysis of the Births in England, 1939." *Population Studies* (September).

Howard, A. and I. Howard. 1964. "Pre-Marital Sex Among the Rotumans." *American Anthropologist* 66, no. 2 (April):266-83.

Hulse, Frederick S. 1963. "Convention and Reality in Japanese Culture." In *Japanese Character and Culture*, edited by Bernard Silberman. Tucson: University of Arizona Press.

Illsley, Raymond, and Derek Gill. 1968. "New Fashions in Illegitimacy." *New Society* (November 14):709-11.

International Labor Office. 1972. *Yearbook of Labor Statistics 1971*. Geneva: International Labor Office.

Issawi, Charles. 1947. *Egypt: An Economic and Social Analysis*. London: Oxford University Press.

Jaffe, F. 1972. "Low-Income Families: Fertility Changes in the 1960s." *Family Planning Perspectives* 4 (January):43-47.

Jamaica, Department of Statistics. 1947. *Jamaica, Quarterly Digest of Statistics*. September, Kingston: Government Printing Office.

James, William H. 1970. "Incidence of Spontaneous Abortion." *Population Studies* 24:245.

Japan, Bureau of Statistics. 1965. *Population Census, Summary of 1% Tabulation Results*. p. 19.

———. 1964. *Statistical Abstract*, p. 295, table 9.

———. *Statistical Yearbook*, 1940, 1950, 1955, 1960, 1965.

Japan, Division of Health and Welfare. *Japan, Vital Statistics*, 1940.

Japan, Ministry of Health and Welfare. *Annual Report*, 1955 *through* 1964.

———. *Report on Public Health Administration*, 1962 *through* 1967.

———. *Vital Statistics*, 1950, 1955, 1960, 1964.

Jeger, Lena M. 1951. *Illegitimate Children and Their Parents*. London: National Council for the Unmarried Mother and Her Child.

Jenkins, W. W. 1958. "An Experimental Study of the Relationship of Legitimate and Illegitimate Birth Status to School and Personal and Social Adjustment of Negro Children." *American Journal of Sociology* 64:169-73.

Johnson, David R., and Phillips Cutright. 1973. "Problems in the Analysis of Latin American Illegitimacy." In *Comparative Social Research: Methodological Problems and Strategies*, edited by M. Armer and A. Grimshaw, pp. 377-415. New York: John Wiley & Sons.

Johnson, Warren R. 1968. *Human Sexual Behavior and Sex Education*. Philadelphia: Lea and Febiger.

Johnston, Kenneth. 1968. "Divorce: the Financial Facts." *New Society* (March 14):379.

Jones, W. C.; H. J. Meyer; and E. F. Borgatta. 1966. "Social and Psychological Factors in Status Decisions of Unmarried Mothers." In *The Unwed*

Mother, edited by Robert W. Roberts, pp. 201-17, New York: Harper & Row.

Kadushin, Alfred. 1968. "Single Parent Adoptions: An Overview of Some Relevant Research." Mimeographed. Madison, Wisconsin: University of Wisconsin, School of Social Work, (May).

Kammerer, Percy G. 1918. *The Unmarried Mother.* Boston: Little, Brown.

Kampmeier, R. H. 1968. "Venereal Disease in the Teenager." *Medical Aspects of Human Sexuality* 2, no. 3:14-21.

Kantner, John F., and Melvin Zelnik. 1972. "Sexual Experience of Young Unmarried Women in the United States." *Family Planning Perspectives* 4, no. 4 (October):9-18.

———. 1973. "Contraception and Pregnancy: Experience of Young Unmarried Women in the United States." *Family Planning Perspectives* 5, no. 1 (Winter):21-35.

Kasanin, M., and Sieglinde Handschin. 1941. "Psychodynamic Factors in Illegitimacy." *American Journal of Orthopsychiatry* 11.

Keovichit, S. n. d. "Attitude Toward Family Planning in Four Areas of Bangkok: Preliminary Findings." Unpublished manuscript at Faculty of Public Health, Mahidol University, Bangkok.

Kerr, Madeline. 1951. *Personality and Conflict in Jamaica.* Liverpool, England: University Press.

Khlentzos, Michael T., and Mary A. Pagliaro. 1965. "Observations from Psychotherapy with Unwed Mothers." *American Journal of Orthopsychiatry* 35.

Kinsey, Alfred, et al. 1953. *Sexual Behavior in the Human Female.* Philadelphia and London: W. B. Saunders Co.

Kiser, Clyde V. 1958. "Fertility Trends and Differentials Among Nonwhites in the United States." *Milbank Memorial Fund Quarterly* 36, no. 2 (April):190-96.

Kiser, Clyde V.; Wilson H. Grabill; and Arthur A. Campbell. 1968. *Trends and Variations in Fertility in the United States.* Cambridge, Massachusetts: Harvard University Press.

Kitaoka, J. 1957. *Over-Population and Family Planning in Japan.* Economic Series, no. 14. Tokyo: Science Council of Japan (January).

Knodel, J. 1967. "Law, Marriage and Illegitimacy in Nineteenth Century Germany." *Population Studies* 20, no. 3 (March):279-94.

Komarovsky, Mirra. 1962. *Blue Collar Marriage.* New York: Random House.

Kovar, Mary Grace. 1970. "Interval from First Marriage to First Birth." Paper presented at the annual meetings of the Population Association of America, Atlanta, Georgia, April 16-18.

Koyama, Takashi. 1961. *The Changing Social Position of Women in Japan.*

Geneva, Switzerland: UNESCO.

Krause, Harry D. 1971. *Illegitimacy: Law and Social Policy.* New York: Bobbs-Merrill.

Kumar, Joginder. 1969. "Demographic Analysis of Data on Illegitimate Births." *Social Biology* 16, no. 2 (June):92-108.

Kvaraceus, W. C. 1945. "Prenatal and Early Developmental History of 136 Delinquents." *Journal of Genetic Psychology* 66:267-71.

LaBarre, Weston. 1969. "The Triple Crisis: Adolescence, Early Marriage and Parenthood, Part II—Fatherhood." In *The Double Jeopardy, the Triple Crisis —Illegitimacy Today.* New York: National Council on Illegitimacy.

Lader, Lawrence. 1966. *Abortion.* Boston: Beacon Press.

Landis, Judson T., and Mary G. Landis. 1968. *Building a Successful Marriage.* Englewood Cliffs, New Jersey: Prentice-Hall.

Laslett, Peter. 1965. *The World We Have Lost.* London: Methuen.

———. 1967. "The Extent of Bastardy in Restoration England." Mimeographed paper presented by Professor Laslett at a Colloquium of the Department of Demography, University of California, Berkeley.

———. 1973. "Long-term Trends in Bastardy in England." *Population Studies* vol. 27, no. 2 (July):255-86.

League of Nations. 1939. *Study on the Legal Position of the Illegitimate Child.* Document No: C.70.M.24.IV.

———. 1929. *Study of the Position of the Illegitimate Child Based on the Information Communicated by Governments.* Document No: C.P.E.141(1).IV.

Lee, Luke T. 1971. "Law and Family Planning." *Studies in Family Planning* 2, no. 4 (April):81-98.

Lee, Luke T., and Arthur Larson. 1971. *Population and Law.* Durham, North Carolina: Rule of Law Press.

Leffingwell, Albert, M. D. 1892. *Illegitimacy and the Influence of Seasons Upon Conduct.* London: Sonnenschein.

Leoy, Ruben. 1965. *The Social Structure of Islam.* Cambridge University Press.

Liebow, Elliot. 1967. *Tally's Corner.* Boston: Little, Brown.

Linner, Birgitta. 1967. *Sex and Society in Sweden.* New York: Pantheon.

Loesch, John G., and Nahman H. Greenberg. 1962. "Some Specific Areas of Conflicts Observed During Pregnancy: A Comparative Study of Married and Unmarried Pregnant Women." *American Journal of Orthopsychiatry* 32.

London Times. May 8, 1964, p. 8c, May 26, 1966, December 6, 1966, February 22, 1967, July 2, 1967, p. 11, col. 5.

Lorimer, Frank. 1954. *Culture and Human Fertility.* Geneva, Switzerland: UNESCO.

———. 1963. "Issues of Population Policy." In *The Population Dilemma*, edited by P. M. Hauser, pp. 143-77. Englewood Cliffs, New Jersey: Prentice-Hall.

Lowrie, Samuel H. 1965. "Early Marriage: Premarital Pregnancy and Associated Factors." *Journal of Marriage and the Family* 27, no. 1 (February).

Lynn, D. B., and W. L. Sawrey. 1959. "The Effects of Father-absence on Norwegian Boys and Girls." *Journal of Abnormal Social Psychology*, 59 (1):258-62.

MacIver, R. M. 1952. *Social Causation*. Boston and New York: Ginn.

Malinowski, Bronislaw. 1930. "Parenthood, the Basis of Social Structure." In *The New Generation*, edited by V. F. Calverton and S. D. Schmalhausen, pp. 113-68. New York: Macauley.

Martz, Helen E. 1963. "Illegitimacy and Dependency." *Health, Education and Welfare Indicators*. Washington, D.C.: Bureau of Family Services, Welfare Administration, U.S. Dept. H.E.W., September.

Matsumoto, Y. S. 1960. "Contemporary Japan, the Individual and the Group." In *Transactions of the American Philosophical Society*, New Series, vol. 50, pt. 1.

May, Geoffrey. 1931. *The Social Control of Sex Expression*. New York: Morrow.

May, Rollo. 1950. *The Meaning of Anxiety*. New York: Ronald Press.

McCandless, Boyd R. 1967. *Children: Behavior and Development*. New York: Holt Rinehart & Winston.

McClosky, Herbert, and John H. Schaar. 1965. "Psychological Dimensions of Anomy." *American Sociological Review* 30, no. 1 (February):14-40.

McDaniel, E. B. 1967. "Short Summary of a Family Planning Survey of a Village in Northern Thailand (Ban Pong)." Mimeographed. (September).

Merton, Robert. 1957. *Social Theory and Social Structure*. Glencoe, Illinois: Free Press.

Metge, Joan. 1967. *The Maoris of New Zealand*. London: Routledge and Kegan Paul.

Miller, Daniel R., and Guy E. Swanson. 1958. *The Changing American Parent*. New York: Wiley.

Mischel, Walter. 1961. "Father-absence and Delay of Gratification: Cross-Cultural Comparisons." *Journal of Abnormal and Social Psychology*, 63:116-24.

Momeni, Djamchid A. 1972. "The Difficulties of Changing the Age at Marriage in Iran." *Journal of Marriage and the Family* 34, no. 3 (August):545-51.

Monahan, Thomas P. 1960. "Premarital Pregnancy in the United States." *Eugenics Quarterly* 7, no. 3 (September):133-47.

Muller, Charlotte. 1971. "Socioeconomic Outcomes of Restricted Access to Abortion." *American Journal of Public Health* 61, no. 6 (June):1110-18.

Muramatsu, Minoru. 1960. "Effect of Induced Abortion on the Reduction of Births in Japan." *Milbank Memorial Fund Quarterly* 38 (April):152-66.

———. 1970. "Role of Induced Abortion in Fertility Control in Postwar Japan." *Bulletin of the Institute of Public Health* 19:97-107.

Murdock, George. 1949. *Social Structure*. New York: Macmillan.

Myrdal, Alva. 1945. *Nation and Family*. London: Kegan Paul.

National Assistance Board. *Report for the 17th of November to July 4, 1949*. London: Minister of Pensions and National Insurance.

———. *Report for 1962*. London: Minister of Pensions and National Insurance.

National Council on Illegitimacy. 1965. *Illegitimacy—Data and Findings for Prevention, Treatment, and Policy Formulation*. New York: National Council on Illegitimacy.

———. 1967. *Unmarried Parenthood*. New York: National Council on Illegitimacy.

———. 1968. *Unmarried Parents and Their Children*. New York: National Council on Illegitimacy.

Nelson, George R., ed. 1953. *Freedom and Welfare, Social Patterns in the Northern Countries of Europe*. Ministries of Social Affairs of Denmark, Finland, Iceland, Norway, Sweden.

New York Times. 1967. July 15, p. 1, col. 2.

Nielsen, Kathryn M., and Rocco L. Motto. 1963. "Some Observations of Family Constellations and Personality Patterns of Young Unmarried Mothers." *American Journal of Orthopsychiatry* 33.

Nimkoff, M. F. 1965. *Comparative Family Systems*. Boston: Houghton Mifflin.

O'Neil, Agnes E. 1971. "Illegitimacy in Canada: Bridging the Communications Gap." *Canadian Journal of Public Health* 62, no. 2 (March-April):156-58.

Otterbein, Keith. 1965. "Caribbean Family Organization: A Comparative Analysis." *American Anthropologist* 67, no. 1 (February):66-79.

Packard, Vance. 1968. *The Sexual Wilderness*. New York: David McKay.

Pakter, J., and F. Nelson. 1965. "The Unmarried Mother and Her Child." In *Illegitimacy—Data and Findings for Prevention, Treatment and Policy Formulation*, p. 33. New York: National Council on Illegitimacy.

Parade. 1967. "Parent Shortage." (October 1).

Pauker, Jerome D. 1969. "Girls Pregnant Out-of-Wedlock—Pregnant Because They are Different or Different Because They are Pregnant?" In *National Council on Illegitimacy, The Double Jeopardy, The Triple Crisis—Illegitimacy Today*. New York: NCI.

Pearl, R. 1939. *The Natural History of Population*. London: Oxford University Press.

Pearson, John S., and Phyllis L. Amacher. 1956. "Intelligence Test Results and Observations of Personality Disorder Among 3594 Unwed Mothers in Minnesota." *Journal of Clinical Psychology* 12.

Peristiany, J. G., ed. 1965. *Honour and Shame: The Values of Mediterrannean Society*. London: Weidenfeld and Nicolson.

Perlman, Helen Harris. 1964. "Unmarried Mothers." In *Social Work and Social Problems*, edited by N. Cohan. New York: National Association of Social Workers.

Pilpel, H., and N. Wechsler. 1971. "Birth Control, Teen-Agers and the Law: A New Look, 1971." *Family Planning Perspectives* 3, no. 3 (July):37-45.

Planned Parenthood-World Population. 1969. *Methods of Contraception in the United States*. New York: Planned Parenthood-World Population.

———. 1970. *Voluntary Sterilization for Men and Women*. New York: Planned Parenthood-World Population.

Podell, Lawrence. 1968. "Fertility, Illegitimacy, and Birth Control." Preliminary Report No. 6 in *Families on Welfare in New York City*. New York: City University of New York, Center for Social Research.

Pohlman, Edward. 1967. "Unwanted Conceptions: Research on Undesirable Consequences." *Eugenics Quarterly* 14, no. 2 (June):143-54.

———. 1969. *The Psychology of Birth Planning*. Cambridge, Massachusetts: Schenkman.

Population Investigation Committee & Royal College of Obstetricians and Gynaecologists. 1948. *Maternity in Great Britain*. Oxford University Press.

Population Reference Bureau. 1967. "One Minute to One Year—The Dangerous Age." *Population Profile*. Washington, D.C., September 19.

———. 1972. "The Population Year in Review: 1971." *Population Profile* (January).

Prachuabmoh, V., and J. T. Fawcett. 1967. "Fertility Control in Rural Thailand: Some Results of a Demonstration Project in Photharam District." *Proceedings of the International Union for the Scientific Study of Population*. Sydney, Australia: August 21-26.

Pratt, William F. 1965. "Premarital Pregnancies and Illegitimate Births in a Metropolitan Community—An Analysis of Age and Differentials." Paper presented at the annual meetings of the Population Association of America, April.

———. 1965. *A Study of Marriages Involving Premarital Pregnancies*. Ph. D. dissertation, University of Michigan. Ann Arbor, Michigan: University Microfilms.

Presser, Harriet B. 1970. "Voluntary Sterilization: A World View." *Reports* on *Population/Family Planning* 5 (July):1-36.

Presser, Harriet B., and Larry L. Bumpass. 1973. "Demographic and Social Aspects of Contraceptive Sterilization in the United States: 1965-1970." In *Demographic and Social Aspects of Population Growth*, edited by C. F. Westoff and R. Parke, Jr., Washington, D.C.: U.S. Government Printing Office.

Queen, Stuart A., and Robert W. Habenstein. 1967. *The Family in Various Cultures*. Philadelphia: J. B. Lippincott.

Rainwater, Lee. 1966. "Some Aspects of Lower Class Sexual Behavior." *Journal of Social Issues* 22, no. 1 (January):96-108.

Research Unit, Deparent of Health of Puerto Rico. 1967. *Master Sample Survey of Health and Welfare*. July.

Reed, Ellery F., and Ruth Latimer. 1963. *A Study of Unmarried Mothers Who Kept Their Babies*. Cincinnati, Ohio: Social Welfare Research.

Reeder, L. 1965. "Social Isolation and Illegitimate Pregnancy." Paper read at conference of the Society for the Study of Social Problems, San Diego, California, August.

Reiss, Ira L. 1960. *Premarital Sexual Standards in America*. New York: Free Press.

———. 1964a. "The Scaling of Premarital Sexual Permissiveness." *Journal of Marriage and the Family*. 26, no. 2 (May):188-98.

———. 1964b. "Premarital Sexual Permissiveness Among Negroes and Whites." *American Sociological Review* 29 (October):688-98.

———. 1967. *The Social Context of Premarital Sexual Permissiveness*. New York: Holt Rinehart & Winston.

———. 1969. "Premarital Sexual Standards." In *The Individual, Sex and Society*, edited by C. Broderick and J. Bernard, pp. 109-118, Baltimore, Maryland:Johns Hopkins Press.

———. 1970. "Premarital Sex as Deviant Behavior: An Application of Current Approaches to Deviance." *American Sociological Review* 35, no. 1 (February):78-87.

Rivera, Julius. 1971. *Latin America, A Sociocultural Interpretation*. New York: Appleton-Century-Crofts.

Roberts, George W. 1957. *The Population of Jamaica*. Cambridge University Press.

———. 1968. "The Present Fertility Position in Jamaica." In *World Views of Population Problems*, edited by E. Szabady, pp. 259-75, Budapest, Hungary.

Roberts, George W., and L. Braithwaite. 1961. "A Gross Mating Table for a West Indian Population." *Population Studies* (September):198-217.

Roberts, Robert W., ed. 1966. *The Unwed Mother*. New York: Harper & Row.

Robinson, W. S. 1950. "Ecological Correlations and the Behavior of Individuals." *American Sociological Review* 15 (June):351-57.

Rodman, Hyman. 1963. "Lower-Class Value Stretch." *Social Forces* 42, no. 2 (December):205f.

———. 1966. "Illegitimacy in the Caribbean Social Structure: A Reconsideration." *American Sociological Review* (October):673-83.

———. 1971. *Lower-Class Families, The Culture of Poverty in Negro Trinidad.* New York: Oxford University Press.

Roemer, Ruth. 1967. "Abortion Law: The Approaches of Different Nations." *American Journal of Public Health* 57, no. 11 (November):1906-12.

Rosen, Harold. 1967. *Abortion in America.* Boston: Beacon Press.

Russett, Bruce, et al. 1964. *World Handbook of Political and Social Indicators.* New Haven, Connecticut: Yale University Press.

Safilios-Rothschild, Constantina. 1972. "'Honor' Crimes in Contemporary Greece." In *Toward a Sociology of Women*, edited by Safilios-Rothschild, pp. 84-95, Lexington, Massachusetts: Xerox College Publishing.

Sauber, Mignon, and Elaine Rubinstein. 1965. *Experiences of the Unwed Mother as a Parent.* New York Community Council of Greater New York.

Schacht, L. E., and H. Gershowitz. 1963. In *Proceedings of the Second International Congress of Human Genetics*, 1961, vol. 2, pp. 994-97. Rome.

Schachter, J., and M. McCarthy. 1960. "Illegitimate Births: United States, 1938-57." *Vital Statistics, Special Report* 47, no. 8:229.

Schofield, M. 1965. *The Sexual Behavior of Young People.* Boston: Little Brown.

Scott, John Finley. 1971. *Internalization of Norms.* Englewood Cliffs, New Jersey: Prentice-Hall.

———. 1972. "Ascription and Mobility." In *Issues in Social Inequality*, edited by G. W. Thielbar and S. Feldman, pp. 580-97. Boston: Little Brown.

Sears, Pauline S. 1951. "Doll-play Aggression in Normal Young Children: Influence of Sex, Age, Sibling Status, Father's Absence." *Psychological Monographs* 65, whole no. 323, no. 6.

Selvin, Hanan C. 1958. "Durkheim's Suicide and Problems of Empirical Research." *American Journal of Sociology* 63:607-19.

Shapiro, Sam; Herbert S. Levine; and M. Abramowicz. 1971. "Factors associated with early and late fetal loss." *Advances in Planned Parenthood VI.* Excerpta Medica International Congress Series.

Shinozaki, Nobuo. 1957. *Report on Sexual Life of Japanese.* Tokyo: Institute of Population Problems, Welfare Ministry, (July).

Shope, David F., and Carlfred B. Broderick. 1967. "Level of Sexual Experience and Predicted Adjustment in Marriage." *Journal of Marriage and the Family* 29, no. 3:424-27.

Shorter, Edward. 1971. "Illegitimacy, Sexual Revolution, and Social Change in Modern Europe." *Journal of Interdisciplinary History* 2, no. 2 (Autumn):237-72.

Shorter, Edward; John Knodel; and Etienne van de Walle. 1971. "The Decline of Non-martial Fertility in Europe, 1880-1940." *Population Studies* 25 (November):375-93.

Shryock, Henry S., and Jacob S. Siegel and Associates. 1973. *The Methods and Materials of Demography*. Washington, D.C.: U.S. Bureau of the Census.

Siegman, A. W. 1966. "Father Absence During Early Childhood and Antisocial Behavior." *Journal of Abnormal Psychology* 71:71-74.

Silberman, Bernard S., ed. 1962. *Japanese Character and Culture*. Tucson: University of Arizona Press.

Simms, Madeleine. 1972. "The Future of the Abortion Act." *Midwives Chronicle and Nursing Notes* (January):6-10.

Simons, Betty; Elinor F. Downs; Madeline M. Hurster; and Morton Archer. 1966. *Child Abuse: A Perspective on Legislation in Five Middle Atlantic States, and A Survey of Reported Cases in New York City*. New York: Columbia University School of Public Health and Administrative Medicine.

Singh, J. A. L., and R. Zingg. 1942. *Wolf Child and Feral Man*. New York: Harper & Bros.

Sklar, June, and Beth Berkov. 1973. "The Effects of Legal Abortion on Legitimate and Illegitimate Birth Rates: The California Experience." *Studies in Family Planning* 4, no. 11 (November):281-92.

Smelser, Neil J. 1963. *Theory of Collective Behavior*. New York: Free Press.

———. 1968. *Essays in Sociological Explanation*. Englewood Cliffs, New Jersey: Prentice-Hall.

———. 1971. *Sociological Theory: A Contemporary View*. New York: General Learning Corp.

Spitz, Rene A. 1964. "Hospitalism." In *The Family: Its Structure and Function*. edited by Rose Coser, pp. 399-425. New York: St. Martin's Press.

Stephens, W. N. 1961. "Judgments by Social Workers on Boys and Mothers in Fatherless Families." *Journal of Genetic Psychology* 99:59-64.

Stinchcombe, Arthur. 1968. *Constructing Social Theories*. New York: Harcourt, Brace & World.

Stoetzel, Jean. 1955. *Without the Chrysanthemum and the Sword*. New York: Columbia Press.

Stolz, L. 1954. *Father Relations of War-Born Children*. Stanford: Stanford University Press.

Stycos, J. M., and K. W. Back. 1964. *The Control of Human Fertility in Jamaica.* New York: Cornell University Press.

Svalastoga, Kaare. 1954. "The Family in Scandinavia." *Marriage and Family Living* 16 (November):374-80.

Sweden, Statistiska Centralbyran. 1970. *Befolkning Forandringar, 1969* Stockholm.

Taeuber, Irene B. 1958. *The Population of Japan.* Princeton, New Jersey: Princeton University Press.

Tanner, J. M. 1966. "The Secular Trend Towards Earlier Physical Maturation." *Tydshrift voor Geneeskunde* 44:531-36.

Teele, J. E., and W. M. Schmidt. 1970. "Illegitimacy and Race." *Milbank Memorial Fund Quarterly*, 48 (April), pt. 2.

Tekse, Kalman. 1968. *A Study of Fertility in Jamaica.* Kingston, Jamaica: Dept. of Statistics, October.

Terkelsen, Helen E. 1964. *Counseling the Unwed Mother.* Englewood Cliffs, New Jersey: Prentice-Hall.

Terman, Lewis M. 1938. *Psychological Factors in Marital Happiness.* New York: McGraw-Hill.

Tietze, Christopher. 1965. "Induced Abortion and Sterilization as Methods of Fertility Control." In *Public Health and Population Change*, edited by M. C. Sheps and J. C. Ridley. Pittsburgh, Pennsylvania: University of Pittsburgh Press.

———. 1972. "Report of the Swedish Abortion Committee." *Studies in Family Planning) 3, no. 2 (February):28.*

———. 1973. "Two Years' Experience with a Liberal Abortion Law: Its Impact on Fertility Trends in New York City." *Family Planning Perspectives* (Winter).

Tietze, Christopher, and H. Lehfeldt. 1961. "Legal Abortion and Eastern Europe." *Journal of American Medical Association* 175:1149-54.

Tietze, Christopher, and Sarah Lewit. 1972. "Joint Program for the Study of Abortion (JPSA): Early Medical Complications of Legal Abortion." *Studies in Family Planning* 3, no. 6 (June):97-124.

Timasheff, Nicholas S. 1960. "The Attempt to Abolish the Family in Russia." In *A Modern Introduction to the Family*, edited by N. Bell and E. Vogel, pp. 55-63. Glencoe, Illinois: Free Press.

Tomasson, Richard F. 1971. "Sexual Permissiveness and Illegitimacy in the Five Nordic Countries." Paper delivered at the American Sociological Association Meetings, August 30-September 2, Denver, Colorado.

Trout, Louise K. 1956. "Services to Unmarried Mothers." *Child Welfare* 35.

United Nations, *Demographic Yearbook.* New York: United Nations, annual.

United Nations, Bureau of Social Affairs. 1969. *Growth of the World's Urban and Rural Population*, 1920-2000. Population Studies No. 44. New York.

United Nations Economic and Social Council (UNESCO). *Yearbook.* New York: United Nations, annual.

UNESCO, International African Institute. 1956. *Social Implications of Industrialization and Urbanization in Africa South of Sahara.* Paris: UNESCO.

United Nations Sub-Commission on Prevention of Discrimination and Protection of Minorities. 1967. *Study of Discrimination Against Persons Born Out of Wedlock.* New York: United Nations.

United States Bureau of the Census. 1961. "Marriage, Fertility and Childspacing, August, 1959." W. Grabill and R. Parke, Jr. *Current Population Reports.* Series P-20, No. 108. Washington, D.C.: U.S. Government Printing Office, July tables 16 and 17.

United States Bureau of the Census. 1969. "Marriage, Fertility and Childspacing: June 1965." *Current Population Reports.* Series P-20, No. 186. Washington, D.C.: U.S. Government Printing Office, tables 17 and 18.

United States Department of Health, Education, and Welfare. 1968a. *Trends in Illegitimacy, United States, 1940-1965.* Public Health Service Publication No. 1000-Series 21-No. 15. Washington, D.C.: U.S. Government Printing Office. February.

———. 1968b. "Visits for Medical and Dental Care During the Year Preceding Childbirth, United States 1963 Births." *Vital and Health Statistics,* Series 22, no. 4. Washington, D.C. May.

———. 1970. "Interval Between First Marriage and Legitimate First Birth, United States, 1964-1966." *Monthly Vital Statistics Report,* vol. 18, no. 5. Washington, D.C.: National Center for Health Statistics, March 27.

———. 1971. "Monthly Vital Statistics Report." *National Natality and Infant Mortality Surveys: 1964-1966,* vol. 20, no. 5 supp. Washington, D.C.: National Center for Health Statistics, August 2.

———. 1972. *Family Planning Evaluation.* Abortion Surveillance Report, Jan.-Mar. 1971. Washington, D.C.: Center for Disease Control, March.

United States Office of Vital Statistics. *Vital Statistics of the United States,* 1968. Vol. 1. Washington, D.C.: Superintendent of Documents.

University of the West Indies. 1964. *Estimates of Intercensal Population by Age and Sex, and Revised Vital Rates for British Caribbean Countries,* 1943-1960. Census Research Programme, publication no. 8. Kingston, Jamaica, 14-15.

Vasquez, J. L. 1968. "Fertility Decline in Puerto Rico: Extent and Causes." *Demography* 5:864.

Vergara, Julio Morales. 1965. "Analysis Demografico De La Ilegitimidad en Chile." For the United Nations World Population Conference.

Vincent, Clark E. 1961. *Unmarried Mothers.* Glencoe, Illinois: Free Press.

———. 1962a. "Unmarried Mothers: Society's Dilemma." *Sexology* 28:451.

———. 1962b. "Spotlight on the Unwed Father." *Sexology* 28:538-42.

———. 1966. "Teen-Age Unwed Mothers in American Society." *Journal of Social Issues* 22, no 2:22-33.

Vogel, Ezra F. 1963. *Japan's New Middle Class.* Berkeley: University of California Press.

Walsh, Robert H., and Dovie Bryant. 1971. "Social Forces and Premarital Sexual Permissiveness: Further Comments on Reiss's 'Proposition One.' " Paper presented at the American Sociological Association meetings, August 30-September 2, Denver, Colorado.

Welfare Council of Toronto and Its District. 1943. *A Study of the Adjustment of Teen Age Children Born Out of Wedlock Who Remained in the Custody of their Mothers or Relatives.* Tornoto: Subcommittee of the Unmarried Parenthood Committee.

Westermarck, Edward. 1925. *The History of Human Marriage.* Vol. 1. London: Macmillan.

Whelan, Elizabeth Murphy. 1972a. "Illegitimate and Premaritally Conceived First Births in Massachusetts, 1966-1968." *Social Biology* 19 (March):9-28.

———. 1972b. "The Temporal Relationship of Marriage, Conception and Birth in Massachusetts." *Demography* 9, no. 3 (August):399-414.

Whelpton, P. K.; A. A. Campbell; and J. E. Patterson. 1966. *Fertility and Family Planning in the United States.* Princeton, New Jersey: Princeton University Press.

Wikman, K. R. V. 1937. "Die Einleitung Der Ehe." In *Acta Academiae Aboensis Humaniora* 11.

Wimperis, Virginia. 1960. *The Unmarried Mother and Her Child.* London: George Allen & Unwin.

Winch, R. F. 1949. "The Relations Between the Loss of a Parent and Progress in Courtship." *Journal of Social Psychology* 29:51-56.

World Health Organization. 1970. *Spontaneous and Induced Abortion.* WHO Technical Report Series, No. 461. Geneva, Switzerland.

Wynn, Margaret. 1964. *Fatherless Families.* London: Michael Joseph.

Yamane, Tsuneo, and Hisaya Nonoyama. 1967. "Isolation of the Nuclear Family & Kinship Organization in Japan." *Journal of Marriage and Family* 29, no. 4 (November):783-96.

Yarrow, L. J. 1961. "Maternal Deprivation: Toward an Empirical and Conceptual Re-evaluation." *Psychological Bulletin* 58:459-90.

Yaukey, David. 1969. "On Theorizing About Fertility." *The American Sociologist* (May):100-104.

———. 1973. *Marriage Reduction and Fertility.* Lexington, Massachusetts: D. C. Heath.

Young, Leontine. 1954. *Out of Wedlock.* New York: McGraw Hill.

Youssef, Nadia. 1970. *Social Structure and Female Labor Force Participation in Developing Countries: A Comparison of Latin American and Middle-East Countries.* Ph. D. dissertation, University of California, Berkeley.

Zelnik, Melvin, and John F. Kantner. 1970. "United States: Exploratory Studies of Negro Family Formation—Factors Relating to Illegitimacy." *Studies in Family Planning* 60 (December):5-9.

———. 1972. "The Probability of Premarital Intercourse." *Social Science Research* 1, no. 3 (September):335-41.

Zetterberg, Hans. 1964. *On Theory and Verification in Sociology.* Totowa, New Jersey: Bedminster Press.

Index

Abegglen, J., on Japanese factories, 84

Abortion, 108-112; risk, 207; propositions, 210, 242-245

Adoption, of legitimate and illegitimate children, 10

Adulterous illegitimacy, 6, 132-133; blood tests, 132; types, 133

Adultery, legislation in England, 156

Africa: ratios of illegitimacy, 52-55; race, 69; marriage customs, 128

Age distribution of women, 103

Age-specific: proportions married, 125, 127; illegitimacy rates, 61-64; illegitimacy ratios, 61; white and nonwhite U.S. rates, 68-69; rates in Sweden, 169; abortion in U.S., 228-231

Anomie, and individualism, 90

Anxiety, and pregnancy, 72-75

Arab countries: marriage in, 120; family honor, 148-149

Ariga, K., on family in Japan, 247

Arriaga, Eduardo, on union dissolution, 86

Asia, ratios over time, 49-51

Australasia, ratios of illegitimacy, 47-49

Batten, Thelma, on theory and research, 115

Bauman, K., and J. R. Udry, on powerlessness and contraceptive use, 182

Belgium, ratios over time, 36, 42, 43

Bell, R., and J. Chaskes, on coital experience among college women, 138, 142

Benson, Leonard, on fatherless families, 10-11

Berger, Morroe, on family in Middle East, 105, 147; marriage customs, 127, 130

Billingsley, A., and A. T., on Negro family in America, 68, 92

Birth registration, 20; recognizing unlisted illegitimates, 21; reregistration, 21

Blacks in U.S. *See* Negro

Blake, Judith: on Jamaican family, 4, 130, 150; reproductive alternatives, 15; sexual exploitation, 67; union duration, 87; women's ignorance, 97; values in Caribbean, 93-95; U.S. attitudes toward premarital sex, 152-153; U.S. attitudes toward birth control, 173

Blake, J., and K. Davis: on values as cause, 95; on social sanctions, 155

Bogue, Donald, on birth control service, 174

Bowerman, C., et al., on unwed mothers: relationships of, 75; self-image, 108; nonuse of contraception, 179, 181

Bridal pregnancy. *See* Marriage during pregnancy

Briffault, R., on urban Uganda, 130-131

Brinton, Crane, abolish "illegitimacy," 76

British Isles, ratios of illegitimacy, 32-40. *See also* England

Bulgaria, ratios over time, 44-45

Bumpass, L., and C. Westoff, on unwanted births, 161

Bundling, patterned, 192, 193

Burgess, E., and P. Wallin, on premarital coitus, 139

Calderone, Mary, 165

Campbell, Arthur, on youth of unwed mothers, 12

Canada, premarital coitus in, 138, 140

Caribbean, 4; ratios of illegitimacy, 26-31; race, 68; mother revenge, 74; sex ratio, 87-88; urban-rural differences, 89; woman's bargaining position, 97. *See*

childhood, 7, 66; of females, 97; youth, 162

Devereaux, George: on unwed mothers in primitive societies, 12; on preindustrial beliefs about abortion, 210-211

Discrimination, and illegitimacy, 17

Divorce: and sex norms, 91; and illegitimacy, 133-135; among Moslems, 147; in Japan, 248

Dixon, Ruth, on desirability of marriage, 129

Dodd, Peter C., on Arab women and honor, 148-149

Dore, Ronald, on family links in Japan, 248, 249

Durkheim, Emile: on "social facts," 16; on individualism, 90; moral community, 157

Economic factors, in Caribbean illegitimacy, 87-88. *See also* Poverty

Education, 96-98; proportion of youth in school, 97; sex, 98; and premarital coitus, 143, 145; of Negro women, 150; and conception, 161; and pregnancy outcome, 225-226

Employment, of women, 83-84

England: ratios over time, 34, 39, 40; age-specific ratios in, 61; age specific rates in, 62-64; postconception marriage 108-109; historical marriage patterns 131; divorce and illegitimacy, 133-134; premarital coitus, 138-141 passim; teenaged coitus, 161-162; premarital pregnancy, 188-193, 205; probability of legitimation, 193-196; abortion, 236-238; welfare for unwed mothers, 249-250

Europe: ratios of illegitimacy, geographical and cultural groupings, 32-46; marriage during pregnancy, 108, 191-193; abortion, 233-235

Family honor: in Arab countries, 148-149; in Mediterranian countries, 154-155

Fatherless: boys, 10; girls, 11; families and poverty, 86

Fathers: biological vs. sociological role, 2, 3, 4; stability, 7, 10, 11, 87; emotional and financial support, 10; and social services, 13; unemployment of, 83; child support, 185-186

Fecundity, 162-164; and childbearing, 66; and health, 106, 162, 164; and age at menarche, 162-163; and venereal disease, 163-164

Finland, ratios in, 34-36, 41

Foote, C., et al, on hospital abortions, 209

Foote, Nelson, 106

France: premarital coitus in, 139; premarital pregnancy in, 188-189, 205

Francis, O. C., 87

Freedman, Ronald, on abortion and fertility decline, 210

French Institute of Public Opinion, on premarital coitus, 139

Freud, S: mentioned, 72-75, 106, 152

Frisch, R., and R. Revelle, on age at menarche, 162

Furie, Sidney, on welfare and contraception, 173

Furstenberg, Frank, on contraceptive motivation, 180, 181

Garcia, C., on conception, 106

Gebhard, Paul: on coital experience, 150; postmarital coitus, 145; coitus and religion, 157; frequency, 160-162; premarital conceptions, 201; pregnancy outcomes, 224-228, 242-243, 244; abortions, 208-209

Gendell, M. and J. Van der Tak, on unmarried women and fertility, 68, 243

Geographical patterning of illegitimacy, 24-64, 70

Germany, premarital coitus in, 138

Goldsmith, Sadja, on contraceptive clinics for teens, 172-173

Goldstein, Sidney, on premarital pregnancy in Denmark, 196-197

Goldstein, S., and J. Mayer, on status levels and illegitimacy, 82

Goode, William: Caribbean research, 4; on types of illegitimacy, 6-7; African marriage systems, 52; industrialization and illegitimacy, 84; status placement, 84-85; dependence of women, 84, 97; disruption vs. integration, 88-90; values in Caribbean, 93-95; marriage customs, 125-128

Gough, Harrison, socialization scores of unwed mothers, 11, 15, 75

Gough, Kathleen, fatherhood among the